COLOR IN NATURE

PENELOPE A. FARRANT

COLOR IN NATURE

A Visual and Scientific Exploration

BLANDFORD

ACKNOWLEDGEMENTS

I would like to thank the many people who generously allowed me to use their pictures in this book: Chris B. Banks, Robert Berthold, William Farrant, Marilyn Fox, Raymond Hoser, Robert King, Mrs J.M. King, Mrt W.H. King, John Landy, Alan Leishman, Audrie Leslie, John Lush, Lenore McLay, David Malin, (Anglo-Australian Telescope), NASA, Jaime Plaza, Marianne Porteners, Les Rodgers, Julian Seddon,and Steve Wilson.

Many thanks to David Malin and Coral Cooksley at the Anglo-Australian Telescope for their help, to Dennis Hall for research of NASA material, to Jan Smith at the State Library of New South Wales, and to Professor Alan Walker at Sydney University.

I would also like to thank those who read and offered critical comments on the manuscript (Ruth Dircks and William Farrant), or sections of the manuscript (especially Robert King and Stephen Dain). My special thanks also to editors Meryl Potter, for advice and guidance in the earlier stages of the project, and Ingaret Ward in the later stages, to designer Joy Eckermann and publisher Charles Pierson. This book would not have been possible without the support of members of the Colour Society of Australia, in particular Carol Arthur, Stephen Dain and Steve Morton.

NOTE TO READERS
SCIENTIFIC NAMES: For ease of reading, all names of plants and animals in the text have been called by their common names. Anyone wishing to check on their scientific names, should turn to the section Scientific Names of Plants and Animals in each Chapter at the back of the book, p 194, where all scientific names are given, chapter by chapter.

A BLANDFORD BOOK

First published in the UK 1997 by Blandford
A Cassell Imprint
Cassell Plc, Wellington House,
125, Strand, London WC2R 0BB

Text copyright © 1997 Penny Farrant

Distribution in the United States by Sterling Publishing Co., Inc., 387 Park Avenue South, New York, NY 10016–8810

ISBN 0-7137-2351-3

A Cataloguing-in-Publication Data entry for this title is available from the British Library.

Edited by Ingaret Ward
Designed by Christie and Eckermann
Separations by Pica
Printed in Hong Kong

CONTENTS

INTRODUCTION

This book draws together for the first time a wealth of information from many branches of scientific study: astronomy, geology, zoology, botany and physics.

In one book we can examine colour in the natural world — both how colour is produced and the purpose it serves. This book also explores the influence of colour in many areas of our lives.

Dr Farrant's multi-disciplinary approach, together with her involvement in the Colour Society of Australia (New South Wales Division), combine to produce a book that is both erudite and readable. Lectures to the Colour Society of Australia revealed widespread interest in this field and the need for a source book on the subject.

I am happy to recommend this book both to the general reader and to students across a range of disciplines in schools and universities. It is also an excellent source book for libraries.

Stephen J. Dain BSc(Hons), PhD, FBCO, FAAO, FVCO, MIES(ANZ)
Associate Professor, School of Optometry, University of New South Wales
Councillor, Colour Society of Australia (New South Wales Division)
Member, Directorial Committee of the International Research Group on Colour Vision Deficiencies

CHAPTER 1

THE NATURE OF COLOUR AND THE COLOUR OF NATURE

This book explores the question 'What is the role of colour in nature?'. Why is snow white, an egg yolk yellow, a leaf green? If we look at the world around us, we see it has many colours - vivid and subdued, solid and translucent, single and varied. What causes these colours, what animals can see them and how, and why do these colours exist?

The importance of colour to life on Earth probably goes back to the first green organisms that trapped the sun's energy for photosynthesis. All life on our planet depends on this process, in which energy from the sun is converted into chemical energy, and carbon dioxide and water are converted into carbohydrate and oxygen. Photosynthesis of plants and colour vision of animals are probably the two most important adaptations of life on Earth to the colours of the sun's light.

IDEAS ABOUT VISION AND COLOUR

In human civilisation, colours have always played a significant role: even the earliest cave-dwellers used pigments (colouring substances) in their rock drawings 40 000 years ago. Pigments and dyes (colouring substances in solution), made from minerals, animals and plants, were incorporated into pottery, glass and textiles from earliest times.

Early peoples did not understand the exact nature of vision. At first they believed that there was no physical interaction between an object and an observer. Later, Greek philosophers and mathematicians like Aristotle (384-322 B.C.), Euclid (c. 300 B.C.) and Ptolemy (c. A.D. 130) introduced the idea that vision involved rays that travelled from the eye towards an object, with an observer being able to see objects encountered along the path of the rays. Other Greek philosophers, such as Socrates (469-399 B.C.) and Plato (428-347 B.C.), believed that vision consisted of images produced by objects interacting with spirits from an observer's eyes. It was an Arab scholar, Alhazen (c. A.D. 1000), who eventually suggested that the eye detects light and that light is a physical entity. By the time of the European Renaissance, Leonardo da Vinci (1452-1519) believed that light rays sent out by objects were perceived through the eyes. From these last notions, modern concepts of vision were developed by scientists such as Sir Isaac Newton (1642-1727) and Thomas Young (1773-1829).

It was not until the early nineteenth century that ideas about the existence of atoms, the basic building blocks of matter, were introduced by the British quaker scientist John Dalton (1766-1844). Nonetheless, a knowledge of the structure of the atom is essential to understanding the development of the concept of colour (see BOX 1).

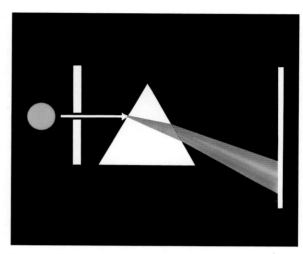

Fig. 1.1 Using a glass prism to refract or bend light, Newton showed that sunlight is a mixture or spectrum of light of different colours.

In ancient times the explanation of colour was metaphysical rather than scientific, with colours being used as symbols for various mysteries of the universe. In the fourth century B.C., Aristotle described the colours of nature in terms of their being mixtures of black and white: e.g. black objects mixed with sunlight or firelight become crimson in colour. Aristotle's systematisation of knowledge dominated scientific thinking for centuries, until eventually challenged by Leonardo da Vinci, René Descartes (1596-1650) and Robert Boyle (1627-1691).

A spectrum of colour

During the Plague in 1666, Newton realised the significance of colours produced when a beam of sunlight passed through a glass prism. He passed a narrow beam of white sunlight through a glass prism to produce the rainbow colours (fig. 1.1). He then blocked off all colours except one and allowed this coloured beam to pass through a second prism: the colour remained unchanged. Finally, he allowed all the colours of light to pass through a second prism orientated in the opposite direction from the first: the colours emerged from the second prism as a beam of white light. What Newton had discovered was that white sunlight is actually composed of a mixture of colours; the glass prism bent or refracted each colour to a slightly different extent, separating them into a spectrum in the process.

Newton recognised seven colours in the spectrum of sunlight: violet, indigo, blue, green, yellow, orange and red (though indigo is no longer recognised as a separate colour in the spectrum). He demonstrated that an observer sees objects as coloured because those objects reflect only some of the light rays that reach them. The discovery of the splitting of sunlight into its spectrum had important repercussions, leading eventually to the development of spectroscopy (see BOX 2).

Particles and waves

Scientists had several theories about how light travelled. Newton believed light consisted of small particles called corpuscles emanating from a light source. His contemporary, Christiaan Huygens (1629-1695), suggested light could be better understood as moving waves. This theory was generally accepted though scientists were still not satisfied they understood how light travelled. In 1900 the German physicist Max Planck (1858-1947) put forward the quantum theory, which said that some aspects of light could be better explained if light were regarded as discrete indivisible packets of energy or quanta. In 1905 Albert Einstein (1879-1955) applied the name 'photon' to this quantum package of light. Nowadays we think of light as sometimes behaving like particles and sometimes behaving like waves: a beam of sunlight is a stream of rapidly moving and vibrating photons which move in waves from the sun. The distance between successive crests of a wave of photons is called its wavelength (fig. 1.2).

Light is a type of radiant energy, i.e., energy emitted by an object that has been heated or otherwise excited. Visible light is not the only type of radiant energy in the universe. Electromagnetic radiation, or radiant energy transmitted through matter or space in an electromagnetic field, comes in many forms. While light is the only part of the spectrum visible to us, other parts are detectable. Many of these are familiar to us and are classified according to their photon energy. In order of increasing energy, the radiation in the electromagnetic spectrum includes: radio waves, microwaves, infra-red radiation, visible light, ultraviolet radiation, x-rays, gamma rays and cosmic rays (fig. 1.3).

All these types of radiation travel at the same speed in a vacuum, regardless of the energy of their photons. The photons with more energy, however, oscillate more frequently and have a shorter wavelength, than photons with lower energy. Wavelengths of light are measured in nanometres, where each nanometre is one-millionth of a metre. Different wavelengths of light are seen as different colours (fig. 1.4).

LIGHT AND COLOUR

Although visible light is only a tiny part of the total electromagnetic spectrum, it forms over 80% of radiation arriving at Earth from the sun. Life on Earth is beautifully adapted to use these wavelengths: e.g. photosynthesis in plants and vision in animals. At longer wavelengths, electromagnetic waves have insufficient energy to stimulate light-sensitive cells; at shorter wavelengths, ultraviolet light is damaging to sensitive animal and plant tissues, with x-rays, gamma rays and cosmic rays being progressively more harmful.

Fig. 1.2 Light can best be thought of as a stream of particles, called photons, which oscillate in different directions, but move together as a wave.

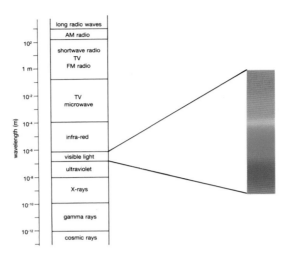

Fig. 1.3 Electromagnetic radiation includes many types of waves with different wavelengths and energies; visible light forms only a small part of this spectrum.

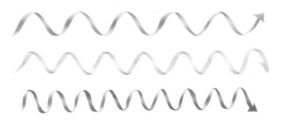

Fig. 1.4 Red light waves have low energy and long wavelength (c. 700 nm), blue light waves have high energy and short wavelength (c. 400 nm), and light of other colours falls in between.

Very few animals can detect all wavelengths in the visible range. Within this part of the electromagnetic spectrum, the eyes of various animals are sensitive to different wavelengths: e.g. humans can detect wavelengths from around 400-780 nanometres. Different wavelengths of light enable us to perceive different colours, from violet and blue (short wavelength, high energy) to red (long wavelength, low energy).

Light travels from a source in a straight line, unless it enters a different medium or encounters an obstacle. Then it may be transmitted, absorbed, reflected, refracted, diffracted, polarised, or scattered, depending on the medium or material encountered (see BOX 3).

SOURCES OF VISIBLE LIGHT

Various objects emit light with wavelengths in the visible range. The most important is the sun: Earth receives only a very small proportion of the sun's radiated energy, which takes about eight minutes to travel 150 000 000 km. Other sources of visible light or luminescence include fire, lightning, auroras and even some plants and animals!

Ultraviolet light (also called black light because it

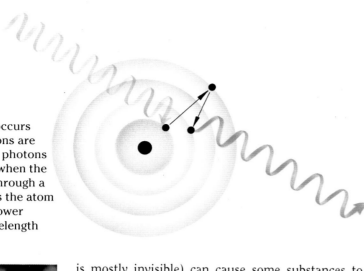

Fig. 1.5 Fluorescence occurs when an atom's electrons are excited by high energy photons (e.g. ultraviolet light); when the electrons drop down through a lesser number of orbits the atom emits photons with a lower energy and longer wavelength (e.g. blue light).

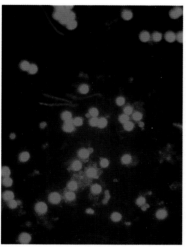

PL. 1.1 Chlorophyll in living algae from a coral shows red fluorescence under ultraviolet light. *Photo: P. Farrant*

slightly longer time after the removal of the ultraviolet light source (though still less than a second).

Bioluminescence is light emission by living organisms: e.g. bacteria, octopuses, shrimps, fireflies and glow-worms. This 'living' light is produced within the cells of the organisms: chemical energy is transformed into light energy during a chemical reaction. The principle of light emission is the same as for other types of luminescence: electrons are excited to a high energy state and emit light as they return to the normal state (see BOX 1).

COLOUR, COLOUR, COLOUR

Colour is involved in almost every aspect of our daily lives. Many specialised fields of study deal with various aspects: physical, optical, chemical, psychological, biological, physiological and neurological.

Colour is a complex subjective sensation existing only when an observer is present to see different wavelengths of light reflected (or altered in some other way) by an object. Most colours around us are produced by selective absorption of some wavelengths of light by dyes and pigments in objects, while the other, reflected wavelengths are perceived as colours: an apple appears red because it reflects red light and absorbs all other colours (fig. 1.6).

Black and white are not strictly regarded as colours. An object appears black if it absorbs or transmits all the incident white light (fig. 1.7), and white if it reflects all the light (fig. 1.8).

is mostly invisible) can cause some substances to emit light. If luminescence persists for only a short while after a light source is removed (less than one-millionth of a second), it is known as fluorescence (fig. 1.5). The sun is a source of ultraviolet light and objects that fluoresce under sunlight emit light during the day, though it is not usually noticeable. Many substances are fluorescent when extracted from living organisms, e.g. the chlorophyll of green plants fluoresces red (pl. 1.1). However, in living organisms themselves the energy is usually directed into chemical reactions so light is not produced.

Phosphorescence is a type of light emission similar to fluorescence, in which ultraviolet light is absorbed by an object then re-emitted as longer wavelength visible light. In phosphorescence the light lasts for a

Fig. 1.6 An apple appears red because it reflects red wavelengths of light; the other wavelengths are absorbed by pigment molecules in the apple skin and their energy is lost as heat.

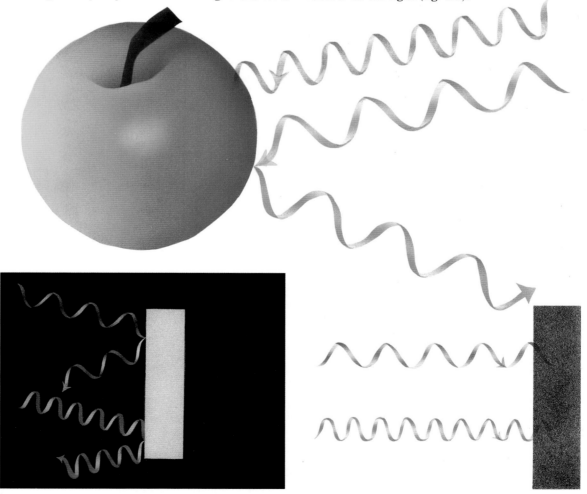

Fig. 1.8 Right: An opaque object appears white if it reflects all wavelengths of light.

Fig 1.7 Far right: An opaque object appears black if it absorbs all wavelengths of light.

BOX 1

ATOMS, MOLECULES AND COLOUR

Atoms, ions and molecules

All matter in the universe consists of atoms. At the centre of each atom is a very dense, positively charged nucleus composed of positively charged protons and neutrally charged neutrons. The number of protons in the nucleus of an atom is different for each type of chemical element, and is known as its atomic number. Chemical elements, such as hydrogen, oxygen and gold, are substances composed of only one type of atom (fig. 1.9).

The nucleus of an atom is surrounded by a cloud of electrons, much lighter, negatively charged particles arranged in orbits. Within a single atom, the positive charge of the nucleus is usually balanced by the negative charge of the electrons because there are usually the same number of electrons as protons. Because electrons are outermost, however, they can be lost or gained by an atom. If an atom or molecule loses or gains one or more electrons, it becomes electrically charged and is known as an ion. The process of ion formation is called ionisation.

Atoms tend to join up with other atoms to share electrons and form a more stable entity with little or no overall electric charge. Such combinations of atoms are known as molecules. Molecules are the natural units of matter, as they are made up of atoms functioning as a unit (fig. 1.10). Within a molecule, atoms are joined together by bonds, regions in which pairs of electrons are shared. In a double bond the adjacent atoms share two pairs of electrons.

other molecules in a chemical reaction or be re-emitted as light. The colour of an object is determined by which wavelengths of visible light provide the energy necessary for readjustment of its electrons. This energy, the exact difference in energy between two orbits, is absorbed, and the remaining wavelengths are reflected and perceived as colour by an observer.

The atomic theory of light maintains that photons are formed when electrons move from a higher orbit to a lower one: each move produces a single quantum. The energy of photons, and therefore whether or not the radiation is visible, and if so the colour of the light produced, depends upon whether electrons move to a nearby orbit or one further away: the further away they move, the more rapidly the photons vibrate and the more energy they possess. Photons with high energy produce short wavelength, violet and blue light, whereas photons with low energy produce long wavelength, red light (fig. 1.11, fig. 1.12).

The most vivid colours of natural substances, whether organic or inorganic, are produced by large groups of atoms that share an electron cloud: in such an arrangement the electrons can be excited to higher states by only a small amount of energy. Many natural dyes and pigments are large molecules whose electrons can easily be excited to higher states by the energy of visible light.

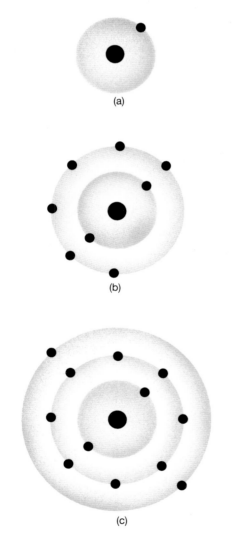

(a)

(b)

(c)

Fig. 1.9 Atoms consist of a central nucleus containing protons (positive) and neutrons (neutral), around which orbit negatively charged electrons. Hydrogen (a) has one proton, oxygen (b) 8 and carbon (c) 12. The orbits in which electrons have least energy are those closest to the nucleus (ground state), but they can gain energy and move to a higher orbit (excited state).

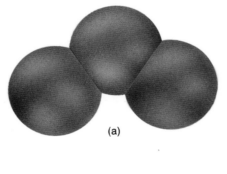

(a)

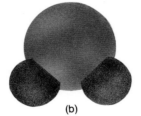

(b)

Fig. 1.10 A molecule consists of a group of one or more types of atoms bonded together. A molecule of ozone (a) contains three oxygen atoms, whereas a water molecule (b) contains a single oxygen atom and two hydrogen atoms.

Excited electrons

Electrons move in a number of orbits at various fixed distances from the nuclei of atoms, ions and molecules. It is the movement of electrons between these orbits that causes electromagnetic radiation to be emitted. Each orbit has a characteristic energy level associated with it so a precise amount of energy is needed to move or excite electrons into a higher orbit; light waves can provide these exact amounts of energy.

When electrons return from an excited state orbit to the ground state, the energy may excite

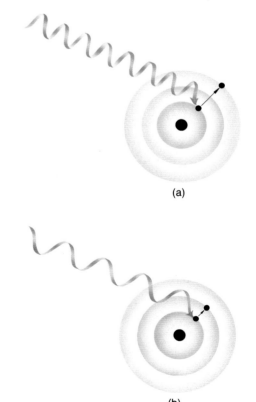

(a)

(b)

Fig. 1.11 Photons of energetic short wavelength blue light (a) will excite electrons into higher orbits than those of red light (b).

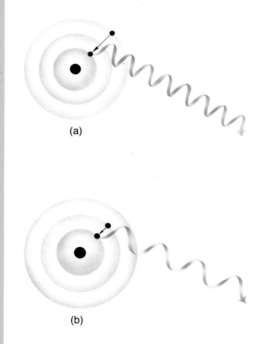

(a)

(b)

Fig. 1.12 Visible light is emitted by an atom when its electrons fall from a higher orbit to one that is less energetic. Short wavelength blue light is produced by electrons falling a longer distance (a) than they do for red light (b).

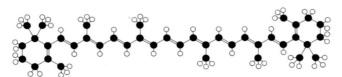

Fig. 1.13 Carotenoids, like this molecule of beta-carotene, owe their yellow, orange and red colours to size and structure.

Coloured organic molecules

Many of the molecules found in living organisms have a number of features that help to reduce the energy needed to excite their electrons and thus provide them with colour (fig. 1.13): they are large; they contain atoms of low atomic number, like carbon, hydrogen, oxygen and nitrogen; their atoms are often arranged in long chains or in systems of rings, with alternating single and double bonds; there is often an imbalance of charge between the ends of the molecules; and they may contain one or more atoms of a transition metal. A transition metal is one of a group of eight elements (titanium, vanadium, chromium, manganese, iron, cobalt, nickel and copper) that have unfilled electron orbits available for electron excitation. Iron atoms in haemoglobin make blood red, while the magnesium atom in chlorophyll colours plants' leaves green (fig. 1.14).

When light is absorbed by an organic molecule, the energy not only provides the plant or animal with colour, but may also trigger chemical reactions because these also depend upon excitation of electrons. The chemical

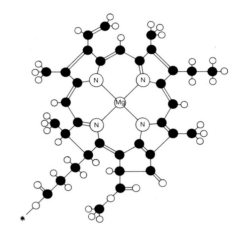

Fig. 1.14 The green colour of chlorophyll *a* is due to its structure.

environment of a molecule may affect its colour. A well-known example of this is the colour change seen in red hydrangeas when alum is added to the soil. As well, there are many substances, inorganic and organic, that can intensify colours in plants and animals through their chemical interactions with pigment molecules.

BOX 2

LOOKING AT THE SPECTRUM: SPECTROSCOPY

The nature of any substance in the universe can be revealed through the colours or spectrum of light it absorbs or emits when heated or otherwise excited: all substances are made up of one or more chemical elements, each of which absorbs or emits photons when its electrons undergo transition from one energy state to another. The spectroscope is used to analyse and measure, and in some cases even produce, spectra. It has been used to reveal many properties of stars, including their chemical composition, velocities, temperatures and magnetic fields, as well as the exact composition of many materials on Earth and the impurities they contain.

Newton's discovery that white light could be split into its component colours by passing it through a prism was the basis for the development of the spectroscope. The first spectroscope was made in 1814 by Joseph von Fraunhofer (1787-1826). The instrument used

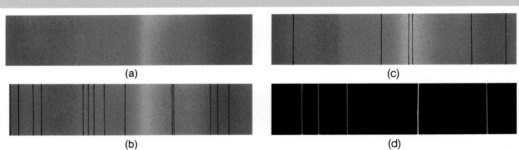

(a)

(c)

(b)

(d)

Fig. 1.15 (a) Continuous emission spectrum of the sun. (b) When examined closely the sun's spectrum is seen to contain a number of dark lines (Fraunhofer lines), each due to absorption by particular elements in the sun's atmosphere. (c) Absorption spectrum of mercury. (d) Emission spectrum of helium.

lenses to spread the spectrum of sunlight. It showed clearly the dark lines, now known as Fraunhofer lines, that cross the sun's spectrum. These lines had been observed in 1802 by William Hyde Wollaston (1766-1828) when he was looking at the colours of the sun's spectrum: at that time he did not know what they were. Each Fraunhofer line is the result of absorption of a certain colour of light by particular elements in the outer, cooler layers of the sun's atmosphere.

A spectroscope spreads out light, either by refraction, where it is passed through a prism, or by diffraction, where it is passed through a

diffraction grating, i.e. a very narrow opening. Two types of spectra can be studied with a spectroscope depending upon whether the substance being examined emits light or not: emission spectra (light emitted by a substance) and absorption spectra (light passing through a substance — see fig. 1.15).

As well as analysing the colours of light in spectra, modern spectroscopes measure the total energy of the photons received for each colour of the spectra: the relative amounts of energy received indicate relative proportions of various elements in the composition of the substance being analysed.

PL. 1.2 Tree ferns, New Zealand. *Photo: L. Rodgers*

PL. 1.3 Blue ocean, Fiji. *Photo: W. Farrant*

The colours an animal sees depend on the type of eyes and brain it possesses. Whereas humans see a range of colours, other animals like dogs and cats detect only a few; despite this, their relatively well-developed brains can utilise the information they receive. On the other hand, the eyes of most birds detect a greater range of colours than human eyes, but birds' brains are poorly developed and the information is used mostly for automatic responses.

COLOURS OF NATURE

Nature presents large areas of earthy colours: greens, blues and browns (pls 1.2-1.4), but is quite sparing with vivid colours, which are usually seen only for short times or over small areas (pls 1.5-1.7). Colours of organisms are often particularly attractive because they are arranged in striking patterns (pls 1.8-1.11). Almost all known colours occur in nature, in minerals, animals and plants: the colours and patterns of invertebrate animals (those without backbones) in particular are surprisingly bright and varied (pls 1.12-1.20). Even the earthy colours are extremely varied: e.g an enormous number of different greens can be seen in the bush (pls 1.21-1.22).

Fig. 1.5 Waratah, eastern Australia. *Photo: P. Farrant*

PL. 1.4 Left: Lake Mungo, Australia. *Photo: P. Farrant*

PL. 1.7 Below: Pouch fungus, New Zealand. *Photo: L. Rodgers*

PL. 1.8 Caterpillar with striking colours and patterns. *Photo: W. Farrant*

PL. 1.9 Fish, Australia. *Photo: W. Farrant*

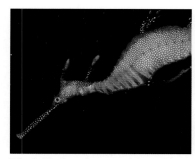

PL. 1.10 Sea dragon, Australia. *Photo: P. Farrant*

PL. 1.11 Pair of coral fish, Maldives. *Photo: P. Farrant*

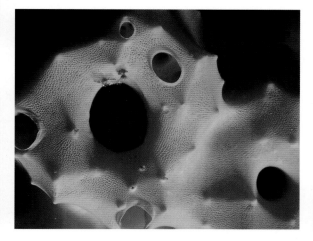

PL. 1.12 Top left: Cuttlefish. *Photo: P. Farrant*

PL. 1.13 Top right: Hydroid, Fiji. *Photo: W. Farrant*

PL. 1.14 Above left: Scallop covered with orange sponge, Vanuatu. *Photo: P. Farrant*

PL. 1.15 Above right: Nudibranchs (sea slugs) often have wonderfully exotic coloration. Lord Howe Island. *Photo: W. Farrant*

PL. 1.16 Left: Pink sponge, Australia. *Photo: P. Farrant*

PL. 1.17 Right: Brittle star on sponge, Maldives. *Photo: P. Farrant*

PL. 1.18 Far right: Feather star, Fiji. *Photo: P. Farrant*

PL. 1.19 Soft coral, Maldives. *Photo: P. Farrant*

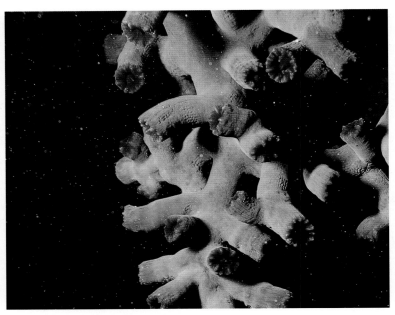

PL. 1.20 Coral, Maldives. *Photo: W. Farrant*

PL. 1.21 Ferns, New Zealand. *Photo: W. Farrant*

PL. 1.22 Lichen, Mt Kosciusko, Australia. *Photo: W. Farrant*

PL. 1.23 Below: Emission and reflection nebulae in Sagittarius. *Photo: Anglo-Australian Telescope*

The striking colours of celestial objects, like the planets, have been revealed by colour photography (pl. 1.23). Earth's atmosphere itself is responsible for producing many fascinating coloured phenomena (pls 1.24, 1.25). Getting down to Earth itself, we need only look around to see the variation in colours of the land and water surfaces (pls 1.26, 1.27) and of the various habitats of the plants and animals that live here (pls 1.28, 1.29). Each of the following chapters will discuss different aspects of colour in our world.

PL. 1.24 Aurora australis, New Zealand.
Photo: A. Leslie

PL. 1.25 Sunrise, Coorong, South Australia.
Photo: M. Porteners

PL. 1.26 Above: Striped rocks,
Mt Kilimanjaro. *Photo: W. Farrant*

PL. 1.27 Left: Azure blue sea,
Great Barrier Reef. *Photo: M. Porteners*

PL. 1.28 Above: Seaweed, eastern Australia.
Photo: P. Farrant

PL. 1.29 Left: Cheetah, Masai Mara, Kenya.
Photo: W. Farrant

The Fate of Light/Light Paths

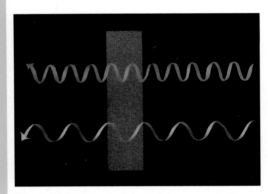

Fig. 1.16 Transmission: light waves of all colours pass through a colourless transparent medium.

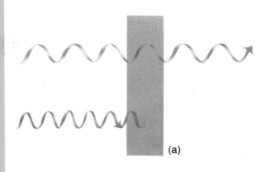

(a)

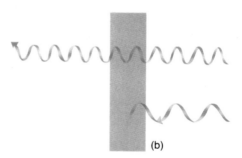

(b)

Fig. 1.17 Absorption: a red transparent medium absorbs all wavelengths of light except red (a); a blue transparent medium absorbs all wavelengths except blue (b)

Transmission (fig. 1.16)

Transmission occurs when light passes through a transparent or translucent medium to an observer, e.g. when light travels through a glass window. A transparent medium like glass allows most of the light through, so that objects can be seen clearly through it. A translucent medium like paraffin wax allows only some of the light through, so objects cannot be seen through it; some of the light is absorbed, some is transmitted, some is reflected and some is scattered from a translucent object. If a transparent or translucent medium is coloured, e.g. a stained-glass window, some wavelengths of light pass through (i.e. are transmitted) but

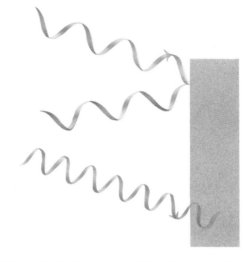

Fig. 1.18 Reflection: red light bounces off an opaque red object, while light of other colours is absorbed.

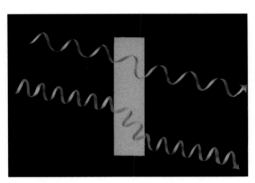

Fig. 1.19 Refraction: when light waves pass from one transparent substance into another, their speed changes and they bend; blue light waves are bent more than red.

some are absorbed. An opaque object is one that does not transmit any light at all, such as a sheet of metal.

Absorption (fig. 1.17)

When light strikes a surface, the energy of some or all of its wavelengths is removed by chemical colorants in the object; the energy absorbed is converted to heat. The remaining energy of the wavelengths of light that have not been absorbed, is reflected back to an observer who perceives it as colour, e.g. the pigments in the surface of a green leaf absorb all colours of light except green, which is reflected back to the observer.

Reflection (fig. 1.18)

When light strikes a surface and bounces off, it is said to be reflected. Most objects do not produce their own light; they are seen because they reflect the light coming from a luminous body, like the sun, toward the eyes of an observer. The colour of an object depends on

which wavelengths of light are reflected and which are absorbed. A red apple reflects only the red light that reaches it from a light source; all the other colours are absorbed at its surface. The smoother a surface, the more regular is the reflection of light from it and the shinier it appears. A rough surface appears dull because light waves are reflected irregularly from it, in many directions. Reflection is responsible for us being able to see the colours of plants and animals, and the colours of the planets and the moon. Both reflection and refraction are involved in the formation of rainbows.

Refraction (fig. 1.19)

When light passes obliquely from one transparent medium into another transparent medium of different density, such as from air to glass, it is deflected or bent away from its original path because its speed changes in the new medium, i.e. it is refracted. Different wavelengths or colours are refracted at slightly different angles because of their different energies: red (long wavelength, low energy) is deflected least. Refraction is the reason that a coloured spectrum is seen when white light passes from the air into a glass prism. Refraction also accounts for the apparent displacement of a straw in a glass of water or a seastar in a rockpool. Refraction is involved in many atmospheric phenomena, such as rainbows and halos.

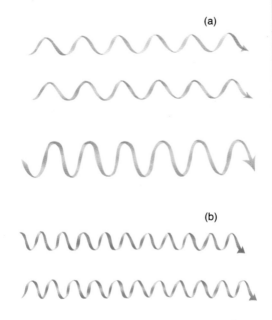

(a)

(b)

Fig. 1.20 Interference: when two light waves are in phase, they interfere positively to reinforce each other and produce a wave with double the intensity of colour (a). When two waves are out of phase they cancel each other and no colour is seen (b).

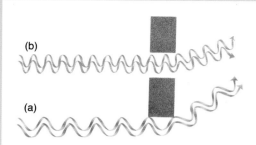

Fig. 1.21 Diffraction: light waves passing an opaque object or through a narrow opening tend to bend around the corners rather than continue straight ahead; red light (a) is diffracted more than blue (b).

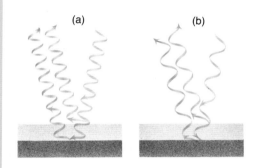

Fig. 1.22 Iridescence: when a light wave is partially reflected and partially transmitted at the surface of a thin layer of transparent material (e.g. a bubble), the two parts of the original wave may interfere with each other when the transmitted wave is reflected from a lower layer and re-emerges at the surface. In this case the blue waves are in phase and their colour is reinforced (a) but the red waves are out of phase and their colour is cancelled (b).

Interference (fig. 1.20)

When light waves from a source separate, follow different paths and then recombine and interfere with each other, the colour of some wavelengths intensifies. Waves that are in phase because their crests and troughs coincide will combine to produce a single new wave with the same wavelength (and thus colour) but with higher peaks. The colour of the waves that are out of phase will be cancelled. Interference causes the colours seen in a thin layer of oil on a puddle and the colours of soap bubbles. There are two types of interference colours caused by diffraction or by reflection and refraction.

Diffraction (fig. 1.21)

When a light ray passes by the edge of an opaque object it spreads around the corner of the object. The degree of this spreading, or diffraction, depends upon the wavelength of the light. Light rays are also diffracted if they pass through a narrow opening, or a series of tiny lines or slits (called a diffraction grating) whose width is less than the wavelength of the light. Waves of different wavelengths are diffracted to different degrees, so the original ray of light spreads out and breaks up, forming light and dark or coloured bands. These bands occur because the light wave interacts on itself. The parts that have arrived by different routes interfere with each other, either reinforcing each other in the light bands or coloured areas, or cancelling each other in the dark bands.

Iridescence (fig. 1.22)

Interference of many light waves reflected from layers within an object creates iridescence. The light may be reflected from the front and back surfaces of thin layers, from layers of particles or air pockets, or from the faults and boundaries in crystalline materials. This phenomenon is responsible for the metallic lustre of many animals, such as beetles, birds and fish, and for the colours of opals, mother-of-pearl, some crystals and even some plants.

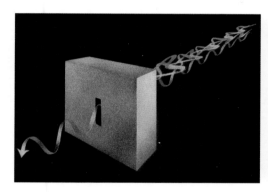

Fig. 1.23 Polarization: in an unpolarised wave of light the photons oscillate in all directions at ninety degrees to the line of disturbance of the wave. In polarised light (e.g. light passing through a polarising filter) the photons all oscillate in the same direction.

Polarisation (fig. 1.23)

Ordinary light waves vibrate randomly in all directions, whereas if they are polarised they vibrate in only one plane. The effect of a polarising filter is easily seen by looking through polaroid sunglasses. The coating on the lenses cuts out many of the light waves that reflect directly off a water surface to cause glare. However, if the head is tilted sideways so the glasses are at right angles, the light coming from the direction of the water surface is no longer polarised and the glare will be seen. Some naturally occurring crystals like tourmaline have the ability to polarise light by allowing through only those waves vibrating in one direction.

Scattering (fig. 1.24)

The term scattering refers to the deflection, or diffraction, of photons of light through collisions with other particles, regardless of the size of the particles. Scattering by large particles, relative to the wavelength of light (Mie scattering), is largely responsible for the colours of clouds and pollution haze. Large particles tend to scatter all wavelengths of light equally in all directions, so the resulting light is a mixture of all wavelengths and is white.

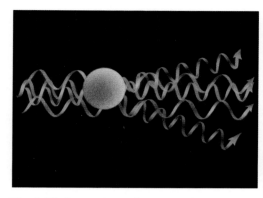

Fig. 1.24 Scattering: when particles in air or water are larger than wavelengths of visible light, they scatter waves only slightly .

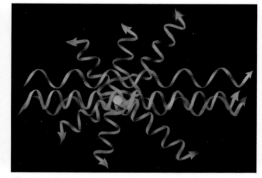

Fig. 1.25 Rayleigh scattering: when particles in air or water are small relative to light wavelength they scatter blue light preferentially.

Rayleigh scattering (fig. 1.25)

Rayleigh scattering, named after its discoverer, British physicist John William Strutt Rayleigh (1842-1919), is a special type of scattering of light by extremely small particles. These are usually air molecules (e.g nitrogen and oxygen), whose size is only a fraction (usually less than 10%) of the wavelength of light. They are too small to selectively absorb light of different wavelengths. Light striking these tiny particles transfers its energy to them, causing them to become excited and re-emit the light in nearly all directions. The smaller the particles, the more intensely they scatter the shorter wavelengths of light: blue light is scattered more intensely than red light, so to an observer the light source appears redder and the surroundings bluer. Ultraviolet light, which has an even shorter wavelength than blue light, is scattered even more efficiently, and this is why we can still get a suntan on a dull day.

Rayleigh scattering creates the blue of the sky and the oceans, the blue of shadows and the blueness of distant mountains. It also accounts for the orange and red of a rising or setting sun.

CHAPTER 2

COLOUR IN THE UNIVERSE

The language of astronomy is particularly colourful: e.g. the universe contains red-shifted galaxies, red giants, white dwarfs and black holes. The universe is the system in which everything exists or happens: apart from Earth, it contains celestial bodies like planets, stars and galaxies, as well as dust, gas and nebulae. These celestial bodies are seen from Earth because of the light they emit or reflect.

Although colour is present in the universe, it is not always apparent, especially to the naked eye. Techniques like colour photography and spectroscopy, however, have shown that the universe is coloured (see BOX 1).

EARTH: JEWEL OF THE SOLAR SYSTEM

Seen from space, Earth is blue, green, white and brown. Clouds in the atmosphere are white, oceans dark blue and continents green and brown (pl. 2.1). These colours can vary with atmospheric circulation and changing amounts of airborne particles and water vapour.

Earth and its atmosphere reflect about 40% of light received from the sun: this fraction (0.4) is known as Earth's albedo. Air molecules in the atmosphere cause Rayleigh scattering of some incoming sunlight (see p.11). This is why Earth's

PL. 2.1 Right: Earth from space: this photo extends from the Mediterranean Sea area to the Antarctic south polar ice cap. *Photo: NASA*

PL. 2.4 Left: Varying amounts of the unlit side of Earth (where it is night) can be seen from space. *Photo: NASA*

atmosphere appears as a blue halo around the planet when viewed from space (pl. 2.2). The moon is not blue when seen from space because it does not have a scattering atmosphere (pls 2.3, 2.4). The albedo of Earth (0.4) is greater than that of the moon (0.07), so Earth appears brighter from the moon than the moon does from Earth.

THE MOON

The moon itself is essentially brownish grey, the colour of its rocky surface: it has large areas of lava plains with dark volcanic iron- and magnesium-containing basalt (pls 2.5, 2.6). Moonlight is sunlight reflected off the moon's surface towards Earth: we see a varying amount of the sunlit side of the moon as it orbits Earth, and this is the reason for its phases. Sometimes, during partial phases of the moon we can just detect the area in shadow when it reflects Earth's bluish white light and this is known as earthshine or ashen light (pl. 2.7).

The colour of the moon as seen from Earth depends on its position in the sky and the airborne particles and water vapour in Earth's atmosphere. A full moon close to the horizon is redder than a pale yellow full moon high in the night sky because of Rayleigh scattering and coloured light reflected from the setting sun.

PL. 2.2 Blue halo of atmosphere surrounds Earth when seen from space. Rain clouds over New Guinea. *Photo: NASA*

PL. 2.3 Far left: Earth's moon does not have a blue scattering atmosphere. Crescent Earth rising into the black lunar sky. *Photo: NASA*

PL. 2.5 Left: We see the moon because sunlight is reflected off its surface. *Photo: NASA*

PL. 2.6 Far left: The moon's surface is brownish grey because of its iron- and magnesium-containing rocks. *Photo: NASA*

PL. 2.7 Left: Earthshine: new moon, normally not visible, lit briefly by light reflected from bright clouds at sunrise. *Photo: L. Rodgers*

PL. 2.8 During an eclipse of the moon, the part blocked by Earth appears red due to scattering by our atmosphere. *Photo: W. Farrant*

Once in a blue moon

The rare phenomenon of a blue moon occurs because of the presence of particular types of particles, such as volcanic dust, high in the atmosphere. The moon appears to be indigo, blue or even green when the particles are relatively large and fairly uniform in size. The particles are exactly the right size to absorb or scatter yellow and red wavelengths, leaving the blue and green wavelengths of moonlight. On the day before or after a blue moon is seen, a blue (or green) sun may also be seen, during the day, for the same reason. During a lunar eclipse, when Earth lies between the sun and the moon, the moon is reddish orange due to Rayleigh scattering of the sun's rays passing through Earth's atmosphere (pl. 2.8).

Moonlight

Coloured objects seen in sunlight do not appear to be coloured when seen by moonlight because light reflected from the moon's surface is insufficient to activate cones in the human eye. Cones are the light-sensitive cells responsible for daytime and colour vision. Rods are the light sensitive cells responsible for vision in the dark: they detect light but not colour (see p. 113).

While we may be incapable of distinguishing a great deal of colour in objects lit by the moon, the moon's light is coloured. It is somewhat redder than sunlight, because of reflection from the brownish grey surface; however, we perceive its light as a cooler, somewhat bluer colour. This is because we associate the moon with cooler night-time temperatures and the sun with the day's warmth.

PL. 2.9 Venus. *Photo: NASA*

PL. 2.10 Mars is red due to particles of limonite, a brown iron oxide that occurs in the planet's surface and atmosphere. *Photo: NASA*

THE OTHER PLANETS

Planets are celestial objects that orbit a star. Apart from Earth, there are eight other planets that orbit the sun in our solar system. Their colours are pale even when viewed through a telescope. However, we have information on their colours from various unmanned spacecraft that have either flown past them or landed during the last few decades.

Mercury and Venus

Small and closest to the sun, Mercury has virtually no atmosphere and so is very hot by day and very cold by night. Its surface is made of bare silicate rocks, similar in colour to the surface of Earth's moon.

From Earth and space, Venus appears brilliant yellow, with faint patterns in its upper clouds. The sky is bright orange because of sulfuric acid in the clouds (pl. 2.9). These reflect sunlight and make the planet easily seen from Earth. The surface rocks are reddish brown, extremely hot and sometimes molten.

The red planet

Mars is known as the red planet because fine-grained orange-brown dust covers its surface (pl. 2.10). This dust is limonite, a brown iron oxide, and large amounts of it occur in the rocks on the planet's surface and in its atmosphere. Yellow clouds are also seen, particularly at the hottest times of the Martian year, when the planet is closest to the sun. These clouds are dust storms, usually small, but which can sometimes cover the entire planet. White clouds and hazes, caused by mists and surface frosts, are also seen near the polar caps and over volcanoes. White polar caps are made of solid water (ice) and solid carbon dioxide (dry ice) and are best seen in summer when not covered by cloud. The average surface temperature on Mars is -23°C.

The Martian sky is permanently pink because limonite particles are suspended in the atmosphere after storms (pl. 2.11). The sky is not blue as on Earth because Martian air is extremely thin and the limonite particles in the air are large relative to the wavelength of light. The particles preferentially absorb blue light and effectively act as mirrors by scattering the remaining wavelengths: the colour of the atmosphere is therefore pinkish, like the particles themselves.

PL. 2.11 The sky on Mars is pink because limonite particles are too large to preferentially scatter blue light. *Photo: NASA*

Jupiter's Great Red Spot

Jupiter is the largest, most massive and colourful planet in our solar system. Viewed through a telescope, Jupiter is surrounded by a variety of coloured bands. These bands relate to different atmospheric conditions and include tropical, subtropical, temperate and polar zones. They show changes in structure and colour with time, e.g. yellow colours sometimes seen near the equator may be storms created at zonal boundaries by opposing winds, like hurricanes on Earth.

Jupiter's upper atmosphere contains hydrogen gas and clouds of ammonia crystals. White and orange clouds form in the highest, coldest parts of the atmosphere. Colours relate to electric charge of particles in the clouds and the amount of sulfur present. Darker brown zones and blue-grey areas are the lowest, warmest parts of the atmosphere; they are made of gases containing ammonium hydrosulfide crystals and water-ice crystals (fig. 2.1).

The Great Red Spot is a relatively stable feature of Jupiter. It has been observed since the seventeenth century and has shown some colour variation though remaining the same in structure. The Red Spot moves gradually and irregularly in longitude and is believed to be a giant, self-sustaining, high-pressure region of atmospheric disturbance, colder than its surroundings. The red colour may be due to red phosphorus. On occasions, white ovals are seen on Jupiter and these are also likely to be atmospheric because they move in a way similar to the Red Spot. Red and blue-green can sometimes be seen on the planet, the result of atmospheric refraction. One of Jupiter's moons, Io, is usually a bright red-orange because of its active volcanoes and the high sulfur content of its surface. However, because sulfur changes colour with temperature, other colours like yellow, green and black are also seen. The smooth surface of Europa, another of Jupiter's moons, is white because of its ice.

Saturn's coloured rings

Saturn is a dull yellow. It has bands but they are not as vividly coloured as those of Jupiter, probably because Saturn is colder. The visibility of dark and bright bands, and the transient spots on Saturn, are

PL. 2.12 The colours of Saturn's rings, thought to be composed of ice, are probably due to various impurities in the ice. *Photo: NASA*

ammonia clouds

ammonium hydrosulfide clouds

water ice clouds

Fig. 2.1 Jupiter's atmosphere contains clouds of bluish water-ice, dark brown clouds of ammonium hydrosulfide and whitish clouds of ammonia.

PL. 2.13 The sun's yellow chromosphere, the coolest part of its atmosphere, is visible during a total eclipse. *Photo: NASA*

furnace. Though they may be white-hot or even blue-hot, most are too far away from Earth for their heat to reach us. We feel only the heat of our closest star, the sun. The sun is a yellow star that emits light in the middle of the visible spectrum. It has a relatively low mass compared to other stars and will eventually become a white star, producing no energy at all.

The sun is made of hydrogen and helium; hydrogen atoms fuse to form helium (with the release of energy) in the central core. The visible colour of the sun is that of its cooler surface or photosphere, which is the source of virtually all light emitted by the sun and received on Earth's surface. Outside the photosphere is the chromosphere, a red rim visible during a total solar eclipse, when the moon blocks the sun's surface. This colour is caused by the emission of red light by hydrogen. The coolest outermost gaseous layer, or atmosphere, of the sun, the corona, extends well out into the solar system, and can be seen as a pearly halo of light during a total eclipse (pl. 2.13). Its colour is similar to that of sunlight as we know it.

Sometimes solar flares occur, as a result of energy being released: charged particles are ejected into the solar system, as the solar wind, and they create disturbances such as auroras.

Starlight

Continually moving particles in Earth's atmosphere cause light rays from stars to bend slightly, by refraction and scattering, so their images appear to move or twinkle, especially near the horizon where the path of their light through the atmosphere is

restricted by a thick haze over the planet's surface. Coloured clouds of pale blues, browns and whites lie longitudinally over the planet (pl. 2.12). Their colours are due to different mixtures of chemicals like methane, ammonia and sulfur. Saturn's rings, thought to be composed of pieces of ice, or ice-covered material, show a variety of colours. One of Saturn's moons, Titan, shows interesting variable colours, including white, yellowish pink and red, caused by organic compounds in its nitrogen atmosphere.

Uranus, Neptune and Pluto

These outermost planets have surface temperatures below −200°C. Uranus' blue-green is probably due to the presence of methane, ammonia and water on its surface, seen through a clear atmosphere of essentially hydrogen and helium. Methane absorbs red wavelengths of light, causing the blue-green of the planet. The overall bluish colour of Neptune, named after the Roman god of the sea, is due to its surface haze: like Uranus, methane on its surface absorbs red light and causes the planet to appear bluish. Neptune has various belts and zones, and white clouds of frozen methane. Pluto is the smallest planet, smaller even than our moon; its colour and the composition of its atmosphere are unknown.

THE SUN AND OTHER STARS

Stars are luminous balls of gas, held together by their own gravity, which produce light by nuclear reactions. Most light in the universe comes from stars, each of which is like an enormous nuclear

PL. 2.14 We can only detect the colours of the brightest stars by eye. Orion at dawn, New Zealand. *Photo: L. McLay*

longest. Slight changes in the colours of twinkling stars are due to the slightly different angles at which different wavelengths of starlight are bent or refracted (pl. 2.14).

Refraction and scattering by Earth's atmosphere also affect star colours. The colour of a setting star, as it appears to move towards the horizon, can be seen in photographs of star trails (pl. 2.15); the trails become dimmer and redder closer to the horizon due to Earth's atmosphere (pl. 2.16).

Stars emit light composed of many wavelengths. Their spectra are continuous or flat, meaning that no particular wavelengths are dominant. Star colours are usually weak pastels or whitish colours, in comparison with the vivid colours of reflective objects like nebulae. While most stars are not strongly coloured, some have only one or two strong spectral colours because of large proportions of one or two elements in their composition: these stars are unusual in being more vividly coloured.

Colour, temperature and composition

The colour of a star is related to its temperature: hotter stars emit more blue light and cooler stars emit more red light. Astronomers have ordered the colours of stars into a sequence: in order of decreasing temperature, the colours are blue and green, white, whitish and yellow, orange and red. Each step in the star colour sequence used by astronomers is known as a spectral class, of which there are seven: O, B, A, F, G, K and M. Each spectral class relates both to the colour of a star and its composition, e.g. white, green or blue class A stars are composed mainly of hydrogen, with some ionised metals.

Dark lines within the spectra of stars are due to the presence of gases in the stars' atmospheres, e.g. the white star Rigel has strong hydrogen lines, and the red star Betelgeuse has a banded spectrum with very weak hydrogen lines.

Coloured dwarfs and giants

The colours and brightnesses of stars also relate to their mass, i.e. the amount of matter they contain. Red stars are generally cooler, duller and less massive than blue or white stars from which they may have evolved, but may be much larger in diameter. Stars which reach the stage of being massive red supergiants may end their lives by exploding as supernovas, explosions in which much of the star mass is blown out into space as a cloud of gas and dust, and the core of the star becomes a very dense neutron star. When a neutron star eventually ceases to shine, it may collapse and form a black hole, with a gravitational field so strong that it can no longer emit any radiation (fig. 2.1).

Stars which do not follow this evolutionary path may degenerate eventually to white dwarfs, stars with low mass and luminosity but high surface temperature. Since they do not produce energy, white dwarf stars eventually cool down to become non-luminous black or brown dwarfs. Brown dwarf stars have extremely low mass and are cool and very dim, emitting mainly infra-red wavelengths: little is known of their eventual fate.

PL. 2.15 Above: Because Earth rotates once every 24 hours, the stars appear to move in circles about the celestial poles. *Photo: M. Porteners.*

PL. 2.16 Left: Time-exposure photograph of the sun; the trail reddens as the sun nears the horizon. *Photo: Anglo-Australian Telescope*

Cluster colours

The colours we see in a star cluster, a group of stars with a common origin, relate to the age of the cluster: for this reason there are certain common combinations of colour and brightness. The bright stars in young clusters are blue and the faint stars red, whereas somewhat older clusters contain red stars, and very old clusters contain only faint white dwarfs (pl. 2.17).

NEBULAE

Nebulae are clouds of interstellar gas or dust lit by stars in them or nearby. They are made of the gas and dust derived from exploding stars, especially red supergiants, e.g. Antares, which produces most of the dust particles in the Milky Way. Gas and dust

Fig. 2.2 Stars are formed from clouds of collapsing gaseous material. The fate of any one star then depends on its mass. Small stars may eventually become red supergiants and form planetary nebulae, eventually become black dwarf stars. More massive stars may end their lives by exploding as supernovae, becoming neutron stars or forming black holes.

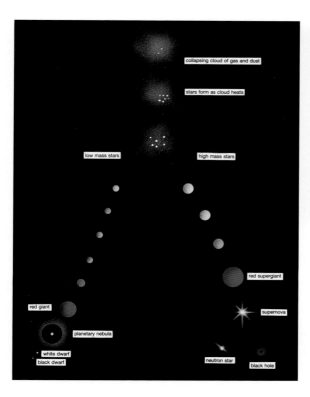

PL. 2.17 The Jewel Box star cluster, containing bright blue stars and a red giant star (Kappa Crucis). *Photo: Anglo-Australian Telescope*

The spectra of emission nebulae are typically emission-line spectra, consisting of one or a small number of different wavelengths: for this reason they are intensely coloured. Emission lines are due to atoms of gaseous material: ionised oxygen causes lines in the ultraviolet and ionised hydrogen in the red and blue-green parts of the spectrum.

Planetary nebulae

A supernova or exploding star produces an emission nebula when the outer layers of the star, usually a red supergiant, expand outwards and are lit by the remnant or neutron star. These nebulae sometimes take the form of rings or discs around the central neutron star and so are known as planetary nebulae. A supernova first appears as a very bright light in the sky, e.g. the 1987 supernova produced orange-yellow light when it was first seen. With time, the glowing shell or nebula of a supernova moves further outwards, the colours whitening with increasing distance from the central star (pl. 2.20).

are continually being recycled in the universe. There are several different types of nebulae.

Emission nebulae

Emission nebulae emit light themselves as a result of ultraviolet light they absorb from nearby hot bright stars. The ultraviolet light ionises hydrogen gas in the nebulae, causing light emission. Emission nebulae are found in parts of a galaxy where newly formed blue and white stars give off enough heat and light to cause the surrounding gas to shine as well, e.g. the star Sigma Scorpii emits enough ultraviolet light to ionise hydrogen so the nearby nebula is red (pls 2.18, 2.19).

PL. 2.18 The Trifid Nebula, in Sagittarius: emission of light by hydrogen causes red, reflection of starlight by particles of dust causes blue. *Photo: Anglo-Australian Telescope*

PL. 2.19 The Orion Nebula, an emission nebula where stars are forming. *Photo: Anglo-Australian Telescope*

Reflection nebulae

Reflection nebulae are clouds of dust and gas which do not contain stars or produce their own light. They are visible on Earth because they scatter or reflect starlight from nearby very hot, bright stars; they also absorb some starlight. Since a coloured object is by definition one that reflects and absorbs wavelengths of light selectively, reflection nebulae produce the strongest colours seen in the universe.

Most reflection nebulae are blue because the stars nearby, whose light they reflect, are usually young and blue (pl. 2.21). The colour of incoming starlight is important in determining the colour of a reflection nebula because the dust grains in nebulae are similar in size to the wavelength of light. Particles this size produce Mie scattering, a type of scattering between Rayleigh scattering and large particle scattering, in which colours are maintained but are slightly bluer. The size of the dust grains is known from the type of scattering observed to occur.

Nebulae do not just reflect or emit light: while a reflection nebula may be basically blue, it may also contain red and pink colours if it emits some light because of heating by a nearby hot star (pl. 2.22). While most reflection nebulae are blue with some red or pink, others exist that are green, yellow and brown: the causes of these colours are unknown.

Interstellar reddening

The colour of a reflection nebula also depends on the thickness of the dust it contains: the reds of reflection nebulae are often caused by interstellar reddening. This occurs when starlight passes through the dust of nebulae. Because dust grains are similar in size to the wavelength of light, they absorb some light emitted by stars, causing them to appear dimmer. The dust particles also scatter some light. In both cases, blue light is lost because its shorter wavelength makes it more vulnerable to absorption or scattering

PL. 2.20 Above: The Helix Nebula: a planetary nebula, formed as a sun-sized star sheds its outer layers at the end of its life. *Photo: Anglo-Australian Telescope*

PL. 2.21 Left: Reflection nebula in Orion; dust particles preferentially scatter blue starlight. *Photo: Anglo-Australian Telescope*

PL. 2.22 The Horsehead Nebula in Orion: its colours are due both to reflection and emission of light. *Photo: Anglo-Australian Telescope*

by dust. Most of the longer wavelength red light passes through relatively unaffected so stars appear redder (pl. 2.23). If the dust of a nebula is very thick, most incoming starlight is scattered many times; as a result the nebula appears very pale with few colours. A growing nebula can also dim the light of the star or stars responsible for its formation. (p1. 2.23 a & b)

Dark nebulae

If the dust of a nebula is very thick and does not contain stars, the nebula may entirely obscure background stars. Such nebulae are known as dark nebulae, e.g. the Coal Sack and the Horsehead Nebula. They appear as dark patches against the starry night sky (pl. 2.24).

COMETS

A comet is an object, composed of gases and dust, which orbits the sun. While many comets have an orbit entirely within the solar system, some have hyperbolic orbits that extend well outside it. We can usually see a comet only when it gets close enough

PL. 2.23a Two star forming regions in Carina, at different distances from Earth: the closer one is pink, but the more distant one is red due to interstellar reddening. *Photo: Anglo-Australian Telescope*

PL. 2.23b Below left: Interstellar reddening of blue light causes the green of the head of this cometary globule. *Photo: Anglo-Australian Telescope*

PL. 2.24 Below right: Dark nebulae like these Bok globules are regions of dust that contain no stars and are so thick that they obscure the light of celestial bodies beyond. *Photo: Anglo-Australian Telescope*

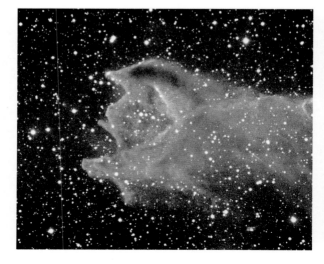

to the sun for its tails to develop. A comet has a nucleus, made up mainly of ices of water, ammonia and methane. As it approaches the sun, heat evaporates the ices to form a gaseous fuzzy head or coma which surrounds the nucleus and emits light because of ionisation of its gases by ultraviolet wavelengths of sunlight. When the comet is even closer to the sun, one or more types of tail form (pl. 2.25).

Falling stars

When dust particles, e.g. from the coma of a comet, meet Earth's atmosphere they burn up to produce the brilliant white, yellow or blue flashes of meteors or falling stars. Meteors are white, yellow or blue-hot because of friction caused by Earth's atmosphere. A meteor shower, best seen before sunrise, is a spectacular sight. Meteors should not be confused with meteorites which originate in the asteroid belt, a region of the solar system between Mars and Jupiter containing dust particles and rocks which orbit the sun: these are also known as the minor planets.

GALAXIES

Galaxies are the largest individual conglomerations of matter in the universe: they consist of celestial bodies like planets, stars and nebulae. Galaxies are so large that light takes thousands of years to travel from one side to the other, and the distances between galaxies are even bigger: light takes millions of years to travel between them. Our galaxy, the Milky Way, contains over 100 000 000 stars and there may be the same number of galaxies in the universe.

Galaxies are classified according to their shape, and there are three basic types: irregular, spiral and elliptical. The shape of a galaxy is thought to depend upon the degree of rotation of the gas cloud from which the galaxy originally formed and from the rate at which stars are formed during the galaxy's lifetime. Irregular galaxies have no distinct shape and are composed mostly of gases. Elliptical galaxies contain mostly old stars and little dust or gas: they are therefore reddish yellow. The most colourful galaxies are spiral galaxies (pl. 2.26).

Red shift

The light from a luminous object that is moving away from an observer at a rapid rate shows a shift in the position of the dark bands of its spectrum, towards the red wavelengths: this phenomenon is known as a red shift. Because the spectra of many galaxies show this red shift, astronomers believe that they are rapidly moving away from us. If a galaxy were approaching an observer on Earth, it would appear bluer. The movement of galaxies away from us provides good evidence that the universe is expanding.

In the next chapter we will look at the colourful effects caused by Earth's atmosphere.

PL. 2.25 Above left: The coma of Halleys comet is tinged blue, while the short yellow tail consists of dust grains that reflect sunlight. *Photo: Anglo-Australian Telescope*

PL. 2.26 Above right: Messier 100, a spiral galaxy: the arms contain blue stars; red or pink patches along the edges of the arms are newly forming emission nebulae; between the arms are dark lanes of dust, sprinkled with stars, which appear somewhat redder or yellower than other stars in the arms of the galaxy because of interstellar reddening. *Photo: Anglo-Australian Telescope*

SEEING STARS

We can study the universe with the naked eye or a telescope (these were the main means of doing so until this century). However, shortcomings exist in both telescopes and the human eye.

It is difficult to see any colour in the night sky by eye, because of limitations in the human eye itself. Even when we look through a telescope we see in colour only those objects that are very bright (pl. 2.27).

Some telescope lenses suffer from the problem of chromatic aberration: the glass bends blue light more than other colours so objects appear blurred by a surrounding rainbow of coloured light (fig. 2.3). An achromatic lens minimises chromatic aberration. As our eyes are not very sensitive to the colour of small sources of light, it is often easier to see star colours if the telescope is slightly out of focus: this makes the images of distant objects larger. Colours of celestial objects are also easier to see against contrasting colours: this is the case for double stars that are relatively close together and different colours.

Spectroscopes, C.C.D.s (charge coupled devices, linked to video screens) and photographic cameras, however, reveal details of colour in the universe that we cannot see through telescopes.

Spectroscopy

As discussed in detail on p. 5, a spectroscope enables us to study the spectra of objects in order to obtain information about their nature. It can tell us about a star's composition, temperature, magnetic field, velocity and direction of travel. Stars, like all substances in the universe, are formed from a variety of different chemical elements. Because stars are so hot, they emit light: each element they contain emits light of a characteristic colour. The only way we can discover what far-away objects in the universe, such as stars, are made

PL. 2.27 It is difficult to detect colour in stars by eye because they are point sources of light, almost at the limit of detection of colour by the eye; as well, there is insufficient light for activating the colour-sensitive cells or cones, in the retina. Orion at dawn. *Photo: L. McLay*

of, is to study the various wavelengths or colours of light they emit. The energy measured for these particular wavelengths gives information on the relative amounts of each element present in them.

Charge coupled devices and videos

These days, most astronomers record information about the universe electronically, using C.C.D.s. The C.C.D. uses a silicon chip to produce images of celestial objects as video signals. A telescope focuses an image onto the C.C.D. Light photons from celestial objects passing through the telescope strike an array of capacitors, generating a charge. Signals are amplified and sent to a video screen. While much useful information can be obtained and recorded, the images are inferior to photographs.

Photographing the colours of the universe

Photography enables us to 'see' colour in the universe because the camera integrates light received from objects over a long time: our eyes are incapable of doing this. Cameras are also able to detect light at levels too low for the human eye to detect. Celestial objects are usually photographed using a telescope to focus an image onto photographic plates.

It is impossible to see the colours of all the stars in a photograph that covers a large portion of the sky. This is simply because stars vary in brightness, are different sizes and are located at different distances from Earth: some will be over-exposed in the photograph while others will be invisible because they are under-exposed.

One ingenious method for showing the colours of stars in a single photograph has been devised by the Australian astro-photographer David Malin. During a half-hour exposure of the sky, the focus of the camera is altered slightly and by the same amount at a regular time interval, say every five minutes. For each star, one of the focus settings will be correctly exposed and show the colour of the star (pl. 2.28).

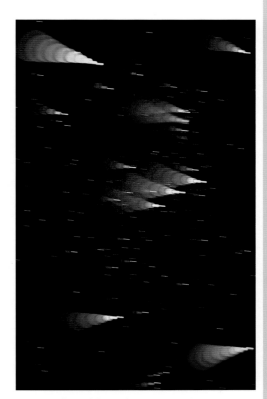

PL. 2.28 David Malin's method of recording star colours in a photograph: one of the colour 'swatches' for each star will be correctly exposed and show its colour. Orion. *Photo: Anglo-Australian Telescope*

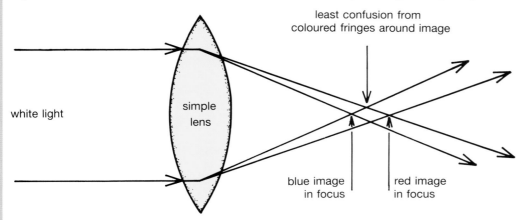

least confusion from coloured fringes around image

white light

simple lens

blue image in focus

red image in focus

Fig. 2.3 Chromatic aberration affects some lenses because the differently coloured wavelengths of light are separated by refraction.

CHAPTER 3

ATMOSPHERIC COLOUR

Earth is surrounded by a gaseous layer called the atmosphere which extends about 400 km above its surface. Composed of nitrogen (78%), oxygen (21%) and other gases like carbon dioxide, it also contains particles, both natural in origin and the result of human activity. Small aerosol particles (suspended in air) include volatile oils produced by plants, volcanic dust, forest fire smoke and metallurgical fumes; larger particles include sea salt, oil, tobacco smoke, fly-ash, insecticides, silt, storm dust, sand, clay, pollen, bacteria and water droplets (pls 3.1, 3.2). Many coloured phenomena occur in or are associated with Earth's atmosphere because of the interaction of sunlight or charged particles with air molecules and with other particles in the air.

BLUE SKY

When we look at a clear blue sky, light travels from the sky towards us (pl. 3.3). Since this light originates from the sun, it must be re-directed in some way. The blue of a clear sky in the middle of the day is due

to Rayleigh scattering, discussed in detail on p. 11 (fig. 3.1). If Earth lacked an atmosphere, there would be no particles to absorb or scatter sunlight and the sky would be black.

Moving molecules

The intensity of the sky's blue varies during the day and from day to day, largely because of the degree of movement of air molecules. Air molecules are constantly moving, as they are never equally distributed in the atmosphere. At a sub-microscopic level, small numbers of molecules coming close to each other create slightly dense pockets of air and leave behind less dense pockets. As this happens all the time, air is never uniform in density; higher density pockets produce stronger scattering and a more intense blue.

When large numbers of dust particles accumulate in the air in dry weather, the sky gradually brightens. Scattering by these particles adds white to the sky and makes the blue less intense. This is because the

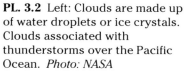

PL. 3.2 Left: Clouds are made up of water droplets or ice crystals. Clouds associated with thunderstorms over the Pacific Ocean. *Photo: NASA*

PL. 3.1 Below: The layers in Earth's atmosphere each consist of fine particles suspended in a stable layer of air. *Photo: NASA*

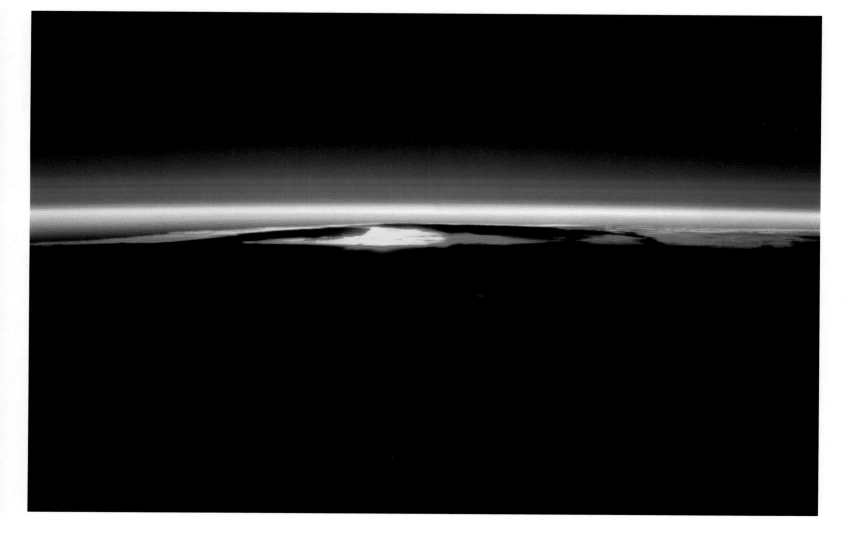

PL. 3.3 A blue sky is due to Rayleigh scattering of blue light from the direct path of sunlight coming to Earth. *Photo: P. Farrant*

particles are large relative to wavelengths of visible light, and no longer scatter blue light preferentially but tend to scatter all wavelengths more or less equally. The blueness of the sky increases noticeably after a heavy rainstorm when rain has washed away larger dust particles from the air.

The sky is bluest in the middle of the day when the path of sunlight through Earth's atmosphere is most direct and comes in contact with fewest particles. About 10% of the light is scattered and the disc of the sun itself appears whitish yellow. At other times of the day, when sunlight passes through a greater distance of Earth's atmosphere, the light is scattered more often and encounters more particles that scatter wavelengths other than blue. This has the effect of whitening the blue of the sky.

Sunrise and Sunset

The colours of sunrise and sunset are also caused by Rayleigh scattering. As more blue light is removed by this process, the sun becomes less blue. At sunset, when light travels through a greater distance of the atmosphere, not only blue but also green wavelengths are scattered by air molecules and dust particles, so that only yellow and red wavelengths reach the observer, and the sun appears redder (pl. 3.4). At sunrise and sunset the sun lights up the sky immediately around it in the same colours (pls 3.5, 3.6). Further away from the sun, colours become less intense and the sky whitens. The whiteness is a result of multiple scattering of sunlight: the more molecules light encounters, the more it is scattered; and more wavelengths become involved, so that eventually all the wavelengths of sunlight are scattered. When all the different wavelengths of

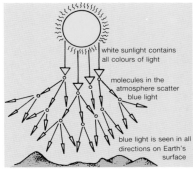

Fig. 3.1 The sky is blue because air molecules are small enough to scatter blue light preferentially (Rayleigh scattering).

PL. 3.5 Above: The colours of sunrise are also due to Rayleigh scattering of blue light. *Photo: W. Farrant*

PL. 3.4 Left: Reds and oranges of a setting sun are due to Rayleigh scattering of sunlight travelling through Earth's atmosphere. *Photo: R. Berthold*

PL. 3.6 The traditional folklore 'red sky at night, shepherd's delight; red sky in the morning, shepherd's warning' is often found to be correct. A red sky usually contains dust or water droplets. Dust is less likely to be present in the air in the morning, so the water droplets may belong to potential rain clouds. *Photo: P. Farrant*

sunlight are present they will mix to re-create white light. As the disc of the sun goes behind the horizon, on rare occasions there may be a flash of green (see BOX 1). Afterwards, the western sky remains coloured for some time with an afterglow due to particles in the atmosphere still scattering the sun's light from below the horizon. Colours in the eastern sky at sunset and twilight are less intense (pls 3.7-3.10).

Sunsets in deserts (pls 3.11, 3.12), during bushfires or after volcanic eruptions can be very red (pls 3.13, 3.14). The colours of a sunrise or a sunset in coastal areas are not usually as spectacular as they are inland: the sun itself may appear orange but overall the colours are whiter. This is because of water droplets in the air, which are relatively large and tend to scatter all wavelengths equally so the colours mix again to re-create white light. Unusually good sunsets in coastal areas sometimes occur when water droplets in the air are very small.

PL. 3.7 Right: The colours in the eastern sky at sunset are paler than those in the western sky because the sun's light has travelled further. Blues and greens are due to scattered light; dust particles in the upper atmosphere scatter sunlight still reaching them and create a glow; and the bluish colour is Earth's shadow, lit along the top by red light from the western sky. *Photo: M. Porteners*

PL. 3.8 Far right: After sunset the colours of the eastern sky merge into the violet of night, as Earth's shadow rises in the sky. *Photo: W. Farrant*

PL. 3.9 As Earth's shadow sets at dawn, the violet colour of the night sky takes on the colours of sunrise. *Photo: M. Porteners*

PL. 3.10 The sky at night is actually blue, though there is not enough light for our eyes to see any colour. *Photo: W. Farrant*

PL. 3.11 Desert sunset in Australia. *Photo: M. Porteners*

PL. 3.12 Dust particles from desert soils increase the amount of blue light scattering and make sunsets even redder. *Photo: M. Porteners*

PL. 3.13 Dust from volcanoes may remain high in the atmosphere for some time, producing some colourful atmospheric effects. *Photo: W. Farrant*

PL. 3.14 Volcanic dust, Mt Aso, southern Japan. *Photo: W. Farrant*

BLUE HAZE

Distant mountain ranges often appear to be covered in a blue haze (pl. 3.15). This happens in parts of the world like the Grand Canyon of the U.S.A. and the Blue Mountains of eastern Australia, where there is extensive vegetation, little human occupation and an atmosphere free of industrial by-products. Air circulation in these areas is good, with efficient exchange between the lower and upper parts of the atmosphere. Ozone from the upper atmosphere combines with terpenes to produce tiny particles that selectively scatter the blue wavelengths of sunlight and create the blue haze. Terpenes are naturally occurring molecules, containing hydrogen and carbon, that occur in the oils produced by some plants like eucalypts. Larger particles in the air, such as water vapour or salt (coastal regions), cause a blue haze to be whitened (pl. 3.16).

PL. 3.15 Above: Distant blues are due to Rayleigh scattering by molecules of air and small molecules of plant origin. *Photo: R. Berthold*

PL. 3.16 Left: In coastal areas a blue haze is often whiter because of water and salt in the air; these particles tend to scatter all wavelengths of light equally to produce white. *Photo: P. Farrant*

PL. 3.17 Although mist consists of colourless water droplets, it appears white because the droplets scatter all wavelengths of light. *Photo: W. Farrant*

PL. 3.18 Lens-shaped clouds on the tops of cool mountains are bright white because they contain small water droplets. *Photo: W. Farrant*

CLOUDS, MISTS AND FOG

Clouds, mists and fogs usually appear white, even though they contain colourless water droplets (pl. 3.17). As particles in the air become larger in size relative to wavelengths of light, Rayleigh scattering is replaced by non-selective scattering, in which all wavelengths of light are scattered equally and white light results. The difference in colour between the two types of scattering can be seen when looking at smoke: smoke composed of very tiny particles is blue, whereas it becomes whiter with increasing particle size. Black smoke not only scatters light but also absorbs it.

Clouds, consisting of water droplets or ice crystals, occur in the lower part of Earth's atmosphere, the troposphere, which extends 10-20 km above Earth's surface (fig. 3.2). Slight differences in the size of particles in a cloud will affect the intensity of light scattered and hence the cloud's brightness, because the intensity of scattered light depends on the ratio of surface area to volume of the particles. Bright, white, recently formed clouds are made of small

droplets, which have greater total surface areas relative to their volumes and scatter white light more intensely (pl. 3.18). Older, less white clouds have larger and fewer water droplets and these absorb more light. The brightness of a cloud is also related to the relative positions of the observer, the sun and the cloud. If a cloud reflects the sun's light straight to the observer, it appears to be very bright white. Seen from the other side, the same cloud will appear dark grey because it is in shadow (pl. 3.19). Clouds are often other colours (pl. 3.20) and many effects are produced by clouds that alternately block and filter sunlight (pl. 3.21).

Mother-of-pearl clouds

Mother-of-pearl or noctilucent clouds occur very high in the atmosphere (30-80 km above Earth's surface) and display faint iridescent light of different colours, especially silvery blue and gold. These clouds are seen only at night, for about two hours just after sunset or just before sunrise, usually at latitudes of 60-80°. They are high enough above Earth's surface to remain sunlit because they are out of Earth's shadow (which causes the darkness of night) for some time after the lower clouds have become dark.

The colours of mother-of-pearl clouds are formed by the diffraction of light (see p. 10) by ice crystals or droplets of water of extremely uniform size. Rays of sunlight are bent around the edges of the crystals or droplets, spreading out into their spectral colours

PL. 3.19 Grey parts of clouds are in shadow. *Photo: P. Farrant*

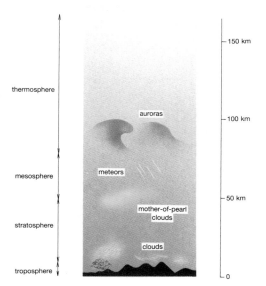

Fig. 3.2 Layers of Earth's atmosphere.

because the different wavelengths are bent by different amounts. These crystals and droplets form in the upper troposphere when water vapour, carried upwards in cold air currents from the polar regions, condenses around tiny particles of dust; these have come from the breakup of meteors in the thermosphere (the region of the atmosphere about 80 km above Earth's surface) or from volcanoes.

BROWN HAZE

We are familiar with the brown haze seen over large cities, e.g. Los Angeles and Tokyo frequently seem to be enveloped by it. Brown hazes result from human activities: increasingly dense population centres emit pollutants into the atmosphere, where they interact with light. Car exhaust is one of the major pollutants, producing gases like nitrogen dioxide, hydrocarbons and carbon monoxide, as well as particulate matter like carbon. Nitrogen dioxide, a toxic brown gas, makes photochemical smog brown.

The gases and particles (smoke, dust, fly-ash, oils, lead) that cause air pollution are generally large relative to the wavelength of light and so they are not effective as Rayleigh or blue-light scatterers. They scatter all wavelengths of sunlight to create an opaque haze that would be white if it were not coloured brown by nitrogen dioxide. Though pollutant particles may be in the same size range as naturally produced airborne particles like volcanic dust, they generally occur at lower atmospheric levels and are more noticeable. Unlike most natural particles, many pollutant particles are attracted to water droplets in the atmosphere, coating them and preventing them from evaporating. This increases their light-absorbing ability and causes the unpleasant glare of pollution haze.

COLOURED HALOS

Sometimes when the sun or moon is behind high, thin cirrostratus clouds or an ice fog high in the

atmosphere, a bright ring or halo of light can be seen around it. The ring, which appears at some distance from the sun or moon, is generally white but may be coloured, usually with an inner edge of red. Halos are seen in cold climate areas where the atmospheric temperature is low enough for clouds to contain ice crystals instead of water droplets. Halos are caused by refraction of sunlight or moonlight by ice crystals falling through the air. The ice crystals act like tiny prisms, dispersing light into spectral colours (pl. 3.22).

Whereas ice takes the form of snowflakes in the lower part of a cold atmosphere, at higher levels hexagonal ice crystals are commonly shaped like pencils and plates. When a ray of sunlight passes symmetrically through a pencil crystal, the light is refracted by a minimum angle of 22° (fig. 3.3).

As light cannot be refracted at angles below the minimum angle, no light reaches the inner region

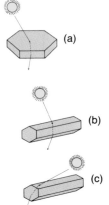

Fig. 3.3 High above Earth's surface, ice crystals are usually plate- (a) or pencil-shaped (b, c). Due to the hexagonal shape of these crystals, sunlight is always refracted by at least 22°.

of a halo and so this is dark. Red is the innermost colour in a halo because it is the least refracted and it is the brightest colour in a halo because of the concentration of light rays refracted at or near 22°. Orange and yellow are the next colours away from the sun or moon, usually followed by white. White occurs because some of the red, orange and yellow wavelengths are bent at larger angles as well as the minimum angle so all the wavelengths start to overlap and produce white light.

Other halo phenomena are caused when differently shaped or differently orientated ice crystals appear in the atmosphere (fig. 3.4). Bright areas of the sky that look like setting suns, one on each side of the real sun, are variously known as mock suns, false suns, sun dogs or parhelia. They are seen when light is refracted by hexagonal plate ice crystals: these do not fall in random orientations but mostly with their flat surfaces horizontal like leaves falling from a tree. Only the sides of a halo are produced because the crystals at the top are not orientated correctly to refract light through the minimum angle. Mock suns may be bright and white, or they may show any or all of the colours of the spectrum: this depends upon the elevation of the sun at the time.

COLOURED CORONAS AND IRIDESCENT CLOUDS

Whereas a halo is a ring of light at some distance from the sun or moon, a corona is an aureole or disc of light whose border is immediately adjacent to the sun or moon (pl. 3.23) or even sometimes Jupiter or Venus. The differences arise because a halo is caused by the refraction of light, and a corona results from diffraction of light (i.e. interference). The colours of a corona are delicate and they shimmer because the clouds are usually thin, moving and discontinuous.

Coronas are seen when a thin layer of cloud lies between the moon or sun and an observer. If water droplets or ice crystals in these clouds are large

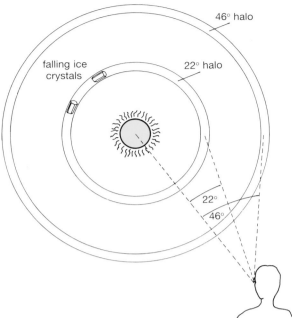

Fig. 3.4 Hexagonal ice crystals falling through the atmosphere can cause a 22° halo, sometimes a 46° halo, and various other phenomena, depending on their orientation and whether they are plate- or pencil-shaped.

relative to the wavelength of light, they will diffract the moonlight or sunlight, i.e. deflect light rays and spread them out into bright and dark rings. Longer red wavelengths are diffracted most, producing the largest pattern of rings. The corona consists of an aureole of intense white light, edged with blue on the inside and red on the outside; white occurs in the middle because of mixing of spectral colours produced by water droplets of different sizes. There may be one or more rings of spectral colours. In general, the larger the water droplets or ice crystals, the smaller the corona. The most spectacular coronas are produced by thin altostratus, cirro-cumulus, or

PL. 3.22 Right: A halo around the sun is due to refraction of sunlight by ice crystals.
Photo: L. McLay

PL. 3.23 Below: Lunar corona: interference colours are due to diffraction of light by thin cloud in front of the moon.
Photo: P. Farrant

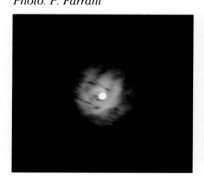

cirrus clouds because these contain the most uniformly sized droplets: more uniform particles produce purer colours.

Thin discontinuous clouds that move across the sun during the day commonly have beautiful iridescent colours, ranging from the spectral colours to soft pastel pinks, blues and greens. The colours of these iridescent clouds are the result of diffraction of sunlight by water droplets of very different sizes within the cloud. Instead of the diffraction patterns being circular as they are in a corona, they follow contour lines corresponding to the size of the droplets in the cloud. The colours may follow the shape of the cloud itself if the droplets become smaller towards the edge and evaporate there. The colours of iridescent clouds are most intense closest to the sun, corresponding to the brightest (first order) ring of diffracted light. Colours other than the spectral colours are due to overlapping colours of different diffraction orders.

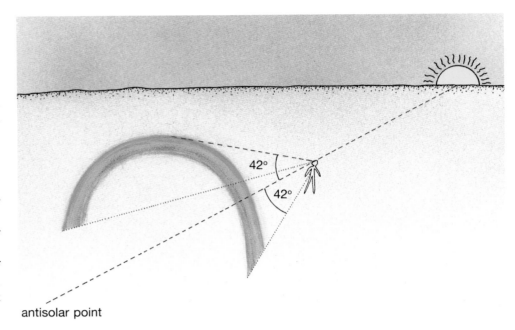

antisolar point

RAINBOWS: TRICKS OR TREATS?

Humans have always regarded a rainbow as a special treat: of all the coloured displays of the atmosphere, it is the best known and the phenomenon most frequently associated with colour (pl. 3.24). Rainbows show the white light from the sun split into its component wavelengths: indeed, we usually refer to these as the colours of the rainbow rather than the spectral colours. Rainbows appear before or after a rainstorm, when the sun is shining but when it is not too high in the sky, early in the morning or late in the afternoon (especially in the afternoon when rainstorms are more frequent) and will only be seen by an observer facing away from the sun (fig. 3.5). Rainbows are least likely to be seen in very cold regions of the world where water in the atmosphere freezes into ice crystals: the water needs to be in droplet form for a rainbow to occur. Sometimes rainbows can also be seen in the spray from a garden hose or in waterfalls. They also occur in moonlight, though we cannot detect the colours because of low night-time light levels.

A rainbow is caused by both refraction and reflection of sunlight by raindrops (see BOX 2). The raindrops must be less than 4 mm in diameter and held in suspension in the atmosphere but too far apart to appear as cloud. Each raindrop acts like a tiny prism, refracting or bending light rays as they enter it. Light is then reflected from the back of each drop and refracted again when it emerges from the drop. Different wavelengths of sunlight are refracted at different angles so that the original white light is split into its spectral sequence of component colours: red, orange, yellow, green, blue and violet. An infra-red component is also present, and has been photographed with special film, though we are unable to see it with the naked eye.

A rainbow actually forms as a full circle, but the only way to see the full 360° circle is from an aeroplane: if an observer is standing on Earth's surface, at least the lower half of a rainbow is always hidden beneath the horizon.

Fig. 3.5 A rainbow is usually seen before or after a morning or afternoon rainstorm, by an observer facing away from the sun when it is low in the sky.

Colour and brightness

A rainbow varies in brightness depending on the viewing angle of the observer. Each colour in a rainbow is due to a different set of raindrops and no two people ever see the same rainbow, but rather the light refracted and reflected by a particular set of drops at a particular time from where they are standing. At any one moment, a rainbow is formed by a particular set of raindrops, but because the drops are falling, the same rainbow seen a few moments later will be formed from a new set of drops.

The intensity of the colours in a rainbow also

PL. 3.24 Rainbow, caused by reflection and refraction of light by water droplets that are too widely spaced to appear as cloud. *Photo: M. Porteners*

where the colours overlap. Eventually, when droplets are very small, colours merge to produce a white fog bow (pl. 3.25). Sometimes too, when droplets are very small and the sun is close to the horizon, a red bow occurs: this is a white bow lit by the setting sun.

Sometimes bows may be seen early in the morning on horizontal surfaces, such as ponds, lawns or even the sea. These are known as dew bows and they are formed in a similar way to rainbows, with sunlight being refracted and reflected by drops of dew.

GLORIOUS COLOUR

At a high altitude above the clouds, say on a mountain or in an aeroplane, observers may see their shadow (or the aeroplane's shadow) projected onto cloud and surrounded by a series of coloured rings. This phenomenon is appropriately called a glory or brockenspectre, after the Brocken, a mountain in Germany where the phenomenon is often seen. For a glory to be seen, the observer must be facing away from a rising or setting sun, and the cloud must contain small water droplets of uniform size. The glory is a diffraction phenomenon, in which the sun's rays, coming from behind the observer, are bent by water droplets and spread into concentric rings of spectral colours. The coloured rings of the glory will form with red on the outside because it is diffracted most. The colours of a glory are bright

PL. 3.25 Above: White fog bow, produced by very small water droplets; the colours merge to produce white light.
Photo: M. Porteners
PL. 3.26 Below: Aurora australis seen from southern New Zealand. *Photo: A. Leslie*

depends on the size of the raindrops. Larger droplets are better at separating different wavelengths, so colours are distinct and bright, especially near the bottom of the rainbow. With a smaller droplet size, the bows start to overlap and colours become paler and less distinct. A bow may then have a red outer edge and a blue inner edge, with white in between

because diffracted light waves interfere constructively with each other: rays of light diffracted by different parts of the rims of individual droplets are reinforced when their wave peaks coincide. All the colours overlap in the centre of the rings to produce a bright white light, and the observer's shadow is seen on this white centre, surrounded by the coloured rings.

HEAVENLY COLOURS

An aurora is a luminous display in the polar sky. The phenomenon is correctly known as the aurora australis in the southern hemisphere and the aurora borealis in the northern hemisphere. The two are commonly called the southern lights and the northern lights respectively.

Auroras may be no more than faint glows on the horizon or patches further up in the sky, but they can also be kaleidoscopes of vividly coloured, flaming, flickering or pulsating displays that appear as rays, coronas, arcs or curtains and which may take up a good deal of the southern or northern night sky (pls 3.26, 3.27). Auroras are spectacular not only because of their colours, but also because of their movement.

Auroras are more likely to be seen around latitudes 65-75° north or south (about 2 500 km from the north and south magnetic poles). In these regions, known as the auroral zones or auroral ovals (fig. 3.6), an aurora can be seen on almost any clear dark night. Auroras are seen less frequently nearer the equator or the poles and they appear less structured, colourful, and dramatic.

Flares and fields: the solar connection

Auroras feature in many ancient legends and derive their name from Aurora, the Roman goddess of dawn, probably because their light resembled dawn breaking in the night sky.

Auroras are associated with sunspot activity and solar flares, which occur when parts of the sun's surface are particularly active and emit energy in the form of charged particles of the solar wind. The

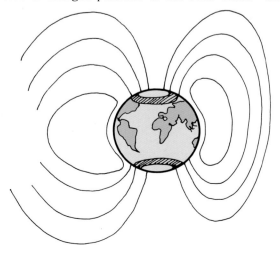

Fig. 3.6 The positions of the auroral zones, at around latitudes 65-75° north and south, are due to Earth's magnetic field: lines of magnetic force bend inward at these regions, and the solar wind reaches well into Earth's atmosphere.

PL. 3.27 Lightning and aurora. Lightning occurs when there are enormous differences in electrical potential between different regions of a cloud: fast-moving electrons hit and ionise air molecules, causing light to be emitted. The light may be bluish because of the high temperature or faintly pink if atomic hydrogen is formed.
Photo: L. McLay

PL. 3.28 Auroras can take the form of arcs that cross the sky in an east-west direction because of Earth's rotation. *Photo: NASA*

nitrogen produces blue and violet. Changes in air pressure, which falls as height above Earth's surface increases, help to determine colours. Oxygen atoms emit red light at very low pressures high in the atmosphere (around 260 km above Earth's surface), whereas at higher pressures lower in the atmosphere they produce yellowish green light, the commonest colour of auroras. Nitrogen molecules or pairs of ionised oxygen or nitrogen atoms, produce the blues and reds that sometimes occur at heights of around 100 km above Earth's surface.

All these colours may be present in an aurora, but even though auroras occur high in the sky (100-300 km above Earth's surface), the curvature of Earth limits the extent of the aurora and the colours seen by an observer far away from an auroral zone. If only the top part of the 250-300 km directly above Earth's surface at the auroral zone is visible, the observer may see only the red part of the aurora. An observer closer to the auroral zone will see more of the aurora and therefore more colours.

Whereas the glows and patches seen in non-polar parts of the world are usually red, the commonest colours of auroras at higher latitudes are yellowish green in the main body of the aurora and red in the upper and lower edges (pl. 3.29). An entire aurora can be seen only from outside Earth's atmosphere, and in 1981 this spectacle was first photographed from a satellite. Seen from space an aurora appears as a glowing ring around Earth's magnetic pole (pl. 3.28).

solar wind travels in all directions and a portion reaches Earth's atmosphere a couple of days after a flare. Here the wind's path is altered by Earth's magnetic field; huge lines of magnetic force envelop Earth entirely except for small gaps near the polar regions: the solar wind is directed towards the regions beneath these gaps, and it is here that auroras appear.

On reaching Earth's atmosphere, the high-energy particles of the solar wind collide with air molecules, and these collisions produce an aurora. When an atmospheric molecule like oxygen or nitrogen is hit by one or more charged particles emitted from the sun, it is ionised or ripped apart into electrically charged atoms. When these excited atoms, or ions, return to their original molecular state, light is emitted in the visible part of the spectrum.

This light has characteristic colours for each element: oxygen produces yellowish green and red;

A PYRAMID OF LIGHT

A weak pyramid of light, the same colour as sunlight, may appear in the western evening sky just after sunset or in the eastern sky just before dawn. This phenomenon is known as zodiacal light because it occurs in the plane of the ecliptic, the plane of the apparent path of the sun around Earth (actually the

---

THE GREEN FLASH

The green flash is a brilliant green light seen on the top rim of the sun's disc at either sunrise or sunset, lasting only momentarily as the disc slides above or beneath the horizon. The phenomenon can be seen only in exceptional atmospheric conditions. It is best to look for it at sunset because at sunrise it is difficult for an observer to judge exactly where the top of the rim is going to appear.

The green flash is caused by refraction of sunlight by Earth's atmosphere. When the setting sun nears Earth's horizon, its light passes through an increasingly longer, denser path of atmosphere, which alters its speed: this causes refraction or bending of the light. Short wavelengths of sunlight (blue and green) are bent more than long wavelengths (orange and red) and this makes the disc of the setting sun separate, imperceptibly, into a vertical spectrum of coloured discs, with the red image lowermost in the sky. As the separate images overlap almost entirely over the area of the sun's disc, only the colour of the top of the rim can be distinguished, and only under exceptional circumstances: the horizon must be low, the air very clean and there must be a shallow layer of warm air under a layer of cool air. The sun's rim then appears green because the blue image of the sun's light is scattered away from the path of sunlight by air molecules (Rayleigh scattering): the green image of the sun appears momentarily as a fleeting flash (fig. 3.7). A red flash can sometimes be seen on the lower rim

of the setting sun when it drops down from behind a low cloud: this is the lowermost image of refracted sunlight. Similar coloured flashes can sometimes be seen when the moon or the larger planets like Jupiter and Venus rise or set.

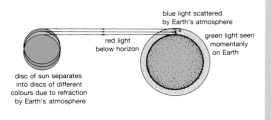

Fig. 3.7

BOX 2

DOUBLE SPLENDOUR

Primary and secondary bows

A double rainbow can form because light rays can travel along a number of paths into and within raindrops. The brighter rainbow is known as the primary bow and the other the secondary bow. A primary bow is violet on the inside and red on the outside, and is produced when rays of sunlight are each reflected once inside the individual raindrops. A secondary bow is red on the inside and violet on the outside, and forms when light is reflected twice inside the raindrops (pl. 3.30).

In a primary bow, light rays entering the tops of each raindrop are first refracted, then reflected off the back wall of the raindrop, and refracted again as they leave. The rays of light leaving the raindrop are concentrated together at an angle of 42° from their original path (fig. 3.8). In a secondary bow, the light rays are reflected twice inside each raindrop: because the rays change direction once more than they do in a primary bow, the colours are reversed in order when they emerge from the raindrops. Light rays emerging to form the secondary bow are concentrated at an angle of 51°, so this bow is larger than the primary bow, but is less intense because the light has been doubly reflected (fig. 3.9).

PL. 3.30 Double rainbow: the secondary bow is fainter, lies to the outside of the primary bow, and has the colours in reverse order (red on the inside). A darker area of sky separates the two bows. *Photo: R. King.*

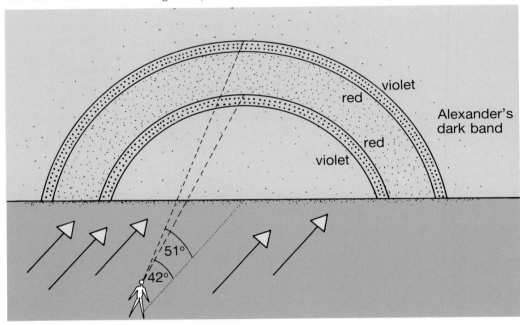

Fig. 3.10

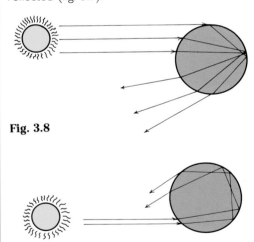

Fig. 3.8

Fig. 3.9

The area between primary and secondary bows is dark because no reflected sunlight reaches this part of the sky: all diffuse light from the primary bow is reflected to its inside, and all the diffuse light from the secondary bow to its outside. This area is known as Alexander's dark band (fig. 3.10).

Supernumerary bows

Any faint bows that occur inside the primary bow are called supernumerary bows or interference bows, because they are the result

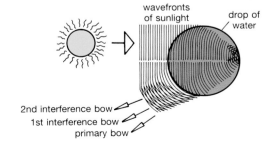

Fig. 3.11

of interference or the reinforcement of colours when the peaks and troughs of different light waves coincide (fig. 3.11). Supernumerary bows are most likely to be seen near the top of a rainbow where the raindrops are smaller and most uniform in size: these drops produce the most distinct interference patterns. Raindrops become more uneven in size and more distorted in shape as they fall downwards through the sky, and so supernumerary bows are less distinct at the base of a rainbow. Supernumerary bows are usually pink and green because they are produced by interference.

PL. 3.29 Auroras can also take the form of veils, curtains, rays (like giant coloured searchlights), and coronas (converging rays). *Photo: NASA*

path of Earth's movement around the sun) that passes through the band of twelve constellations of the zodiac (Aries, Taurus, Gemini, Cancer, Leo, Virgo, Libra, Scorpius, Sagittarius, Capricornus, Aquarius and Pisces): all the planets of the solar system lie near the plane of the ecliptic. Zodiacal light is caused by the scattering of sunlight by interplanetary dust that orbits the sun in the plane of the ecliptic, outside Earth's atmosphere: its spectrum is therefore similar to that of sunlight, but slightly more pink. Zodiacal light may even be part of the sun's corona or outer atmosphere, since its intensity varies with solar activity.

Though zodiacal light is present year-round, usually it can be seen only when the ecliptic is nearly vertical. Zodiacal light is most intense in the tropics, where twilights are short and the ecliptic is close to vertical all year. At mid-latitudes the best viewing times are at the spring and autumn equinoxes: in the evenings of February and March, and the mornings of September-November for the northern hemisphere; and in the evenings of August and September and the mornings of March-May for the southern hemisphere.

A similar phenomenon is the counterglow or gegenschein, which is also produced when sunlight is scattered by dust particles orbiting the sun. The counterglow appears as a faint glow on the ecliptic at a point directly opposite the position of the sun, and is best seen on a moonless night when the ecliptic lies high above the horizon. It can be seen almost overhead in the northern hemisphere at around midnight during December and January, and in the southern hemisphere during June and July.

From the colours of Earth's atmosphere, we now turn to the colours of the land and water surfaces of Earth itself.

CHAPTER 4

THE COLOURS OF THE EARTH'S SURFACE

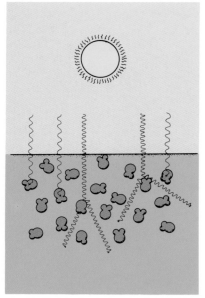

Fig. 4.1 Water molecules absorb long wavelength red light and scatter short wavelength blue light. This is why clear ocean water is blue.

The blue of the oceans is the dominant colour of Earth (pl. 4.1). About two-thirds of the planet is covered by water, over 95% in oceans and over half that in the Pacific. The greens and browns we see are continents and islands (pl. 4.2). Lakes and rivers occupy some surface area of the continents, but the most noticeable features are high mountain chains and vast flat plains. Mountains and basins occur on the ocean floor as well, but we do not see these because they are covered with water.

BLUE WATERS

The colour of natural waters like oceans, lakes and rivers, is caused by several physical processes: scattering and absorption of sunlight by molecules of water itself (fig. 4.1); scattering and absorption of light by microscopic organisms and particles, such as sediment, in the water; and reflection of sunlight, both from the surface and beneath it. The time of day, time of year, latitude, amount of cloud cover and other atmospheric conditions, and the smoothness of the water also determine the amount and colour of light arriving at the ocean surface, and the relative proportions that are reflected or pass through the surface into the water below. As much

as half the light may be reflected from the surface without reaching the water underneath.

Clean, calm ocean water under a clear summer sky will reflect as little as 3% of sunlight reaching its surface. Some blue light entering the water is scattered back through the surface from beneath and this is why the surface of a calm blue ocean appears luminous (pl. 4.3). The water appears blue, both at and beneath the surface, because a great proportion of available light passes into the water and because the water contains little else beside water molecules. The salts dissolved in ocean water make no difference to its colour because they are transparent to visible wavelengths of light which pass through them unchanged.

Water molecules

Water molecules are each made up of one oxygen atom and two hydrogen atoms, with an associated electron cloud that is distributed so it gives a slight negative charge on one side of the molecule and a slight positive charge on the other. Red wavelengths of light have the right amount of energy to be absorbed by molecules with this structure. The molecules are also small enough to scatter blue

PL. 4.1 Right: About two-thirds of Earth's surface is covered by water. Canary Islands, in the Atlantic Ocean: the dark appearance is due to black volcanic rocks and dark soils; three of the islands have given rise to cloud banks on their lee sides. *Photo: NASA*

PL. 4.2 Left: Only about one-third of Earth's surface is covered by land. *Photo: NASA*

wavelengths. This is the same process of Rayleigh scattering that causes the blue of the sky (see p. 11). Water molecules behave in the same way as air molecules in the atmosphere that scatter blue wavelengths to create blue colour. Air molecules, however, have a different chemical nature and they absorb little if any light. Rayleigh scattering occurs only when the water (or air) is extremely clear, e.g. the Sargasso Sea in the North Atlantic, which is usually very clear and blue. Little sediment and few nutrients to support marine life enter this sea from rivers or land run-off, and therefore little planktonic plant and animal life exists.

The colour of water beneath the ocean surface depends partly upon the colour of light at the surface, at any particular time. However, as the light from the surface travels down through the water, its colour changes with increasing depth. If the water is clear, blue wavelengths are scattered most and absorbed least, and so these penetrate furthest below the water surface. Red wavelengths are scattered least and absorbed most. By the time light rays have penetrated 10 m below the surface of a clear blue ocean, around 80% of the incident sunlight is absorbed (pl. 4.4). By 30 m below the surface all red wavelength light is absorbed. Below that depth, even in relatively shallow seas, red animals appear black because there is no red light left to reflect off them, and the colours of other animals appear increasingly blue. Divers must use torches if they want to see the real colours of the underwater world, and a flash is necessary to photograph true colours. Further below the surface of blue oceans and lakes, where virtually no light penetrates at all, even the blue light is absorbed and the water appears black.

COASTAL WATERS

Nearer the coast, ocean water can look brown, yellow or green. These colours are caused by particles larger than water molecules, which are suspended in the water. Particles close to the surface scatter most light back out of the water and so they greatly reduce underwater visibility with increasing depth. As these particles are different sizes, they absorb different wavelengths of light — this selective absorption is largely responsible for the colours of the water surface and of light transmitted through the water.

Coastal waters contain particles of dissolved and suspended material washed from land by rivers and run-off. These particles absorb and scatter light reaching the water surface. They absorb short wavelength blue and green light readily because of their chemical nature. The particles absorb long wavelengths least, so red and yellow wavelengths of light travel most easily through water (pl. 4.5). The amount or concentration of particles influences colour: the more particles in the water, the easier it is for wavelengths of light longer than blue to travel deeper into the water (fig. 4.2). On the other hand, coastal waters can look green when the concentration of particles is lower (pl. 4.6). In these conditions, absorption of short wavelength blue light by suspended particles, and absorption of long wavelength red and yellow light by water molecules, is probably about equal (fig. 4.3).

The nature of the suspended particles is as important as their concentration in determining colour. Water can contain planktonic plants and animals, decayed plant and animal material, bacteria and sediment. The larger the suspended particles, the more equally all wavelengths of light are scattered and the whiter the water appears. Rough water on a sandy beach picks up particles of sand and holds them in suspension, so all light is scattered and very little absorbed, and the water appears white or milky.

Red tides

Sometimes coastal waters can appear blue, green, yellow, red or brown because of the presence of millions of tiny floating organisms that make up

PL. 4.3 Luminous blue ocean near Broome, Western Australia. *Photo: R.J. King*

Fig. 4.2 Yellowish coastal water absorbs blue light. Red and yellow pass through.

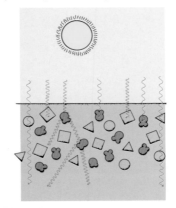

Fig. 4.3 In green coastal waters there is equal absorption of blue and red light.

PL. 4.4 Even at only a few metres below the surface of the ocean, most of the red light has been absorbed by water. *Photo: R. Berthold*

PL. 4.5 Above right: Yellow substance in coastal waters preferentially absorbs blue light and lets red and yellow light pass. *Photo: R. Berthold*

PL. 4.6 Above left: Green coastal waters owe their colour equally to yellow substance and blue light scattering. *Photo: P. Farrant*

PL. 4.7 When particular species of algae suddenly become abundant in tropical waters, the ocean surface appears brownish red, and the bloom is called a red tide. These algae produce toxins that can poison fish and shellfish, as well as the people who eat them. *Photo: R.J. King.*

plankton. Plankton contains both plants and animals, including the eggs and young of many fish and bottom-dwelling animals. Planktonic organisms move long distances by drifting with ocean currents (pl. 4.7).

Large numbers of planktonic algae or microscopic plants are known collectively as phytoplankton. These are found in coastal waters where nutrients like nitrogen and phosphorus are plentiful. The colour of water containing phytoplankton depends on the dominant organisms present and their pigments. Large concentrations of phytoplankton, densest near the surface and decreasing with depth as light decreases, are called algal blooms. These develop when sea temperature is warm, nutrient concentrations high and there is little water movement. Algal blooms can be blue-green, red, yellow-green, brown or even a milky colour.

Yellow substance

All plants, including phytoplankton, contain green pigments or chlorophylls, essential for photosynthesis. When plant pigments break down, they produce yellow substance or Gelbstoffe. Much of the yellow substance of lakes and coastal ocean waters comes from terrestrial plants, which break down in the soil and contribute to humus. Humus, an important component of soil because it contains many of the nutrients essential for plant growth, is a fairly stable mixture of plant and animal remains that have been partially decomposed by micro-organisms. Humic acids and iron compounds are washed out of humus in the soil by rainwater and eventually reach lakes and coastal ocean waters in rivers and run-off.

Muddy sediments, or sediments and yellow substance in combination, can also make water look yellow-brown, e.g. the coastal waters of southern Asia. These are areas of high rainfall, and large rivers carry much sediment into the oceans. When the ocean is yellow-brown on the coasts of more arid lands, as on the Californian coast, the colour is more likely to be due to yellow substance alone: local rivers carry little sediment and nutrient-rich upwelling of deep ocean water supports large concentrations of plankton.

FRESHWATER LAKES

In clear, sunny conditions, large clean lakes are deep blue because their water is virtually pure and the water molecules scatter blue wavelengths (Rayleigh scattering) and absorb red wavelengths. Lakes like this have little plankton or sediment in the water. Lakes are clear and blue if they hold a large volume of water relative to the amount of water entering them from rivers and run-off; if there is little surrounding vegetation; if there is relatively low rainfall; or if water entering them is well filtered. Two of the best known clear, deep blue lakes are Lake Tahoe in California and the Blue Lake in the crater of Mount Gambier in South Australia. These lakes can be a striking deep blue if the weather is fine, but like all bodies of water, they will be a different colour after rain or in cloudy conditions.

Other lakes may be brown, caused by sediment or other particles, or by humic acids and iron compounds, leached out of soils and ultimately originating from the breakdown of chlorophyll as vegetation decays (pl. 4.8). Some lakes like Lake Matheson in New Zealand, can be almost black. Lakes like this tend to occur in heavily vegetated areas with high rainfall.

The green of many small lakes and dams is often caused by green plants, usually microscopic algae (pl. 4.9). Lakes in farming areas are often green because of algal blooms. Water that runs off from farms carries fertilisers and farm animal wastes, which contain nutrients like phosphorus and nitrogen that algae use. Some lakes and waterways are red, due to microscopic algae (pl. 4.10) or floating ferns (pl. 4.11).

GLACIAL LAKES

Glacial lakes occur in high altitude areas like the Andes of South America and the mountains of the South Island of New Zealand, where glaciers formed during the Ice Ages are retreating. As glaciers melt, they leave behind many rocks and boulders; any depressions fill with rainwater and lakes form. Unlike the deep luminous blue of large clear lakes, the water in glacial lakes is blue or green but opaque. This is caused by large amounts of suspended silt near the water surface, which reflect scattered blue light from the sky. Lake Tekapo and Lake Pukaki in New Zealand are both good examples of large glacial lakes that can appear vividly blue in favourable weather (pl. 4.12). The water in glacial lakes, however, is never very clear because it always contains suspended sediment.

A rapidly flowing glacial river appears whitish because the suspended silt scatters all wavelengths of light (pl. 4.13). The river becomes gradually bluer as the water slows down and fine silt particles at the surface reflect more blue from the sky (pl. 4.14).

BLACK AND WHITE RIVERS

Rivers are often described as being clearwater, whitewater or blackwater rivers. All these terms can be illustrated by looking at one river system, the Amazon, the largest in the world. The Amazon begins high in the Andes Mountains, where torrential rainfall erodes the mountain slopes. Vast quantities of sediment are carried thousands of kilometres across South America. The sediment particles totally scatter all wavelengths of sunlight, so the Amazon is called a whitewater river, despite the fact that it is milky brown due to the colour of silt particles.

Of all the tributaries of the Amazon, the Rio Negro is the largest and most famous. It is called a blackwater river because of its colour, which it owes to the large amounts of organic matter from the surrounding jungle that absorb all wavelengths of light. The debris that falls on the jungle floor does not decompose fully because the jungle soil is sandy and does not support enough micro-organisms (bacteria, fungi, invertebrate animals) to break down debris into its component molecules like humic acids and iron compounds. As well, sand does not have the chemical properties that enable other soils to filter out and hold particles of decaying vegetation, so they are washed away by heavy rain (pl. 4.15).

PL. 4.8 Some swamps and ditches in vegetated areas contain water that is naturally brown because of iron-containing molecules derived from the surrounding soil. If the water remains still, iridescent colours may be seen because of the arrangement of iron molecules in parallel layers on the water surface.
Photo: P. Farrant

PL. 4.9 Left: The green of this small waterhole on Ayers Rock in Australia is due to a bloom of microscopic algae. *Photo: R. J. King*

PL. 4.10 Below: Pink lake in Australia: the colour is due to carotenoid-containing microscopic algae.
Photo: J. M. King

PL. 4.11 Below left: The red colour of this river backwater is due to a floating fern.
Photo: P. Farrant

PL. 4.12 Glacial lake, Norway: such lakes may be vivid blue on fine days when the fine silt particles at the water surface reflect blue light from the sky. *Photo: R.J. King*

PL. 4.13 Below: The water in glacial rivers and lakes is always opaque because of the large amount of suspended silt. *Photo: P. Farrant*

PL. 4.14 Below right: The clear water of a stream meets the opaque water of a glacial lake in New Zealand. *Photo: P. Farrant*

PL. 4.15 The Rio Negro in Brazil is the most famous blackwater river. *Photo: P. Farrant*

Some smaller tributaries of the Amazon come from areas that are older, more stable and no longer being rapidly eroded, such as the Brazilian and Guiana Highlands: little sediment is washed into the rivers and so they are quite transparent. These are clearwater rivers (pl. 4.16).

SNOW AND ICE

Some lakes become covered with ice in winter when air temperatures are cold enough to freeze surface layers of water (pl. 4.17). This ice often appears bluish because it reflects blue light from the sky and the effect is accentuated by the low amount of run-off from surrounding land. There is little yellow substance and little phytoplankton growth in lakes at this time of year.

Snow appears white because rays of sunlight that pass from the air into transparent ice particles and from the ice particles into air bubbles trapped between them, are refracted and reflected. Light is scattered in all directions, causing the particles to appear white (pl. 4.18).

REFLECTIONS

The colour of a body of water depends on light reflected from its surface and, to a lesser extent, from the bottom, as well as light scattered from below the surface (pl. 4.19). Reflected colours depend upon the angle of view, e.g. the sea will reflect sky colours to an observer looking at it obliquely, but an observer looking straight down can see through into the water below, providing it is clear. Reflections from the shore often cause striking coloration, especially in lakes which are protected and therefore calmer. Colours of reflections of objects in lakes, ponds and puddles are more intense than the colours in the objects themselves because surrounding brightness is reduced: less surrounding sky is included in the field of view (pl. 4.20).

When reflections are displaced because the water surface is disturbed, the sea at the horizon has the same colour as the part of the sky around 20-30° above the horizon and this is why the colour of the sea at the horizon can be darker than the colour of the sky at the horizon. During the day, the sea

PL. 4.16 Left: Clearwater rivers have well filtered water flowing into them from the surrounding land. *Photo: P. Farrant*

PL. 4.17 Below: On a sunny day, the bluish appearance of ice in a glacier is due to blue light scattered from the sky. *Photo: P. Farrant*

horizon seems to have a blue edge, due to Rayleigh scattering by air molecules and the greater clarity of the water out to sea.

Reflection of light from the bottom of oceans, lakes or rivers influences water colour only if the water is very shallow, e.g. a sandbank causes that part of a river or the sea to appear yellower than the surrounding, deeper areas (pl. 4.21).

SHADOWS

Shadows occur on surfaces not reached by rays of light, because of obstructions blocking the light source. Shadows of objects in daylight are bluish: the sun's yellowish light does not fall on these areas and they receive only scattered blue light from the sky (fig. 4.4). This is especially noticeable on snow where there are no other colours. Shadows may become greenish or yellowish at sunset, as the sun and surrounding sky redden.

Shadows of clouds tend to appear purple or violet on calm turbid coastal water because of colour contrast with surrounding green water. Shadows on a water surface are areas receiving less incident light, and therefore they cannot scatter back as much light

PL. 4.18 Left: Snow is white because of refraction and reflection of light within the air pockets between ice particles. *Photo: P. Farrant*

PL. 4.20 Below: Reflections on Lake Mathieson in New Zealand. *Photo: W. Farrant*

PL. 4.19 Above: The reflection of the setting sun on the ocean appears triangular as it widens towards the horizon because of many individual images that are each a reflection from the side of a small wave facing the observer. *Photo: W. Farrant*

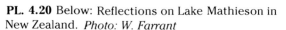

PL. 4.21 Above: Lighter blue water inside a coral reef is due to reflection of sunlight from coral sand in shallower water. *Photo: R. Berthold*

PL. 4.22 Right: Molecules arranged in an orderly manner, give sulfur crystals a regular and symmetrical structure. *Photo: P. Farrant*

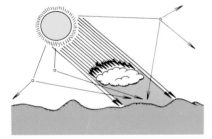

Fig. 4.4 The area in shadow beneath the cloud is bluish because it receives blue wavelength light scattered by molecules in Earth's atmosphere, but no direct sunlight.

PL. 4.23 Rocks that are brown or red usually contain iron; iron is the most common contaminant of rocks. *Photo: R. Berthold*

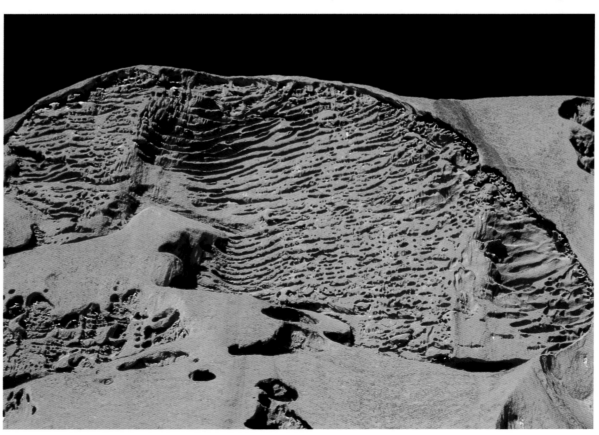

as surrounding areas. Shadows stand out particularly well on turbid water surfaces because particles in the water absorb much of the light and even less light is scattered back. These shadows may have noticeably coloured edges if the water is slightly muddy and particles in the water are small enough to scatter blue light.

REFRACTIONS

White objects on the bottom of a clear shallow stream may sometimes appear to be blue on top and red underneath. When light rays pass through tiny wave crests on the surface of clean rivers or pools, the crests act like tiny prisms and light is refracted: blue wavelengths bend more than red wavelengths because of their different energies, so the light rays are edged with blue and red (fig. 4.5).

EARTH'S CRUST: CONTAMINATION CREATES COLOUR

Minerals are naturally occurring solid chemical compounds, e.g. gold, asbestos, ruby and salt, and they are the materials of which all Earth's rocks, pebbles and sands are composed. There are about 2 500 known minerals, made from less than 100 elements, and their colours are often spectacular in variety and intensity.

When minerals exist as homogeneous, regularly shaped, symmetrical structures, they are known as crystals. Some crystals are colourless and transparent, many have deep saturated colours and others are quite opaque (pl. 4.22).

Most rocks are mainly composed of colourless minerals. Quartz, a hard mineral that is pure silica, is one of the most abundant minerals on Earth. In its pure form quartz is colourless, though with small amounts of contaminants like iron and manganese

BOX 1

PRECIOUS STONES

We describe some minerals as precious because we value them as ornaments or jewellery. Gemstones are usually cut and polished, either to display their colours or enhance their reflectivity. Opaque gems, like turquoise and agate, are cut with a curved upper surface as this is the best way to display their colour and pattern. Transparent and translucent gems, like emeralds and amethyst, however, are cut with facets or flat faces to display their clarity and brilliance. Gems like rubies, sapphires and emeralds owe their popularity to strong colours of red, blue and green, while diamonds are valued for their sparkling quality; they are particularly efficient at refracting or splitting white light.

Diamonds are made of pure carbon, crystallised at high temperature and pressure, and the crystals have a number of internal faces or planes of weakness. Each outside facet of a diamond splits light into its component colours, and the internal faces amplify the different colours of light and reflect them out of the stone in many different directions. Although diamonds are usually colourless, rare examples have pale colours like yellow, red, orange, green, blue or brown.

Most gems, but not all, are crystals. Some of the other materials classed as gems include obsidian, amber, opals, pearls and some corals.

Pearls and corals are crystalline in structure and are produced by animals: pearls by molluscs and corals by colonies of coelenterates. The other materials are non-crystalline: obsidian is a naturally occurring black volcanic glass; amber is a fossil resin or gum produced by pine trees; and opals are formed by silica settling out of water.

Opals: a play of colour

Opals are probably the most colourful of all gemstones (pl. 4.24a). The colours — white, yellows, browns, reds, oranges, blues, greens, greys and black — seem to come from within, creating a 'play of colours', in which the colours change rapidly as the opal is turned slightly from side to side. Opals may be almost transparent to quite opaque, though the translucent opals which show the greatest variety and depth of colours are the most sought after.

Opals are formed when water evaporates from hot underground pools that contain dissolved silica. As the water cools, silica molecules move together to form tiny spheres which settle to the bottom of the pools in tightly packed layers. As more water evaporates, the spheres harden and eventually water is left only in the spaces between the spheres. It is the structure of opals that is mainly responsible for their brilliant iridescent colours. Each colour is caused by a different deposit of silica and water packed in regular layers. Within any one deposit, the size of the silica spheres and the amount of water between them, is uniform.

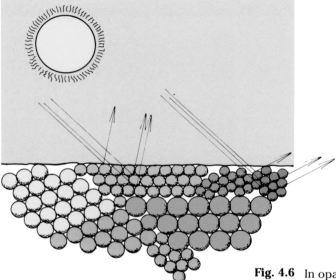

Fig. 4.6 In opals, light waves reflected from different layers of evenly spaced silica spheres produce iridescence. The 'play of colours' seen as an opal is turned is due to differently oriented layers and different sizes of spheres.

The size of the silica spheres determines colour: small spheres produce blues and violets, whereas larger spheres produce other colours. Light waves entering an opal are refracted or bent into their spectral wavelengths, and these are reflected from various layers within the structure (fig. 4.6).

Whereas the silica and water structure of opals causes their iridescent colours, mineral contaminants cause background colours. Mineral contaminants are present in minute amounts and they selectively absorb some wavelengths of light and cause the more uniform black, grey and milky white colours through the stone. The term opalescence refers to the colours reflected from milky opals.

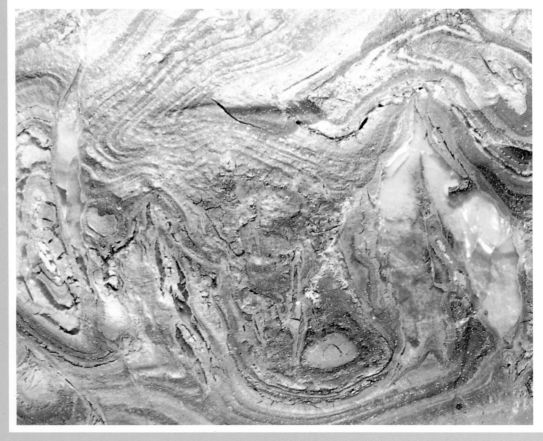

PL. 4.24a Opals often show a range of vivid colours; their iridescence is caused by layers of silica. *Photo: R. Berthold*

PL. 4.24b Copper in malachite and azurite causes the green and blue of these two minerals. *Photo: P. Farrant*

PL. 4.25 Copper is an essential part of the mineral malachite. *Photo: P. Farrant*

PL. 4.26 Haematite owes its colour to the element iron. *Photo: P. Farrant*

Fig. 4.5 Sunlight is refracted (bent) by tiny wave crests, separating into its component wavelengths. This is why a white object on a shallow stream bed appears edged with blue (left) and red (right).

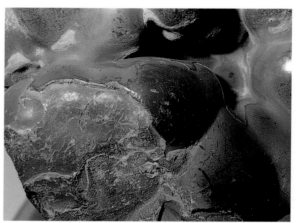

it can be purple (amethyst) or pink (rose quartz). Feldspar is also a very abundant mineral, and the various forms of feldspar are aluminium silicates of potassium, sodium and calcium. Feldspars are usually light in colour, the potassium forms ranging from white to cream, pink, reddish white and yellowish, with the sodium or calcium forms being white, brownish and grey.

Most vivid mineral colours are caused by only a few elements that absorb certain wavelengths of light strongly. These elements are often contaminants, occurring in small quantities unnecessary to the chemical composition of the mineral. They usually belong to the eight transition elements: titanium, vanadium, chromium, manganese, iron, cobalt, nickel and copper. Different transition elements absorb the energy from different wavelengths of light and so they produce different colours.

Iron is probably the commonest contaminant of rocks, and is responsible for red, brown and ochre colours (pl. 4.23). The actual colour iron imparts to a rock depends upon the number of electrons it shares with other atoms. Different electron configurations cause absorption of different wavelengths of light and thus they produce different colours. The mineral structure of a rock, the amount it is heated, its water content and exposure to air, will all affect the type of compounds that iron forms with other elements. Thus any one kind of rock, like sandstone, can vary in colour not only between different locations but also in one place.

Minerals, crystals and gems

The colour of a mineral can change with increasing amounts of a contaminant: an increasing amount of iron in white tremolite causes this mineral to become green and then blackish green, the green forms being known as actinolite. Different types of contaminant elements can also make minerals different colours: rubies and sapphires have the same crystalline structure, but iron and titanium respectively cause their different colours. Chromium gives the colour to dark green jade, iron colours light green jade, and copper gives the colour to turquoise. The same element can produce quite different colours in different minerals (pls 4.24-4.25). Whereas chromium in corundum produces rubies, chromium in the otherwise colourless or whitish mineral beryl produces green emeralds. Valuable minerals, like rubies and emeralds, are called gems (see BOX 1).

The streak is the colour of a mineral in finely powdered form, and is the same colour that is seen when the surface of the mineral is scratched. The streak of a mineral can also be important in its identification because its colour is not necessarily the same as the colour of the whole mineral. The iron-containing minerals haematite, magnetite and limonite have streaks that are red, black and yellow-brown respectively, even though in rock form they all appear black and opaque (pl. 4.26).

Lustrous minerals

Highly lustrous, metallic minerals like gold, silver and copper, have such smooth, opaque surfaces, they reflect almost all light back towards an observer and this is why they are shiny (pl. 4.27). Their respective colours are caused by the small amount of light of various wavelengths absorbed by their surfaces. Gold is frequently alloyed with other metals, especially silver, which can change its colour, e.g. to red-gold or silver-gold; white gold is usually an alloy of gold and nickel. Many metallic elements like silver and copper tarnish when exposed to air: the freshly exposed surfaces become darker, usually grey, brown or black. This is caused by the metal reacting with oxygen in the air, so only the surface of the metal is affected. The change in the chemical nature of the surface means that different wavelengths of light are absorbed and the surface changes colour.

Colour in minerals can also be caused by peculiarities in their physical structure. The needle-like inclusions of rutile in quartz make the mineral blue. These particles are orientated in a regular manner within the quartz and they can reflect and scatter light rays that pass into the mineral. Other transparent minerals like sapphire and tourmaline seem to change in colour or intensity when they are turned around. This is because of the way in which the crystals are orientated in particular directions or axes: either different wavelengths of light are absorbed in different directions, or different amounts of the same wavelength light are absorbed in different directions.

Owing to the electromagnetic nature of ionic crystals, some are sensitive to heat or light and may change colour accordingly, e.g. heat treatment can change the dark royal blue or black of Australian sapphires and make them resemble beautiful cornflower blue sapphires found in India. A number of minerals, including fluorite, calcite and scheelite, fluoresce (emit coloured light) when exposed to ultraviolet radiation: the colours emitted by fluorite include blues, purples, greens and yellows. The colour of fluorescence by minerals under ultraviolet light can be useful in their identification.

Iridescent minerals

Labradorite, a kind of feldspar, shows changing colours of bright blue, green and gold against a grey background, as the mineral is turned. Labradorite itself is colourless and is composed of iron and titanium. The colours are caused by the presence of tiny amounts of black magnetite, in the form of tiny platelets, beneath the mineral surface. The magnetite occurs in parallel layers, and the colours are produced by the interference of light waves reflected from layers at different depths within the labradorite. This iridescence also accounts for rainbow colours seen on the surfaces of limonite and haematite. Thin layers of hydrated iron oxide in the surfaces of these minerals cause interference. Rainbow colours can also be seen in some transparent minerals that have thin cracks inside them, but in these the colour is produced by refraction: light is split into its different wavelengths or colours as happens when it passes through a prism.

COLOURS OF ROCKS

Only a few of the many minerals on Earth are rock forming and these are mostly silicates, compounds of silica with other elements. Silica (SiO_2) is the basic component of sand. Sands and pebbles are fragments of rocks, and their colours therefore resemble the rocks from which they came (pl. 4.28, pl. 4.29). When rocks, pebbles and sands are wet, their colours are intensified (fig. 4.7). The colour of rocks is also influenced by organisms growing on their surfaces (pl. 4.30, pl. 4.31). There are three main types of rock: igneous, sedimentary and metamorphic.

Igneous rocks

Igneous rocks include volcanic rocks - formed when volcanoes erupt and throw out gases, ash and lava, which cool and solidify on contact with air, land and

PL. 4.29 Some black sands, like these in Tahiti, are derived from dark volcanic rocks. *Photo: P. Farrant*

PL. 4.27 Left: Lustrous minerals like pyrite (iron hydroxide) reflect most light back from their smooth surfaces. *Photo: P. Farrant*

PL. 4.28 Below: Light-coloured sands often owe their colours to the sandstones from which they are derived or to heavy non-metallic brown and yellow minerals such as garnet. Fine white sands are derived from weathering and erosion of rocks or from the breaking up of calcareous coral reefs. *Photo: M. Porteners*

PL. 4.30 Above: The rocks on this hillside are covered with red-coloured algae. *Photo: P. Farrant.*

PL. 4.31 Right: Red-coloured algae, green plants, and lichens on rock. *Photo: P. Farrant*

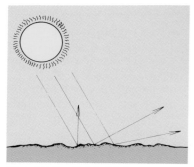

Fig. 4.7 Sunlight shining on a dry surface is reflected in various directions if the surface is not smooth; this whitens the surface colours. After rain, when water fills the surface depressions, sunlight is reflected in one direction and the colours of the surface are intensified.

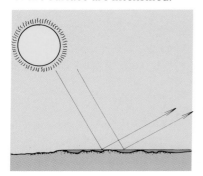

PL. 4.32 Hexagonal basalt columns, Sounkyo Gorge, northern Japan. *Photo: W. Farrant*

water at Earth's surface; and plutonic rocks - formed from magma cooling slowly beneath Earth's surface. The colours of igneous rocks are rarely striking and depend upon minerals present: the darker the rock, the more magnesium, iron and calcium it contains; light-coloured igneous rocks contain more pale minerals like quartz and feldspar.

The two commonest igneous rocks are granite and basalt. Basalt is volcanic, dark, evenly coloured, usually black or dark grey, sometimes with a bluish or greenish tinge (pl. 4.32). Its colour is caused by various combinations of small-grained minerals containing aluminium, iron, magnesium, calcium, sodium and potassium. Olivine basalt contains a significant amount of the greenish mineral olivine.

Granite is plutonic, and speckled because the grains are large enough to be clearly visible; it is commonly white, grey or pale pink, sometimes pale yellow or red (pl. 4.33). Its colour is determined mainly by the relative amounts of the minerals feldspar and quartz, though there are usually dark minerals, such as tourmaline, rutile and graphite, scattered in amongst these. Although granite is a light coloured rock, exposure to the atmosphere results in weathering, a process in which chemical changes to the surface of the rock cause the colours to darken.

Other types of igneous rocks contain different minerals and amounts of silica and therefore differ in colour: e.g. dolerite is greenish black because it contains the mineral augite, which owes its dark greenish black colour to a high iron and magnesium content.

Sedimentary rocks

Sedimentary rocks are formed when mud, sand particles and parts of dead animals and plants sink to the bottom of a body of water, accumulate, and become compressed. Sandstones vary considerably in colour according to content: white, grey or cream indicate quartz; pink indicates a high content of feldspar; grey, green or blue usually indicates fragments of igneous rocks; red or yellow may indicate iron-containing clay minerals, haematite and limonite. Solutions bearing these minerals wash through the rock, the minerals coat the sand grains and so the sandstone appears coloured.

Limestone and chalk are also sedimentary rocks but are composed mainly of calcite (calcium carbonate), a white mineral that is one of the few non-silicate minerals abundant in rocks. Calcite may precipitate directly out of seawater and fall to the bottom of the ocean, where the rock forms; or the shells of tiny organisms living in the water may fall to the bottom and accumulate there. Chalk differs from limestone in being composed mainly of the calcite shells of micro-organisms. Limestones are normally white, but if sand or mud grains also occur among accumulating sediments, they may be grey, white, yellow, red and even black (pl. 4.34).

Metamorphic rocks

Metamorphic rocks are created when heat and pressure change the composition and form of igneous or sedimentary rocks. The process takes place when

Earth's surface folds to form huge mountains or when hot igneous rock intrudes upwards into a layer of sedimentary rock. Marble is perhaps the most beautiful metamorphic rock, with many attractive colours. Under heat and pressure the calcite of limestone recrystallises into larger grains to form marble. Pure calcite produces white marble, while contaminants such as iron oxides in the original limestone cause other colours. The swirls and veins so typical of marble occur where these contaminants were present as bands in the original sedimentary rock. The iron oxide haematite makes marble red, the iron hydroxide limonite makes marble yellow and brown, minerals like serpentine make green marble, and grains of bituminous substances cause marble to be grey or black.

Relatively low pressure and heat, usually over those areas close to where mountain building is occurring, can change rocks like shale and mudstone, composed of fine clay, into slate. Slate is well known as a building material, its sheet-like structure making it useful for flat surfaces, like floors and roofs. Slate often shows a variety of different colours, which range from light pink to orange, blue, green and black. Different colours are caused by the different types of clay minerals and other components such as volcanic ash. Fossilised plant and animal remains can often be seen in slate.

SOIL COLOURS

Fragments of minerals like quartz, feldspar, mica, calcium carbonate and oxides of iron, manganese and aluminium, are responsible for colour in soil in the same way that minerals cause colour in rocks. Soil also contains water, air and organic matter, both living (e.g. fungi, bacteria, burrowing animals and plant roots) and dead (humus, derived predominantly from plant fragments). The major colorants of soils are carbon compounds from humus and various types of minerals derived from the weathering of rocks: together these two components take up about 60% of the volume of soil, with air and water filling the remainder. Humic acid, or humus material dissolved in water, causes most of the dark brown and black colours in soils. Compounds of minerals like iron, manganese and aluminium produce the reds, ochres and yellows.

Soils usually occur in layers above an underlying bedrock. Leaching (the removal of minerals by water) often affects the topsoil if rainfall is high. If the soil itself is wet, conditions become anaerobic (deficient in oxygen), and in cool conditions the humus cannot decompose fully and dark peat is formed.

Compounds of iron, in particular goethite and haematite, are the most important mineral colorants of soil. Goethite is one of the commonest minerals and is found in a wide variety of types of soil in many climatic regions: it is the yellow-brown pigment known as yellow ochre. Red ochre is haematite, the principle ore of iron, and this mineral is common in arid and tropical regions where organic matter decomposes so rapidly that goethite does not form. Soils formed in hot, dry deserts are usually sandy

and shallow, and do not support much vegetation (pl. 4.35, pl. 4.36). Elsewhere goethite and haematite often occur together.

Soil in the tropics

Red lateritic soils form in the hot, wet tropics by the weathering of rocks like basalt. The soils are usually much deeper than the shallow soils of deserts and they contain compounds of iron and aluminium, clay minerals and some silica, e.g. bauxite is a laterite formed by weathering of aluminium-rich rocks. The red terra rossa soils of the Mediterranean region are derived from iron-rich material overlying limestone bedrock, from which the calcium carbonate has leached out. Soils with a high content of calcium carbonate are usually white or grey.

In certain parts of the world that are not very humid, and where the weathered rock is calcareous, the soil can be very dark brown or black: this type of deep, well drained soil owes its colour to a combination of silty clay minerals and black organic humus. In temperate regions with deciduous forests, the soils are brown because they are composed of a mixture of clay minerals, free iron oxides, and large amounts of organic material. In colder regions of the world, where the decomposition of conifer and heath vegetation into humus proceeds very slowly because of the temperature, the clay minerals and iron and aluminium oxides in the soil are leached downwards in the soil when it rains. Here they form a dark, orange-brown layer of soil, leaving behind a grey leached topsoil.

Waterlogged soils

Grey soils and soils mottled with reds and yellows are typical of areas that are periodically waterlogged. A change in soil colour from red to yellow to grey is caused by the action of anaerobic bacteria on iron compounds in soil: as a result of these changes, iron moves out of the waterlogged area, leaving grey patches behind. The only remaining red patches tend to follow the tracks of plant roots, since the roots absorb water. Black streaks of iron sulfide in the soil are a further indication of the activity of anaerobic bacteria. The colour of a soil can therefore indicate its suitability for growing crops. Grey, dull-coloured soils or mottled soils with grey dominating are avoided because they are prone to waterlogging and are poorly aerated. Uniformly bright, especially brown, soils, are most suitable because they are usually well drained.

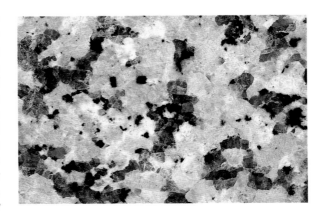

PL. 4.33 Granite is a coarse-grained, light coloured rock; its colour depends upon the relative proportions of various minerals. *Photo: P. Farrant*

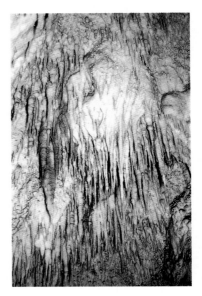

PL. 4.34 Stalactites and stalagmites in underground caves are often brown, red and yellow because of iron compounds dissolved in the ground water that first dissolves the limestone and then evaporates to form these structures. *Photo: P. Farrant.*

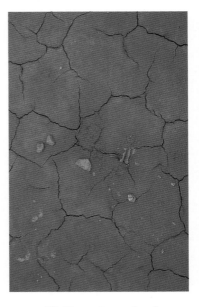

PL. 4.35 The colour of red desert soils in Australia is usually due to iron-containing haematite. *Photo: R.J. King*

PL. 4.36 Sandy desert soil at Lake Mungo, Australia. *Photo: P. Farrant*

PL. 4.37 The red-hot flames of bushfires are produced when vegetation composed of rather volatile compounds (of mainly carbon, nitrogen and sulphur) burn at temperatures of around 600 to 1000°C. When heated even further some substances become white-hot because they emit light from the entire visible spectrum. *Photo: R.J. King.*

COLOUR AND HEAT

Some materials change colour when they are heated, and this is usually an irreversible chemical reaction; e.g. when clay is heated, water is lost and the clay structure changes. Sometimes, however, the colour change is reversible: e.g. zinc oxide is white when cold and yellow when hot. When some substances are heated to very high temperatures, they become red-hot, emitting infra-red radiation and some visible light (pl. 4.37).

Many substances change colour when they react with oxygen from the air, in a process known as oxidation. An example of oxidation is tarnishing, in which the freshly exposed surfaces of metals like silver or copper change colour with exposure to air. When a substance burns, the energy of the heating process excites its electrons, and the electrons subsequently release their energy as visible light of different wavelengths as they revert to more stable arrangements.

The colours of Earth's land and water surfaces depend as much on their organic components, i.e. living plants and animals, and their remains, as their inorganic components. The physical nature of Earth's surface and the organisms that inhabit it interact with and modify each other in several ways to produce different habitats. These are examined in the next chapter.

CHAPTER 5

COLOURFUL HABITATS

PL. 5.1 Tropical rainforests are complex biomes in which the vegetation forms many layers. *Photo: M. Porteners*

PL. 5.2 Epiphytes, plants that grow upon other plants, are common in tropical and temperate rainforests. *Photo: P. Farrant*

PL. 5.7 Left: The fruiting bodies of forest fungi, like this pouch fungus, are often brightly coloured. *Photo: L. Rodgers*

Earth's biomes — forests, grasslands, deserts, mountains, polar regions, oceans, lakes and rivers — which provide the habitats for plants and animals, differ in many respects. They occur at different latitudes and altitudes and over a range of different climates, soil types and light regimes. In each, the plants and animals are adapted to survive in particular conditions.

THE BRILLIANT COLOURS OF TROPICAL RAINFORESTS

Some of the most varied and colourful plants and animals are found in the tropics, those parts of the world between 23° north and 23° south of the equator. Constantly hot and humid areas support tropical rainforests, complex biomes with many layers (pl. 5.1).

At the top of the forest, the crowns of tall evergreen and some deciduous trees interlock to form a canopy layer that intercepts much incoming sunlight and creates a perpetually hot, humid environment beneath. The greens of the canopy foliage are as diverse as the plant species. Some taller trees emerge through the canopy, while vines and creepers grow from below, binding foliage into a continuous canopy. Beneath the canopy are layers of understorey plants: climbers, smaller trees, bamboos, ferns, herbs and epiphytes (plants that grow on other plants, pl. 5.2). Different plant layers provide a variety of habitats for lichens, mosses, algae and fungi that often grow in the moistest and shadiest places, as well as for the forest animals (pl. 5.3).

As little as 2% of sunlight arriving at the rainforest canopy reaches the forest floor. Some of this is direct sunlight, in the form of sunflecks, while some is sunlight reflected from clouds, leaves and tree trunks. Another component is green light that has filtered through canopy leaves. The plant pigment chlorophyll, which is essential for photosynthesis, absorbs energy from the red and blue wavelengths of light. The light that passes through the leaves is thus deficient in these wavelengths and hence appears green. Light reaching the floor is therefore dimmer and its colour has been altered slightly. It contains relatively more far-red wavelength light (infra-red light just outside the visible range of humans) than red wavelength light. The relative excess of far-red light is known to affect some plants, e.g. it can inhibit germination of some seeds. Only when there is a break in the canopy will such seeds receive enough light for long enough to become well-established.

Colour adaptations: leaves

The leaves of some rainforest plants such as figs, philodendrons and spathiphyllums, are shiny green and pointed, and water drops slide off quickly. Some leaves have such shiny surfaces they appear almost metallic and are known as tin leaves, e.g. the giant caladium has leaves like burnished copper (pl. 5.4). In the shaded environment below the canopy, plant leaves have several features that enable them to capture more light energy: the leaves may be broader, softer and thinner than canopy leaves, and darker green, due to an increase in the amount of chlorophyll present (pl. 5.5). Some plants even produce differently coloured leaves at different levels, e.g. coffee and cocoa plants produce small, yellowish green leaves in sunlight and larger, greener leaves in shade (pl. 5.6). These are known as sun-leaves and shade-leaves respectively. In an environment with a relatively high amount of far-red light, such plants have long stems and few leaves and branches. In normal light, leaves are oriented to intercept as much

PL. 5.3 Left: Algae, mosses and ferns are common in moist parts of tropical forests. *Photo: P. Farrant*

PL. 5.4 Right: Many forest floor plants have shiny pointed leaves, which allow water drops to slide off easily. *Photo: P. Farrant*

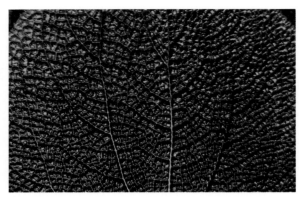

PL. 5.5 Forest floor plants often have dark green leaves; bumpy surfaces mean that parts of a wet leaf can still absorb light. *Photo: P. Farrant*

PL. 5.6 Coffee, a tropical plant that has flowers and fruits on its stems, has larger, greener leaves in the shade. *Photo: R. Berthold*

light as possible yet at the same time to minimise self-shading.

The rainforest floor can be very dark and wet, often splashed with the vivid colours of mushrooms and toadstools, the fruiting bodies of fungi (pl. 5.7). Some fungi are even bioluminescent. We can only guess why this should be so. One possibility is that the light given off may attract animals, which break open the fruiting bodies and release or distribute fungal spores. Some plants that live in the gloom of the forest floor have leaves with blue or green iridescence (see p. 82).

The leaves of even the tallest forest trees do not remain green forever, but eventually die and fall. Though some rainforest trees are deciduous, mostly leaves are replaced periodically in flushes. Falling leaves are rarely vivid, but new growth is often red or pale yellow, before green chlorophyll dominates. Red pigments may protect sensitive young leaves from ultraviolet light, which might otherwise destroy important molecules in their cells (pl. 5.8).

Colourful flowers

Tropical rainforest plants often produce flowers and fruits in flushes, synchronously on the one plant, or synchronously with other plants of the same or even other species over a large area. Flowers are often brilliantly coloured, especially those in the canopy that are pollinated by birds such as hummingbirds or sunbirds, e.g. tulip trees. These flowers are often red or orange, colours easily seen by the birds. Flowers pollinated by birds are often relatively large, robust structures, conspicuously displayed. Flower display may be further enhanced if the species is deciduous, e.g. the cuipo, a Central American tree, which has masses of tiny red flowers after its leaves have fallen.

Flowers lower down in the forest are more likely

PL. 5.8 Left: New leaves of rainforest plants may by pink, red or bluish before their chlorophyll develops fully. *Photo: M. Porteners*

PL. 5.9 Above: Many rainforest trees that do not reach the canopy produce flowers and fruits on their trunks. *Photo: P. Farrant*

PL. 5.10 Right: Birds that live in the rainforest canopy, like this pigeon, are often large, colourful and conspicuous. *Photo: L. Rodgers*

PL. 5.11 Above: Snakes that live in trees, like this python, are often green and well-camouflaged. *Photo: R.T. Hoser*

PL. 5.12 Right: Possums and other nocturnal mammals have poor colour vision and are usually not brightly coloured. *Photo: W.H. King*

especially those that are not tall enough to reach the canopy, display their flowers on their stems (pl. 5.9). Stem-flowering plants include cocoa trees, breadfruit trees and many figs. Flowers produced singly or in small groups often have strong perfume as well as attractive colours.

The diversity of insects and flowers is so great in tropical forests that many plants are pollinated exclusively by particular animals; this is especially true of some plants that produce small, inconspicuously coloured flowers over a long time, e.g. the long-tongued hawk moth pollinates the Madagascan orchid and is the only moth with a tongue long enough to reach the nectar in the flower's spur. Other plants, however, are visited by a variety of pollinating animals: e.g. the flowers of Australian lillypilly trees may be pollinated by insects, birds, bats or pygmy possums. As there is little air movement in the forests, very few plants are wind pollinated and most, even the grasses, rely on insects, birds and other animals.

Animal life

Many rainforest animals have vivid, glossy or iridescent colours. Insects are the most numerous and varied animals here and show the greatest variety of colours. Some brilliant blue butterflies can be seen even from low-flying aeroplanes as they dart back and forth in the canopy. Many butterflies and other insects that are poisonous have bright warning colours, while others such as stick insects, flower mantises and katydid leaf insects, have colours that blend in, and shapes that mimic forest foliage and flowers. Iridescent colours that change with the angle of view make many insects and birds hard to follow as they flit about, and this may confuse potential predators. Tropical forests are renowned for spectacularly coloured birds (pl. 5.10), which are usually large, e.g. bowerbirds, pittas, cassowaries and birds of paradise; smaller birds, such as robins and treecreepers, tend to be inconspicuous and brown. Even though brightly coloured birds may be difficult to see on the dim forest floor, males especially become very conspicuous during their lavish courtship displays on higher branches, e.g. the blue bird of paradise from Papua New Guinea, which hangs upside-down, fans out its breast feathers and moves its tail feathers so that they catch the light and shimmer with a variety of iridescent blues. Conspicuous, colourful birds living in the canopy are usually species that can escape rapidly, such as parrots.

Predatory animals in the rainforest, which sneak up on prey, tend to have camouflage coloration. Tree snakes, praying mantises, eagles, owls and many other predators match the colours of their background (pl. 5.11). The chameleon is well known for its ability to change colour to suit its surroundings. Mammals, such as rodents on the forest floor and possums in the canopy, are usually rather drab in colour because they have poor colour vision and are usually nocturnal (pl. 5.12). In general, species that do not see in colour are not themselves brightly coloured, and at night even animals with colour vision cannot see in colour because of limited available light.

to be white or yellow, colours that stand out in the dim green light and attract butterflies, moths, other insects and even slugs, for pollination. Some gourd vines produce white or yellow flowers on separate vines that intertwine: the vines are actually separate male and female plants that produce flowers with only male or only female fertile parts. Many forest plants have synchronous flowering and many,

THE SUBTLE COLOURS OF SUBTROPICAL FORESTS

In the southern hemisphere, subtropical and temperate forests tend to be either rainforests or scattered evergreen woodlands with dry summers and cool, moist winters. Like their tropical counterparts, temperate rainforests are basically evergreen, characterised by a variety of emergent and canopy trees, vines and understorey plants. The plants produce colourful flowers and fruits, which are fed upon by many brightly coloured insects, birds and other animals (pl. 5.13).

In Australia, woodland colours are subtle. Being drier than other forests, less water is available for plants. Instead of soft, bright green leaves, eucalypts have leaves adapted to reflecting sunlight and conserving water, with a waxy coating that gives them a grey or bluish green colour. The leaves also hang downwards, which again minimises water loss and also allows sunlight to pass through to the forest floor (pl. 5.14). The resulting huge variety of shrubs and grasses in the understorey usually provides woodlands with a multitude of different shades of foliage greens, as well as multi-coloured barks, flowers and fruits. While often small, the flowers of these plants give a showy display, especially in spring, but also at other times of the year if pollinating animals are present or if conditions are good.

THE RICH COLOURS OF DECIDUOUS FORESTS

At middle latitudes, the colours of forests change more dramatically with the seasons. Less sunlight reaches the forests, especially in winter when the sun is lower in the sky and days are shorter. Seasons are marked and rainfall is spread fairly evenly throughout the year. Although there are deciduous forests in the southern hemisphere, seasonal colours are most marked in northern hemisphere forests: in Europe, eastern U.S.A. and south-eastern China (pl. 5.15).

These forests have fewer tree species than rainforests; species include oaks, maples, elms, birches, magnolias and larches. Leaves tend to be broad, soft and juicy and they are shed each year. There are few epiphytes, but many mosses, algae, fungi and lichens.

Deciduous forests are renowned for their magnificent autumn colours: yellows, bronzes, golds, oranges, reds and purples. These are the colours of dying leaves — trees do not retain broad leaves through winter when the water supply below ground is frozen and unavailable. The annual leaf fall in temperate deciduous forests means that a large amount of the organic matter accumulates and the soil is usually rich and brown.

Leaf fall heralds a period of death and dormancy for forest plants and animals. With no leaves to eat, insects either die or pass into a dormant stage of their life cycle. While some birds such as woodpeckers can survive by feeding upon dormant insects under tree bark, most other birds (such as flycatchers which rely on insects and berries) migrate to other places. Many other animals, such as

PL. 5.13 Above: The red flowers of the deciduous Australian flame tree become conspicuous when the tree is leafless in summer. *Photo: P. Farrant*

PL. 5.14 Left: Lack of a closed canopy in a woodland allows the growth of a well developed understorey of shrubs. *Photo: P. Farrant*

PL. 5.15 Autumn leaf fall in a deciduous forest, Germany. *Photo: R.J. King*

PL. 5.16 Anemones carpet the forest floor before the trees have their new leaves. Germany. *Photo: R.J. King*

PL. 5.17 In spring, the new growth of many plants is yellowish green, sometimes flushed with pink. *Photo: R.J. King*

hedgehogs and bears, build up fat reserves during the summer and hibernate when vegetation no longer provides shelter. Others, such as squirrels, store seeds during summer and go below ground for winter. Without colourful animals and green vegetation, the forest is silent and bare, with snow on the ground and ice on lakes and streams. The animals that remain in the open in winter are predators such as wolves and cats, scavengers such as foxes and crows, and others that gather in herds such as deer and bison, none of which needs camouflage coloration. Food becomes scarce and many animals change their diet to survive. Some animals vulnerable to predators also stay in the forest during winter, but their coats change to white for camouflage.

Spring sees many plants flower quickly. While light still reaches the ground before leaves appear on the trees, bulbs such as snowdrops and bluebells that survived winter beneath the soil, carpet the forest floor in whites, pinks, blues or yellows (pl. 5.16). Then the forest trees change into the fragile colours of new growth (pl. 5.17). Light green leaves, often flushed pink with protective pigments, burst forth as buds open. As the weather warms and snow and ice melt, the forest floor turns brown as the decaying leaf litter is exposed. Green mosses, colourful lichens, fungi and algae grow in moist shady parts of the forest. Shade-tolerant plants such as orchids and wood anemones flower, too.

With plenty of foliage and flowers to feed upon, insects such as butterflies, moths and flies emerge from well-camouflaged eggs and cocoons, and migratory birds arrive to feed on insects, flowers and fruits. Some birds have brightly coloured breeding plumage, especially in yellow or white which are the most conspicuous colours in the greenish light, but most, such as thrushes and blackbirds that live on the forest floor, tend to be brown or dark and well camouflaged against leaf litter: these birds attract mates with their song. Large and small animals that spent winter underground, such as reptiles and mammals, also reappear. Most are ground-dwellers, such as bears and mice, but some are climbers, e.g. squirrels. With the courtship displays and ensuing birth of young animals in the spring, the forest becomes a colourful and noisy place. Young animals are often well camouflaged, but some, especially birds, get their adult colours when they moult in summer. At this time, too, brightly coloured male birds change

PL. 5.19 Far left: Yews are evergreen trees that produce bright red fruits. *Photo: R.J. King*

PL. 5.18 Left: Evergreen forests in winter are green and white, the colours of the trees and snow. *Photo: P. Farrant*

to more drab coloration resembling that of the females.

In summer, tree foliage becomes a deeper green because leaves have plenty of chlorophyll; they absorb sunlight and produce the food upon which the whole forest depends. The forest floor beneath is now shady, the light is greenish and there are few flowers. Leaf-eating insects such as caterpillars, ants and grasshoppers are very numerous at this time of year.

EVERGREEN CONIFEROUS FORESTS

At higher latitudes and altitudes of the northern hemisphere, forests are evergreen and coniferous.

PL. 5.20 Below: Ice tunnel through iceberg, Casey, Australian Antarctic Territory. *Photo: J. Seddon*

These forests stretch across North America, Siberia, northern Europe and Scandinavia, areas with short, cool summers and long, cold winters of heavy snow and little sunshine. Owing to the harsh climate and poor soil of these regions, coniferous forests are even less diverse than broadleaf forests. Sometimes a single tree species dominates the forest and thus a single shade of green covers the countryside. Species include pines, spruces and firs, which all produce their seeds in cones.

The leaves of conifers are tough and reduced to needles so they will not lose precious water during winter when the water in the soil is frozen. Though there are huge numbers of needle-like leaves on individual trees, they intercept less light than those of broad-leaved trees because there is less light available at these higher latitudes and because the trees themselves grow straight and are densely packed together in the forest. The leaves are too thick to allow any green light to be transmitted through, though many conifers have leaves with a waxy coating to prevent water loss, and this gives them a bluish green appearance and makes the light on the forest floor slightly bluish. The forest floor, though shaded and sheltered all year, is relatively dim and there are few understorey plants. Accumulations of continuously falling leaves lie on the floor for a long time because the process of decay is hampered by cold. The slowly decomposing leaf litter produces acidic conditions that inhibit the growth of other plants: the forest floor is thus dim and brown except in winter, when covered by a thick blanket of snow (pl. 5.18).

Coniferous forests are far less colourful than deciduous forests, with fewer species of plants and hardly any flowers (pl. 5.19). The few animals are mostly migratory and come in summer to feed on the swarms of insects such as flies and mosquitoes.

POLAR WHITE

Differences between seasons are most pronounced in the polar regions that form 10% of Earth's land surface. Here winters are cold and dark. In summer there is sunlight all day. Because the sun never rises very high but seems to slide around the horizon, light here has a greater proportion of yellow and red wavelengths, rather like the colours of morning or afternoon sky at lower latitudes. This is because the sunlight travels through a greater thickness of Earth's atmosphere. Sunrises and sunsets are often vivid and gloriously pink.

In winter it is dark most of the day and night. Ice forms on the ocean surface, and freshwater lakes may freeze completely. Animals other than warm-blooded birds and mammals, such as cold-blooded frogs, lizards and snakes, are rare in polar regions at any time of year. Most birds are migratory and do not spend winter here, and while some of the few mammals hibernate, most move to lower latitude forests for shelter. The small numbers of birds and mammals remaining in polar regions through winter are camouflaged: predators such as polar bears are white year-round and prey species such as hares and ptarmigan change to white for winter.

Antarctica and the Arctic

No large herbivorous animals live in Antarctica, which is even colder than the Arctic. There are no trees and little plant life except for mosses, lichens, algae and several flowering plants. Some parts of the land surface are not covered with snow in summer, so yellow, red or grey rocks introduce some colour to the landscape. Some of the most striking colours of Antarctica are the intense blues and greens that are often seen in ice caves (pl. 5.20).

In regions within the Arctic circle (further north than 60°N), away from the north pole where there is no land, some plants (mosses and lichens) can live beneath the winter snow, so there is still food for animals such as reindeer at this time of year. In summer, the landscape becomes far more colourful when birds and other animals return, insects emerge and flowers come out. Plants are low-growing perennials, scattered where there are pockets of soil. They tend to be cushion-like, and grow slowly and along the ground rather than upwards, due to harsh conditions. These plants have a variety of differently coloured leaves: bright green; dark green and leathery; bluish green if waxy or hairy; and sometimes even reddish, with pigments that screen excessive light reflected from remaining patches of snow. The variety of colours results from different adaptations of plants for survival in their habitats.

Single-celled algae growing in snow may contain a red pigment, haematochrome, that masks their green photosynthetic pigments and protects them from excess ultraviolet radiation. Small crustaceans living in Arctic and alpine lakes are often red, too, coloured with sunscreening pigments, while in the clearest lakes of all they are pigmented with an even darker pigment, melanin, which screens all but 10% of the ultraviolet radiation.

The flowers of Arctic plants are not generally vividly coloured: many are white and pollinated by flies; others are inconspicuous and wind pollinated. Some colour comes from the spore capsules of mosses, which become pinkish brown as they mature and dry, and lichens coloured with reddish pigments. Occasional splashes of colour are also provided by visiting birds, such as plovers, phalaropes and terns. Most insects and the few reptiles and amphibians are dark coloured so they can absorb all available heat. These cold-blooded animals must soak up the feeble warmth of sunlight which supplies them with energy for survival.

IN THE THIN AIR OF THE MOUNTAINS

With increasing altitude, conditions become colder. Thus coniferous forests can be found on mountains at lower latitudes, and cold deserts and glaciers can be found on top of high equatorial mountains such as Mount Kilimanjaro in Africa. While cold mountains are similar to polar regions in many ways — deriving their colours from snow, colourful rocks and lakes, flowers and the insects and birds that feed on plants — they differ from polar regions in some very important ways. High altitude gives them thinner air and more intense sunlight than low-lying areas at the same latitude. The light is richer in

PL. 5.21 Giant groundsels, Mt Kilimanjaro: hairs on the leaves give many plants a bluish green, grey or silver appearance. *Photo: W. Farrant*

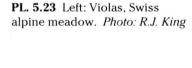

PL. 5.22 Above: Many high latitude or high altitude plants have red pigments that act as sunscreens. Red Tarn, New Zealand. *Photo: P. Farrant*

PL. 5.23 Left: Violas, Swiss alpine meadow. *Photo: R.J. King*

short wavelengths — blue and ultraviolet. These regions are too high to receive sunlight that travels through the lower part of Earth's atmosphere, i.e. light that other, flatter parts of Earth receive at sunrise and sunset and which is richer in orange and red wavelengths (see p. 26).

Plants' leaves at high altitudes are adapted to high levels of ultraviolet light. Many plants such as daisies have greyish or bluish leaves, because they are covered with hairs and waxes that reflect sunlight and reduce water loss (pl. 5.21). Other plants have pigments that act as sunscreens, letting through only useful wavelengths of light (pl. 5.22), e.g. some of the epiphytic bromeliads that grow on the branches of tall trees in mountain cloud forests. These plants have red upper leaf surfaces that act like sunscreens and protect the underlying green photosynthetic tissues from ultraviolet light. The light varies significantly at different times of year, and the quantity of sunscreening pigment alters too, so that photosynthetic production is maximised year-round. If pigments were fixed in quantity, shading of chlorophyll would prevent maximum food production in winter. Some other bromeliads have a powdery, wax-like cover on their leaves that probably also functions as a sunscreen by reflecting excess light.

On mountains at high latitudes, as in polar regions, larger mammals such as deer, and birds such as titmice, move down to the forests below during winter. Other birds, such as swallows and swifts, migrate to warmer places. Insects exist as larvae or pupae during winter and the landscape is white and colourless until snow melts in spring. Summer is

PL. 5.24 High heathland plants often have red, pink or blue flowers that attract birds; this giant lobelia on Mt Kilimanjaro has hidden blue flowers. *Photo: W. Farrant*

the most colourful time in mountain regions. Alpine meadow flowers, e.g. gentians, buttercups, anemones and edelweiss, are usually white, yellow, pink or blue (pl. 5.23). Many flowers of high rocky deserts are yellow or white, while many in high heathlands are pink, red or even blue (pl. 5.24).

GRASSLANDS

About a quarter of Earth's land surface is covered with grasslands, vast open regions where grasses dominate vegetation and there are few trees (pl. 5.25). Grasslands are variously known as steppes in Eurasia, prairies in North America, savannah in Africa, pampas in South America; grasslands also include monsoonal areas in northern Australia, llanos in South America, floodplains in Asia and high plateaus in Mongolia. Some grasslands are moister than others and have taller species of grasses, while others have shrubs and scrubby vegetation, or even scattered trees. All grasslands are characterised by low humidity. Temperate grasslands have warm, dry summers and cool or cold winters, while tropical grasslands usually have one or two rainy seasons with a lengthy dry period. Grasslands lie between the drier deserts and moister forests, and they are usually well away from oceans. They are the habitats most favoured by humans for agriculture, so many have been degraded and turned into semi-desert or desert.

Grassland landscape colours change with wet and dry conditions. During the dry season, vegetation dies down and the landscape is predominantly yellow, red, brown or black: the colour of fertile, fragile soils and stubble from grasses which remain alive even after fires caused by lightning during spectacular storms. Ash, dust and sand in the air during the dry season help to create spectacularly vivid sunrises and sunsets as particles scatter more and more blue wavelengths from the path of the sun's light (Rayleigh scattering, see p. 11). The predominant colour of grasslands during the dry season in tropical monsoon regions is bluish green, because many of the grasses and shrubs have leaves covered with hairs that reflect heat and conserve water (pl. 5.26).

Lush and green

With rain, grasslands become lush and green. Grasses sprout up from growing tips beneath the soil and from dormant seeds, while bulbs, annuals and perennials, such as lilies, daisies and pea plants, produce colourful flowers. All these plants have shallow roots that gather moisture when it rains. The grasses are pollinated by wind and have inconspicuous flowers without coloured petals. Their leaves and seeds (the grass grains) can support huge concentrations of herbivorous animals, from insects to elephants. Grasses grow from points at or below the soil surface, along stems that spread either along, or just under, the ground, so that new upright shoots can be produced continuously. This is why these plants can withstand browsing and trampling by vast herds of mammals such as wildebeest and antelope (pl. 5.27).

Grassland animals usually are coloured and patterned in yellows, browns and reds, making them inconspicuous against their surroundings (pl. 5.28). The landscape is fairly open so there are few places

PL. 5.25 Above: Grasslands are vast open areas with few trees where grasses, consumed by herbivorous animals, dominate the vegetation. *Photo: P. Farrant*

PL. 5.26 Right: Monsoonal regions have distinct and regular wet and dry seasons. Grasses form an important component of the vegetation, but scattered trees, like these bottle trees, as well as shrubs and water plants (in the wet season) may also be present. *Photo: R. Berthold.*

PL. 5.27 Grasses can withstand trampling and being eaten by large herds of mammals like wildebeest. *Photo: W. Farrant*

to hide. Animals that are protected by living in herds are often dark; but many, such as antelopes, underground burrowers such as ground squirrels and mice, and predators such as lions and cheetahs, have colours like the pale shades of background soil and vegetation. Birds of prey, snakes, lizards, and insects such as grasshoppers, also tend to have colours that give them good camouflage.

Mammals other than primates have poor colour vision and are generally not brightly coloured for breeding displays, unlike animals with good colour vision, e.g. birds and lizards. Grasslands support an enormous variety of birds, though perhaps the most spectacular are the large ground birds such as bustards and ostriches, many of which can ruffle their feathers and display colourful patches during breeding (pl. 5.29). The bright colours of birds that live in flocks may help the birds to see each other easily and to keep together (pl. 5.30).

THE DULL COLOURS OF THE DESERTS

Less than one-quarter of Earth's land surface is covered with deserts, areas characterised by very low and unpredictable rainfall. Although deserts usually occur well away from the ocean, they can also extend right to the ocean on the dry side of continents, e.g. in Western Australia and coastal Peru and Chile. Hot deserts are found at tropical and subtropical latitudes, while cold deserts occur in polar regions and on high mountains (pl. 5.31). Because of the low rainfall, both hot and cold deserts have little vegetation and therefore support relatively few animal species. These animals, however, are well adapted to the arid conditions.

Hot deserts receive intense sunlight all year, and because there is little vegetation, the sunlight is not deficient in any wavelengths. For most of the year hot deserts such as the Simpson in Australia and

PL. 5.28 Grassland animals that do not live in groups, such as tortoises, often match the colours of their surroundings. *Photo: W. Farrant*

PL. 5.29 Above: The relatively light colours of this bustard probably help to reflect sunlight and heat. *Photo: W. Farrant*

PL. 5.30 Bees form a significant part of the diet of rainbow birds, whereas most other birds are warned off by a bee's yellow and black coloration. *Photo: W.H. King*

PL. 5.31 Left: The main colours of this high altitude rocky desert are those of the soil and rocks; it supports little plant or animal life. *Photo: W. Farrant.*

Africa's Sahara are yellow, brown, red or grey, the colour of their soils and rocks. Desert soils are little more than weathered rock, as they contain hardly any organic matter. Any rocks in the sand stand out on the bare landscape. The desert sands may be flat expanses, sometimes with white salty patches, or they may be driven by the wind into vast dunes. Sandstorms commonly colour the sky in the same desert colours, producing vivid sunsets because the air is so dry, and wind blown sand erodes the landscape. There is not much shade for desert animals other than at oases, where springs or streams allow lush green vegetation to grow, so many animals seek shelter in underground burrows.

The few plants that live year round in hot deserts either have reduced leaves and green stems that can photosynthesise, such as cacti, or they are grey or blue-green, such as saltbush and bluebush, which have hairs, waxes or salt on their surfaces to reflect ultraviolet light and reduce water loss (pl. 5.32). Cacti produce vividly coloured flowers in yellows, whites, pinks and reds to attract the few desert birds, such as cactus wrens and thrashers, and insects. The desert changes colour dramatically only after rain, when small ephemeral plants such as evening primroses in California and desert peas in Australia, quickly complete their life cycles and clothe the desert soil in blue, yellow, white, red and green (pl. 5.33). Insects such as desert locusts also complete their life cycles quickly and utilise the short-lived vegetation.

Matching the desert sand

Many animals that live in hot deserts are well adapted to a permanent life there. Those that are active during the day often match the desert sand colours: tortoises, sand monitors, spiders, scorpions and many more animals, are pale with patterns in greys, reds or yellows. Many have pale undersurfaces that reflect the radiation from light-coloured sand: this prevents them from becoming too hot. Most mammals, such as kangaroo-rats and jerboas are plain, pale and sandy-coloured, live in underground burrows and become active at night. Animals cannot see in colour at night, so intricate patterning is not needed.

Few animals in hot deserts are brightly coloured, perhaps because food is so scarce that any conspicuous animal is at risk. The few that are, including lizards, birds and beetles, live in burrows and tend to be able to outwit predators in some way. Some poisonous animals, such as the Egyptian cobra, are black. Cold-blooded insects and lizards have dark pigments that absorb the sun's heat and therefore energy. Black pigments also shield internal organs against ultraviolet radiation and strengthen insects' cuticles, making them more resistant to wind-blown desert sand.

Some otherwise camouflaged desert animals can expose small patches of colour, which are normally hidden, to frighten or distract predators, e.g. desert grasshoppers with coloured hind wings. Many desert animals such as desert geckos and some agamid lizards have flattened profiles and cast little shadow to give away their presence. Hairy insects, such as some bees, reflect light and their pale or silver colours

PL. 5.32 Above: Desert spinifex appears silvery green because it has hairs that reflect sunlight. *Photo: M. Porteners*

PL. 5.33 Right: After rain the desert becomes alive with colour, as ephemeral plants quickly grow, flower and set seed. *Photo: P. Farrant*

glitter and make them difficult to follow against the sparkling quartz sands.

THE VIBRANT COLOURS OF CORAL REEFS

Just as tropical rainforests have a great variety of colourful terrestrial birds and animals, tropical coral reefs are colourful underwater environments. The water above coral reefs is shallow and clear, with little suspended matter, organic or inorganic (pl. 5.34). The strong light that illuminates the shallow, sunlit reef waters is more or less spectrally complete, perhaps a little bluer than sunlight, but balanced enough to allow colourful patterns to be clearly visible. A coral reef is vibrant with colour.

Most corals that contain algae living in their tissues have soft brown and green colours because of the photosynthetic pigments of these organisms (pl. 5.35). Other corals without algae, and invertebrates such as seastars, urchins, worms, anemones and clams, are more often brightly coloured because their tissues do not have to transmit light for photosynthesis (pl. 5.36). Tropical coral reef fish are the gaudiest of all, their colours and patterns allowing them to recognise their own and other species (pl. 5.37). Animals such as seasnakes that are dangerous or poisonous, are often conspicuous.

Stripes and spots, even though they are brightly coloured, tend to break up fishes' outlines and thus provide some camouflage. Animals are only conspicuous if they are visible against their backgrounds and in such a colourful environment these fish blend in with their surroundings (pl. 5.38).

THE OPEN OCEAN

Blooms of microscopic plants in the surface waters of the ocean can colour the water green, brownish yellow or even red, depending upon the species. The colours of animals in the open ocean depend upon the depth at which they live. Animals that live on or at the water surface are usually blue or purple, e.g. floating sea slugs, by-the-wind sailors, the Portuguese man-of-war and purple ocean snails. There are also animals that leap out of the water, e.g. blue flying fish, which are coloured with a pigment that not

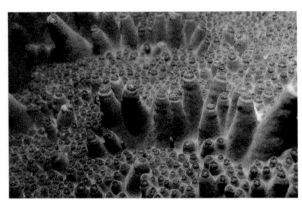

only camouflages them but probably also protects them from the intense ultraviolet radiation at the surface.

Small planktonic animals that live beneath the surface are more likely to be transparent, whereas surface-dwelling fish that are large enough to be conspicuous are disguised with dark blue backs that blend in with the colour of the deep ocean below, pale or silver bellies that blend in with the sunlight when seen from below and bars along the sides to break up their outlines (pl. 5.39). A typical well-

PL. 5.34 Above: Turquoise sea, Great Barrier Reef. *Photo: R. Berthold*

PL. 5.35 Left: Many corals are brownish or greenish because they contain symbiotic algae. *Photo: P. Farrant*

PL. 5.36 Below left: Corals that do not contain symbiotic algae are often more brightly coloured. *Photo: P. Farrant*
PL. 5.37 Below right: Clownfish are brightly coloured but are protected by the anemones they live with: they are somehow immune to the stinging cells of the anemones and in turn help to protect their hosts with aggressive behaviour towards coral-eating fishes. *Photo: P. Farrant*

PL. 5.38 Brightly coloured coral reef angelfish. *Photo: P. Farrant*

PL. 5.39 Fish often match the bluish green colours of their habitat. *Photo: P. Farrant*

from decaying vegetation washed in from the surrounding land; the water is fairly acidic and low in oxygen and supports few plant and animal species. In these waters, red wavelengths of light are transmitted deepest, so camouflaged animals tend to be brown, and conspicuous markings tend to be red, e.g. male sticklebacks in the breeding season.

The eyes of fish are adapted to detect these colours and contain more pigments sensitive to the red wavelengths of light; fish that swim from rivers to the sea adapt by changing their eye pigments during migration. When salmon return to freshwater to spawn, the proportion of blue-sensitive pigments in their eyes decreases and the proportion of red-sensitive pigments increases.

Lakes and rivers can vary in colour in the same way that oceans do, depending on the type of material suspended in the water and the colour of algal blooms.

COLOURS OF THE DARK

Animals live in even the darkest places on Earth: caves and the deep oceans. The luxuriant green vegetation around the mouth of a cave soon dwindles as the light level drops inside. Caves are used by animals as places to hibernate during winter or rest during the day: thus many creatures, such as bats, come and go. Well inside a cave, where there is perpetual darkness and the air or water temperature is constant, there are few animals and rarely any plants. The only plants one is likely to see here (by torchlight!) are the pale yellow seedlings that have germinated from seeds dropped by birds or bats, and which are destined to die for lack of light.

The few types of animals that live permanently in caves - including species of beetles, salamanders, fish, crayfish, harvestmen and millipedes - are not present in large numbers. These creatures are not visible in the darkness and are not camouflaged: they are pale in colour, without any of the pigments of their relatives on the surface, e.g. adult Ozark cave salamanders are pinkish because their blood vessels are close to the body surface for obtaining oxygen. Many cave animals are also blind, slow moving and smaller than related surface species. The cave environment does not provide an abundance of food for energy and growth; energy is probably saved by not producing pigment.

There is not enough food in caves for warm-blooded animals such as mammals and birds to live there permanently, and these animals obtain their food from outside. Some brighter colours are provided by moulds and fungi and the occasional red or orange parasites on otherwise pale larger animals. However, none of these colours can be seen in the dark and the pigments probably have some physiological function. The only colour visible in caves is the coloured light, or bioluminescence, produced by glow-worms, and these insects usually live near the entrance of a cave rather than right inside.

Only some animals can live in the dark, and even these animals depend upon light because they depend ultimately on the food produced by green plants. The next chapter looks at the colours of the most important parts of a plant: its leaves.

PL. 5.40 Southern sealion: marine mammals are often blue or grey, matching the colours of their ocean habitat.
Photo: A. Leslie

camouflaged predatory fish with these colours is the barracuta. Although marine mammals such as whales and dolphins are more conspicuous because of their size, many tend to be blue and grey (and lighter underneath), colours that match the ocean (pl. 5.40).

Deeper in the ocean, where all the red wavelengths have been absorbed by seawater but where some light still reaches, animals tend to be darker: their backs are usually black (or orange or red, which appear black at these depths), and their sides are silvery to reflect surrounding colours. Many species of fish, e.g. some hatchetfish, have rows of blue light organs on their bellies and these are thought to be for camouflage and communication. Hatchetfish have eyes that are sensitive to this blue bioluminescence. On the ocean floor, where no light penetrates, animals tend to be dark, black or red, rather than silvery or bioluminescent.

LAKES

Though the water in some freshwater lakes can be quite blue like ocean water, in most lakes and rivers it is yellow or brown because of the humic acids

CHAPTER 6

LEAVES : BASICALLY GREEN

PL. 6.3 Left: Plants that live low down in tropical rainforests are often dark green, with a large amount of chlorophyll. *Photo: P. Farrant*

Green is the dominant colour of vegetation on Earth (pl. 6.1). The basic green of leaves is due to the green pigment chlorophyll, essential for photosynthesis.

Different leaf surface structures — with variations in thickness, hairiness, waxiness, air content and smoothness — result in many different greens (pl. 6.2). Leaf colour also depends on the age of the leaf, the side of the leaf we are looking at, whether it is wet or dry, the direction of light and wind, and other variables. Many simpler organisms such as algae, which do not even have leaves, show further variation in colour (see BOX 1).

The great variety of leaf colour in nature has a purpose. While plants need to be green for photosynthesis, different greens enable species to adapt to light conditions in their various habitats. The better adapted a plant is to its environment, the better its chance of survival (pls 6.3, 6.4).

Cells: The Building Blocks of Plants

All living organisms are composed of cells, the tiny building blocks of living matter first identified by Robert Hooke (1635-1703). There is an enormous diversity of cells. A mass of similar cells functioning together is called a tissue and a number of different tissues function together in an organ. Mesophyll is the green photosynthetic tissue found in leaves.

Despite the range of cell types, most cells have the same basic components (fig. 6.1). A cell is controlled by its nucleus, and this is surrounded by cytoplasm or general cell contents. Within the cytoplasm are several other types of organelles enclosed by membranes. In mature plant cells a vacuole may take up most of the cell volume. The vacuole contents are known as cell sap; this is turgid and helps support the plant. Plant pigments are produced inside the cell and can occur in cell walls, in plastids or in solution in the cell sap.

PL. 6.1 Right: Bamboo forest, Japan. *Photo: R.J. King.*

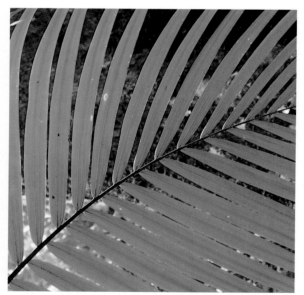

PL. 6.2 Far right above: The fronds of palms that grow in permanently moist tropical habitats are often bright green and shiny. *Photo: M. Porteners*

PL. 6.4 Far right below: The hairs on plants that live in dry open habitats cause these plants to be bluish or whitish green. *Photo: P. Farrant*

BOX 1

THE PLANT KINGDOM

Plants are the chlorophyll-containing organisms that photosynthesise or trap sunlight and convert it into the chemical energy and food that all organisms rely upon. Fungi are often considered with, though not usually classified as, plants; they differ from plants in not containing chlorophyll (pls 6.5 - 6.7). The plant kingdom is divided into a number of groups (pls 6.8 - 6.14), the most advanced of which is the flowering plants or angiosperms. Flowering plants produce flowers containing male pollen and female ovules: after fertilisation, ovules develop into seeds, which are enclosed within fruits (pl. 6.15). The algae, including the seaweeds, are sometimes considered to be a separate group of organisms.

Classification of plants

Like all groups of organisms, flowering plants are divided into further categories. The most useful of the categories of flowering plants are the three lowest ranks of scientific classification: family, genus and species. Every plant belongs to a species: this is the lowest rank and consists of individuals that are capable of interbreeding.

PL. 6.5 Left: The bright colours of fungi like *Amanita muscaria* may warn animals that they are poisonous. *Photo: L. Rodgers*

PL. 6.6 Below Left: Quinones are responsible for many of the yellow, orange, red and purple colours of lichens and fungi. *Photo: W. Farrant*

PL. 6.7 Below right: The yellow fruiting body of the fungus *Cyttaria gunni* is edible, despite its bright colour. *Photo: L. Rodgers*

PL. 6.8 Far left: Red seaweed. Algae are classified according to the combination of pigments they contain. *Photo: P. Farrant*

PL. 6.9 Left: Green seaweed, a species of *Caulerpa*. *Photo: P. Farrant*

PL. 6.10 Far left: Brown seaweed, *Dictyota bartraysei*. *Photo: P. Farrant*

PL. 6.11 Left: Red fruiting bodies of lichens (symbiotic associations of algae and fungi) are often coloured by quinones. *Photo: R.J. King*

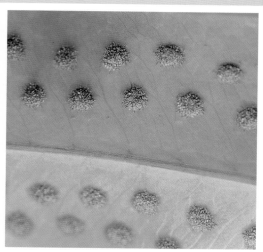

Each species is defined by two names: the name of the genus followed by the name of the species, e.g. corn (*Zea mays*). Each genus contains a number of related species, and further grouping produces families of related genera. Tea (*Camellia sinensis*) belongs to the same genus as many ornamental shrubs (e.g. *Camellia sasanqua*, *Camellia japonica*). In fact there are over 50 species in the genus *Camellia*, and all these (as well as the species in other related genera such as *Stachyurus* and *Stewartia*, each of which contains about six species) belong to the Theaceae or tea family. This family contains about 500 plant species altogether.

PL. 6.12 Above left: Bryophytes, (mosses and liverworts) are plants that have leaves and stems but no conducting tissue. *Photo: R.J. King*

PL. 6.13 Above right: Ferns are plants that have roots, stems, leaves and conducting tissue; they reproduce by spores. *Photo: R.J. King*

PL. 6.14 Right: Deciduous larches are conifers that bear cones and produce seeds. *Photo: R.J. King*

The classification of the sacred lotus *(Nelumbo nucifera)* is as follows:

Kingdom .... Plantae
Division .... Anthophyta
Class .... Dicotyledones
Order .... Nymphaeales
Family .... Nelumbonaceae
Genus .... *Nelumbo*
Species .... *nucifera*

PL. 6.15 Below: Sacred lotus, Indonesia. *Photo: P. Farrant*

CHEMISTRY OF COLOUR

The pigments that give plants their colours are identified on the basis of their chemistry (see BOX 2). Chlorophylls, carotenoids and flavonoids are the most important types of pigments in plants. Each of these groups contains a range of chemically related pigments. All have loose electrons that can absorb wavelengths in the visible range, and this is what creates their colours (see p. 4).

Chlorophyll molecules each contain a central magnesium atom, which is linked to four nitrogen atoms; each nitrogen atom is located at the apex of one of four pentagonal carbon-containing rings. The colour of chlorophyll is caused both by the magnesium atom, which is a transition element and therefore requires relatively small amounts of energy for excitation of its electrons, and by the types of bonds in the structure: a mixture of double and single bonds causes the orbits of the electrons to spread out, so they need little energy to be excited by light. Red and blue wavelengths of light have the right amounts of energy to excite electrons in the chlorophyll molecule, which absorbs these colours and reflects green (pl. 6.16).

The colour of carotenoids is also caused by the large number of double and single bonds joining atoms in the molecule: electrons are spread out because the molecules are long, and again little energy is needed to excite the electrons. In this case the molecules absorb wavelengths in the green, blue and violet parts of the spectrum and reflect yellow, orange and red wavelengths (pl. 6.17).

The structure of flavonoids is based on parent molecules like flavone. Flavone contains three carbon rings, with a mixture of double and single bonds, surrounded by clouds of loosely bound electrons, an arrangement that allows absorption of visible wavelengths of light. The exact colour of individual flavonoids depends upon the side branches they have and the substances with which they are combined. The two types of flavonoids are named after their colours in alkaline solution: blue (anthocyanins) and yellow (anthoxanthins). Flavonoids are water-soluble and are located in the cell sap. Anthocyanins, the most common, are blue, purple or red, while anthoxanthins are cream or yellow.

It is not just the chemical differences of these pigments that cause the range of colours we see. In addition, relative amounts of each pigment, combinations of different pigments (often in different locations in the plant's cells and tissues), physical conditions within the plant's cells and the plant's physical structure, also contribute to its colour.

THE FUNCTION OF PIGMENTS

Plant pigments have different functions. Both types of flavonoids, anthocyanins and anthoxanthins, are important pigments in flowers and fruits, though anthocyanins also occur in leaves. Flavonoids are sensitive to light and absorb specific wavelengths, but this energy is not used for any biological processes in the plant. These pigments provide flowering plants with colours which attract animals that pollinate flowers and disperse their seeds.

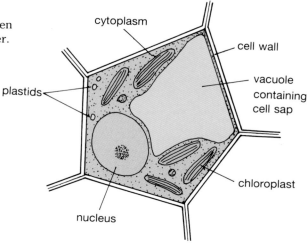

Fig. 6.1 Plant cell.

labels: cytoplasm · cell wall · vacuole containing cell sap · plastids · chloroplast · nucleus

PL. 6.16 Left: A leaf appears green because it absorbs all wavelengths except green; green is reflected back to an observer. *Photo: P. Farrant*

PL. 6.17 Left: Autumn coloration of a deciduous fern is due to carotenoids, yellowish orange pigments that absorb blue and green light. *Photo: R.J. King.*

PL. 6.18 Right: This orchid is pale and has no leaves because it lives on the honey agaric, a parasitic fungus on the roots of forest trees. Most plants have chlorophyll, but if they are kept in the dark they will remain pale. *Photo: L. Rodgers*

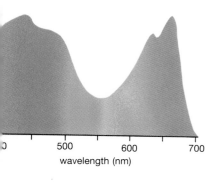

Fig. 6.2 Action spectrum, showing that a photosynthesising plant uses the blue and red wavelengths of sunlight.

x-axis label: wavelength (nm) *ticks:* 500 · 600 · 700

Chlorophylls and carotenoids are sensitive to light, provide the plant with colour, and also act as photoreceptors, i.e. they capture the energy of specific wavelengths of light and transform it into biochemical energy the plant can use for biological processes. The most important of these is photosynthesis.

PHOTOSYNTHETIC PIGMENTS: CHLOROPHYLLS

Photosynthesis is the process by which plant pigments absorb the sun's radiant energy and convert it into chemical energy. This chemical energy is stored in the form of carbohydrates (e.g. starch), which can be broken down later as required to provide the basic molecules for growth and repair, and the energy for all the processes involved in growth, maintenance, repairs and reproduction. Animals that eat plants (and animals that eat these animals) use the molecules and energy for the same processes. The by-products of photosynthesis — water and oxygen — are also crucial for the survival of life on Earth. Photosynthesis is an extremely efficient process: around 30% of light absorbed by a plant is converted into stored chemical energy. Photosynthesis occurs in a plant's chloroplasts (chlorophyll-containing plastids).

Photosynthesis only takes place in the parts of a plant that contain chlorophyll; other pigments merely assist chlorophyll to capture light. The molecules of chlorophyll, other pigments and substances involved in photosynthesis are arranged in an orderly fashion in relation to one another on stacked membranes within the chloroplasts. This arrangement allows the chlorophyll and other pigment molecules to absorb small amounts of light energy and to pass on the energy efficiently to other substances; they can then resume their original states and capture more light energy. Many other substances, apart from carbon dioxide and water, are involved in transferring the energy, but the end result is the formation of carbohydrate, oxygen and water.

Colours of chlorophyll

Several different chlorophylls, all closely related chemically, may be involved in photosynthesis. The most important chlorophyll is chlorophyll *a*, which is found in all but a few parasitic plants. Chlorophyll *a* is a yellow-green pigment (when it is isolated from the plant and from other pigments), whereas chlorophyll *b* is blue-green. The two chlorophylls are usually both present in plant leaves, and in this way they complement each other and together absorb a great deal of the red and blue light used in photosynthesis (fig. 6.2). The colour of the light transmitted through a green leaf, i.e. the light which is not used by the leaf and so passes out the other side, is deficient in these wavelengths. Plants are most sensitive to red and blue wavelengths of light, not only for photosynthesis, but for many other processes. Possibly this is because the two colours are at opposite ends of the spectrum, which is useful for processes stimulated by one colour and repressed by the other.

The overall greenness of plant leaves is determined by the total amount of chlorophyll, and the actual colour of the leaves is determined by relative amounts of chlorophyll *a*, chlorophyll *b* and other pigments: both depend ultimately on the genetics of the plant. However, they can also vary depending on the light in the plant's habitat. If there is no light at all, the pale yellowish precursor of chlorophyll, known as protochlorophyll, will not become green. This pigment needs to be illuminated with sunlight in order to become green chlorophyll. Therefore young seedlings that have germinated in the dark will not become green until they are moved into the light; and they will eventually die if they are not, as protochlorophyll cannot convert light energy into chemical energy. Plants living in different habitats

PL. 6.19 Red seaweeds contain phycocyanin, a pigment which helps capture light in photosynthesis. *Photo: P. Farrant*

tend to have leaves whose colours are best adapted to the light available in those habitats (see chapter 5) but many are also able to alter the amount of chlorophyll if conditions change (pl. 6.18).

Helping chlorophyll

Chlorophylls are essential for photosynthesis, but several other types of pigments help harvest sunlight. These are called accessory pigments because, although they can assist in trapping light, they cannot drive photosynthesis by themselves. Accessory pigments can absorb light energy from wavelengths outside those absorbed by green chlorophyll molecules, because of their different colours. They pass the energy from these other wavelengths on to the chlorophyll molecules for conversion to chemical energy, and in this way help to increase the amount of sunlight harvested for photosynthesis. Like chlorophylls, accessory pigments are not found in all parts of a plant, but unlike chlorophylls, they can also occur in parts of a plant that do not photosynthesise. All plants that photosynthesise contain some accessory pigments. Carotenoids are the most important group of accessory pigments in terrestrial plants, though another group of unrelated pigments is important in algae (pl. 6.19).

COLOURFUL CAROTENOIDS

The orange of carrots, the yellow of buttercups and daffodils, and the red of tomatoes and tulips are all due to carotenoids. While these pigments are common in fruits and flowers, they also occur in leaves where they act as accessory pigments for photosynthesis. Carotenoids only act as accessory pigments when chlorophyll is present and their colours are often masked by the green colour of the chlorophyll.

The two main types of carotenoids are carotenes and xanthophylls, both of which can act as accessory pigments to chlorophyll. Carotenes, usually orange in colour, are oils containing carbon and hydrogen. The best known carotenes are alpha-carotene, beta-carotene and lycopene: the last gives tomatoes their red coloration. Xanthophylls are derived from carotenes. They are therefore very similar in structure but are usually yellow. The xanthophylls include lutein, which is found in green leaves, and fucoxanthin, which is found in brown algae (pl. 6.20).

Most plants contain at least one type of carotene and one type of xanthophyll, though different plants and different plant organs tend to have different ones. In some cases carotenoids do not function as accessory pigments but may provide colours to attract animals that will pollinate flowers or disperse fruits. Carotenoids such as beta-carotene also protect plants' chlorophyll molecules from harmful chemical reactions by absorbing excess light energy.

Additional pigments

Besides photosynthesis, there are other important processes (called photomorphogenic processes) in which plants use light energy for growth, development and differentiation, e.g. stems and leaves bend so they grow towards or away from light and flowers develop when days reach a certain length in the year.

Long wavelength light will not provide enough energy for biological processes, and short wavelength ultraviolet light has so much energy it can damage living tissue, so plants mostly use the visible

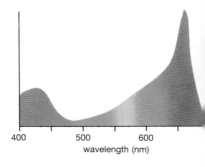

Fig. 6.3 Absorption spectrum of phytochrome.

PL. 6.20 Brown seaweeds contain fucoxanthin, a carotenoid that masks the green chlorophyll. *Photo: P. Farrant*

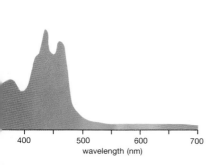

Fig. 6.4 Action spectrum, showing the wavelengths absorbed by blue light receptors as a plant bends towards the light.

wavelengths in between. A number of photoreceptor pigments have evolved that absorb these useful wavelengths of light efficiently. In particular, plants use the blue, red and far-red regions of the spectrum (far-red is the part of the infra-red region just outside the visible range). Each photoreceptor pigment is a particular colour and absorbs a certain range of wavelengths (some or all of which are used to drive biological processes). However, the colours of the photoreceptor pigments involved in photomorphogenic processes occur in such tiny amounts they have no observable effect on plant colour. They only provide a plant with information about its light environment: the colour of light, its intensity, direction and periodicity (intervals of light and dark). There are two important photoreceptor pigments involved in trapping useful wavelengths of light for photomorphogenic processes: a red-light photoreceptor called phytochrome (fig. 6.3) and an as yet unidentified blue-light photoreceptor (fig 6.4).

While pigments from the three main groups (chlorophylls, carotenoids and flavonoids) occur in most plants, there are other pigments that are far less common or which occur in only some plants. These pigments sometimes provide plants with rarer colours, though in many cases the colours are similar to those caused by pigments from the three main groups, e.g. the red of beets is caused by reddish pigments called betacyanins. Some of the yellow

colours in plants' leaves, roots, bark and seeds, are caused by quinones, e.g. juglone, a dark yellowish brown pigment found in walnuts. Some of the yellow, brown and red colours of bark, wood, fruits and leaves are caused by tannins. Tannins are granular substances found in the cell sap, cytoplasm or cells walls of plant tissues.

WHITE LEAVES

White leaf tissue can be caused by air under the leaf surface or by white pigments in the leaf, but it is usually caused by a reduction or total lack of chlorophyll in the leaf. Some plants do not produce any pigments at all and are described as albino. These are usually mutant individuals within a population of normally pigmented plants. Albino plants have yellowish white leaves even when they are exposed to sunlight, because they cannot produce any chlorophyll. Sometimes only one part of a plant is affected. Plants can be partially albino if for some reason they cannot produce the normal number of chloroplasts: this may be caused by a genetic defect or by disease.

VARIEGATED LEAVES

A mixture of two or more colours in the leaves of plants such as cordylines and caladiums is quite common, especially in cultivated varieties. Leaves

PL. 6.21 Parts of a leaf are yellow where there are few chloroplasts and thus a reduced amount of chlorophyll.
Photo: P. Farrant

such as this are described as variegated.

Variegated forms occur in most plant families. If one of the leaf colours is white, this tissue is usually albino, i.e. it completely lacks chlorophyll. A whitish silver colour, e.g. the spots on the leaves of some begonias, is usually caused by pockets of air under the leaf's epidermis. A yellow or light green colour usually indicates that the tissue has a reduced amount of chlorophyll relative to the normal green leaf, and this is because of a reduction in the number of chloroplasts (pl. 6.21).

While white, cream, yellow and green are common colours in variegated plants; so are pinks, purples, reds and browns. Red, purple or pink coloration is caused by anthocyanins which are usually located in the leaf's epidermis, the surface layer above the photosynthetic tissues. The arrangement of different colours depends on the location of affected cells within the plant and the resulting arrangement of cell layers in the areas where new cells are forming.

Plant variegation occurs for several reasons. Mutations probably account for some variegation in nature. Viruses, especially mosaic viruses, can also cause variegation by attacking plant tissues where cell division takes place. Environmental conditions such as nutrient and water stress, changing temperature and light as well as damage by predatory animals may also promote variegation, but it is not known whether these actually cause it. Different agents of variegation mean that colour patterns are not necessarily uniform, even in one plant, e.g. the tricolor variety of the tropical perennial aroid *Aglaonema pictum*, which has attractive leaves splotched with dark green, lime green and silver, is quite variable, and some plants in the natural populations in Sumatra are green, while the others show different amounts of variegation.

Variegated plants in the wild

Variegated plants generally have less chlorophyll and may also be weakened if damaged or infected, so these plants usually do not survive in nature. The larger the area without chlorophyll, the less vigorous the plant. It is only through human intervention that many variegated plants survive. Though some variegation can be passed on through the seed, few variegated plants breed true, i.e. their seeds do not produce variegated offspring but revert back to the original green stock.

Some variegated plants survive and appear to be able to compete in the wild and there are several theories as to how they manage this. Low-growing plants with mottled leaves may be well camouflaged if they grow on a sun-dappled forest floor: they are inconspicuous to the herbivorous animals that feed on them, especially those that lack colour vision. The mottling acts as a disruptive colour pattern, making the shape of the leaf outline difficult for an animal to detect. Mottled leaves may also mimic damage caused by insects, and appear unattractive to leaf-eaters.

YEAR-ROUND RED COLORATION

Some ornamental plants (e.g. varieties of coleus) have leaves that are red or purple year-round (pl. 6.22). These leaves are quite normal and healthy. They have green chlorophyll for photosynthesis but it is masked by other pigments. The permanent red is characteristic of the species, and the plants' ability to produce greater than normal quantities of anthocyanins is hereditary. Though the red coloration may have some function in the species' natural habitat, e.g. it may help to protect chlorophyll from ultraviolet light, it does tend to reduce the

PL. 6.22 Right: Red anthocyanins in the leaves of some plants at high latitude mask their green chlorophyll. *Photo: R. Berthold*

PL. 6.23 Below: Red anthocyanins act as sunscreening pigments in some bromeliads. *Photo: P. Farrant*

PL. 6.24 Leaves can become red due to anthocyanins when they are injured or diseased. *Photo: P. Farrant*

PL. 6.25 Right: Liquidambar: in autumn the green leaves of deciduous trees change colour as they begin to die. *Photo: R. Berthold.*

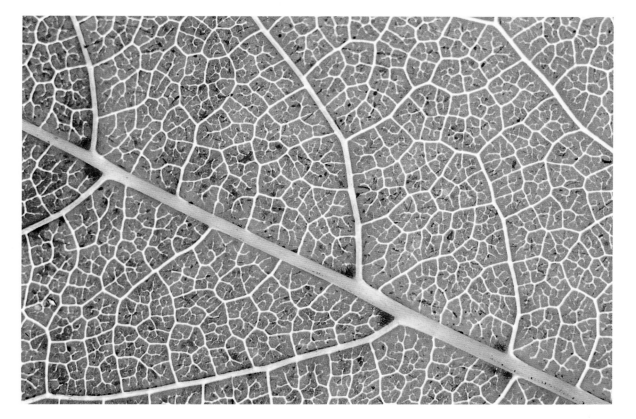

PL. 6.26 Below: The red coloration of the liquidambar leaf is due to anthocyanins. *Photo: R. Berthold*

ability of these species to photosynthesise because less light reaches their chloroplasts (pl. 6.23).

When leaves that are normally green turn red or yellow, it may indicate that the plant is unhealthy, perhaps deficient in some mineral such as phosphorus, potassium or magnesium. Without minerals, cells eventually die because their essential chemical reactions run out of ingredients. Mineral deficiencies usually affect either the young or the old leaves first, depending on the mineral involved. Injury and frosty weather can also make leaves red, though usually only some leaves are affected (pl. 6.24).

DECIDUOUS TREES

All leaves have a finite lifespan and eventually die and fall off the plant. In the tropics, where seasons are not particularly pronounced, plants remain green all year: the colour change of dying leaves is indiscernible because the process is continuous, with only a few leaves changing colour at a time.

The leaves of many temperate deciduous species, however, all die together. The leaves of these plants are generally broad and have a high rate of transpiration (evaporation from leaves); in winter, when the ground is frozen and there is not enough liquid water available to maintain transpiration, the leaves die. The plants themselves survive the winter in a dormant state. In spring, new green leaves sprout, expanding as they photosynthesise, and manufacturing foods that enable the plants to grow. During summer, when leaves are fully grown, carbohydrates made in photosynthesis are transported and used in other parts of the plant. In autumn, decreased light and cooler temperatures mean photosynthesis decreases, and useful materials may be transported from the leaves and stored elsewhere in the plant: the leaves eventually die and fall off the tree. In winter the plant survives on its stored food because there are no longer any green leaves to manufacture carbohydrates.

The process of leaf death in autumn can involve dramatic changes in the colour of leaves, providing conditions are favourable (pls 6.25, 6.26). The main signal responsible for initiating autumn leaf fall is the shortening length of daylight. Other factors contribute and so the event does not always occur at exactly the same time each year. Availability of water and mineral nutrition are also important. Cold weather can start the process: e.g. if a tree is near an artificial light, autumn coloration may be delayed until the first cold spell sets the process in motion.

AUTUMN PIGMENTS

Like other compounds found in plants, chlorophyll molecules continually break down and new ones form. With cooler temperatures in autumn, leaves begin to lose their greenness as their chlorophyll disintegrates and production of chlorophyll eventually ceases. Once chlorophyll starts to break down, the process is enhanced by light, so chlorophyll breaks down more rapidly if the days are sunny.

As the chlorophyll level in leaves declines, the colours of other pigments that the chlorophyll had

initially masked, begin to show through. These other pigments are plastid pigments, orange carotenes and yellow xanthophylls, all of which break down much more slowly than chlorophyll (pl. 6.27).

Many plants also produce red or purple anthocyanin pigments at the time the leaves stop producing chlorophyll. Normally, carbohydrates manufactured during photosynthesis are broken down into sugars, soluble substances that are moved out to supply energy to other parts of the plant, or to storage areas in roots and stems. In autumn, cool night-time temperatures favour more rapid conversion of insoluble carbohydrates into sugars in the leaves. The low temperatures, however, hamper the removal of sugars from the leaves, and the build-up of sugars in the cell sap favours the conversion of colourless flavonoids to coloured anthocyanins. The more acidic the cell sap, the redder these pigments will be, though they will be purple if the sap is neutral, and blue if it is alkaline. Even if some orange carotenes and yellow xanthophylls are still present in the leaves at this stage, red and purple anthocyanins will mask them. The redness at the end of the life of autumn leaves is further enhanced as the orange and yellow pigments break down completely (pl. 6.28).

When there are no more starch reserves for leaves to use, they die. By this stage all pigments have broken down completely, cells have died and tissues have dried out, so the leaves are brown. Brown pigments in the leaves are produced by oxidation of chemicals in the cell walls as the cells die. Oxidation of tannins present in the leaves, may also contribute to brown colours at this stage, as in oaks.

Variation in autumn colours

Both the intensity and range of colours shown by autumn leaves may vary from tree to tree, place to place and year to year. The change of colour begins in colder regions, further north in the northern hemisphere or further south in the southern hemisphere, and at any particular latitude the change

PL. 6.27 Autumn leaves: the yellows are mostly due to carotenoids, which show through when chlorophyll breaks down. *Photo: P. Farrant*

PL. 6.28 Anthocyanins cause the reds and purples of autumn leaves, and the colours intensify as carotenoids break down. *Photo: P. Farrant*

PL. 6.29 Above: Spectacular autumn colour. *Photo: J. Plaza*

PL. 6.30 Right: The new leaves of many tropical plants are pink, red or even blue, due to anthocyanins. *Photo: P. Farrant*

will be seen first in areas that are colder, such as at higher altitudes, or in cooler hollows. In Europe the colour change is reported to travel from north to south over a period of around 2-3 weeks.

The best regions for autumn colours include central Europe, Japan, north-eastern America and eastern Asia (pl. 6.29). These parts of the world regularly experience the conditions needed for good autumn colours: good rainfall in the summer growing season; sunny autumn days (called Indian summers in the U.S.A.) and cool nights with temperatures close to freezing point but without frosts severe enough to kill leaves immediately; calm autumn days without winds so leaves will not be removed from trees prematurely; and sufficient autumn moisture, in the soil or as rainfall, so leaves can continue to grow well into the season. Open, low-lying terrain and soils that are not excessively alkaline also help to produce good autumn colours. In regions where conditions vary, autumn colours tend to be less predictable.

Some species produce better autumn colour than others, particularly if their leaves are naturally high in anthocyanin content, as is the case with Japanese maples. Individuals of the same species vary widely and are selected for cultivation on the basis of their genetic stock. The same tree may show better colours as it ages: during its active growth phase, a plant tends to rapidly use up any excess carbohydrates for growth, so in younger trees conditions in the plant's cells do not favour autumn anthocyanin production.

COLOURFUL NEW FOLIAGE

While tropical plants do not provide a spectacle of autumn colours, their leaves are nonetheless colourful at certain times. The leaves usually die one by one, turning yellow then brown. They are not usually coloured by red anthocyanin pigments because the nights are not cold enough for sugars to be trapped in leaves at night.

New growth of tropical plants often occurs in flushes: new leaves are formed at once, perhaps at intervals of several months. The new growth in tropical plants is sometimes pale yellow or more commonly pink or red, even blue. The pale yellow pigment is undeveloped chlorophyll and red or blue pigments are anthocyanins, which mask the undeveloped chlorophyll if the leaves are red, and probably protect sensitive young leaves from ultraviolet light. Another possibility is that the colour may warn off grazing animals: soft young foliage is favoured by herbivores, so bright colours may suggest leaves are distasteful or poisonous. As leaves mature and their chlorophyll develops, they become green (pl. 6.30).

Even in cooler areas, especially forests, many plants have new leaves coloured red by anthocyanins. Rhododendrons and azaleas have particularly attractive new spring growth called candles because the bracts or leaves around buds are a vivid red. When they break through, leaves may be bronze, pink, silver or gold, depending upon the individual species. The new foliage of deciduous trees in spring is also often red with anthocyanins, though the leaves turn green after a while.

SURFACE COLOUR

Apart from pigments, the physical nature of the leaf surface affects colour. The young leaves of many plants have a hairy covering, and in some species, older leaves also have hairs, especially on their undersides, e.g. the gold or silver of some rhododendron leaves is caused by a cover of tiny hairs (pl. 6.31). Hairs usually help reflect sunlight and reduce water loss, so these types of plants are often found in dry, sunny places, on high mountains or at high latitudes.

Leaves have many different surfaces: glossy, matt, hairy and scaly to name but a few. Textures reflect light differently, creating patterns and colours. Some leaves resemble fine velveteen, e.g. the Philippine spoon lily.

IRIDESCENT GREENS AND BLUES

Some plants that live in the gloom of the rainforest floor have iridescent leaves structurally adapted to capture as much light as possible for photosynthesis. The light that reaches the forest floor is dim and diffuse and most of the photosynthetically useful blue and red wavelengths have been removed by the leaves of plants higher in the canopy. Plants with green iridescence, e.g. cave mosses in Europe and North America, have surface cells which focus the diffuse light onto the chloroplasts in underlying cells (fig. 6.5). The wavelengths useful for photosynthesis are absorbed and the unused green light is reflected directly out of the cells as a concentrated beam of light. For this reason, green iridescence is strongest when viewed directly, whereas at other angles it appears to be pale green or whitish.

Blue iridescence, e.g. in the Malaysian peacock plant, is caused by a different leaf structure, with layers of granules, fibres or air spaces causing blue wavelengths to be reflected intensely, but allowing red wavelengths to be absorbed efficiently and used for photosynthesis. Like green iridescence, blue iridescence appears to prevent the wavelengths of light that are potentially useful for photosynthesis from being reflected away and lost.

Different plants may iridesce with blues of various

PL. 6.31 The colour of a green leaf can be modified by hairs on its surface. *Photo: P. Farrant*

Fig. 6.5 Green iridescence in plants: the outer leaf cells focus light onto chloroplasts in underlying cells. The reflected light is focused into an intense beam at right angles to the leaf surface, with whitish green light at other angles due to backscattering.

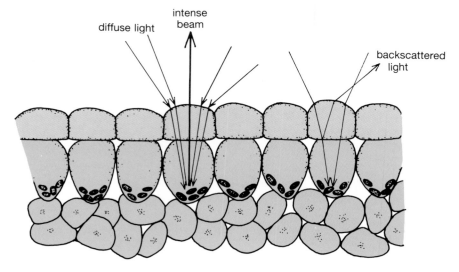

wavelengths; other colours seen when the angle of view changes, are probably caused by the refraction of light from the epidermal cells. The West Malaysian iridescent begonia is a deep blue when leaves are viewed directly, but the colours change with the angle of view, from blue to green and gold.

Low light habitats

Green or blue iridescence in plants is distinguishable from pigment coloration because of its intensity and lustre (pl. 6.32). It occurs in a number of unrelated plant groups, including ferns, mosses, sedges and

Fig. 6.6 Purplish anthocyanin pigments in the lower epidermis of a leaf reflect unused red light back through the photosynthetic tissue, where it has a second chance to be absorbed.

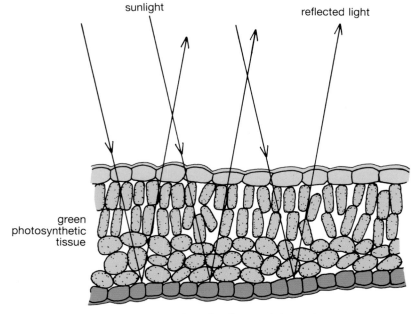

lower epidermal cells containing anthocyanins

PL. 6.32 Above: Blue iridescent seaweed; iridescence is presumed to help plants capture more light for photosynthesis. *Photo: P. Farrant*

PL. 6.33 Right: Discolor begonia: the red undersurface of the leaves reflects red wavelengths back to photosynthetic tissue. *Photo: P. Farrant*

wavelengths of light. Leaves of these plants are red underneath and green on top, a colour scheme that probably helps them to absorb as much light as possible: red light passing through the leaf is reflected by the red pigment back up through the leaf to the chlorophyll in the upper surface, where there is a further opportunity for it to be absorbed (pl. 6.33, fig. 6.6).

LIVING LIGHTS

Some plants can make their own light. The light produced by living creatures is called bioluminescence. Some marine algae (planktonic dinoflagellates) can cause the entire water surface of an inlet or bay to glow at night. The mechanism for creating bioluminescence is similar in plants and animals (and in fungi and bacteria): all these luminescent organisms contain a substance called luciferin which reacts with oxygen in the presence of an enzyme called luciferase, and the chemical energy of the reaction is converted to light energy. The light produced is a cold colour, usually green or blue though some fungi and lichens emit green or even yellow light. The functions of bioluminescence are relatively well understood for animals, but the reasons for plants and fungi producing their own light remain a mystery.

Leaves are basically green so that they can photosynthesise; however, they also show a wide range of other colours. The next chapter looks at the colours of flowers and fruits.

seaweeds, though it is not widespread in plants generally. Many iridescent plants grow in habitats with relatively low light levels, such as rainforests and caves.

Some plants such as epiphytic discolor bromeliads (and also the iridescent begonia and non-iridescent herbs that live on the forest floor), have a further adaptation for efficiently gathering the red

BOX 2

PLANT PIGMENTS

Group	Function/location	Colour-producing & chemical features	Example	Structure
Chlorophylls	photosynthesis; located in chloroplasts of all photosynthetic plants and algae	cyclic structure of carbon rings; carbon chain; double and single bonds; magnesium atom	chlorophyll a	
			chlorophyll b	
Carotenoids	accessory pigments in photosynthesis; protection from light; located in chloroplasts and other plastids	carbon rings; carbon chains; double and single bonds; hydrocarbons (carotenes) or oxygenated hydrocarbons (xanthophylls)	beta-carotene (carotene in carrots)	
			lutein (carotene in green leaves)	
			lycopene (carotene in tomatoes)	
			fucoxanthin (xanthophyll in brown algae)	
Flavonoids	ornamental pigments in flowers, fruits, stems, leaves; located in cell sap of vacuoles	derivatives of glucosides (carbon rings + sugars): anthocyanins from anthocyans, anthoxanthins from flavones or xanthones	pelargonidin (anthocyanin in geraniums)	
			delphinidin (anthocyanin in delphiniums)	
			cyanidin (anthocyanin in red roses)	

		quercetin (anthoxanthin in onion skin)	
		gentisin (anthoxanthin in yellow gentians)	
Betacyanins	ornamental pigments in some groups of plants; located in cell sap	derivatives of glucosides (carbon rings + sugars); large molecules	bougainvillein (in bougainvilleas)
Phycobilins	accessory pigments for photosynthesis in red and blue-green algae; water soluble, in vacuoles	linear structure; of carbon rings double and single bonds	phycoerythrin (from red algae)
			phycocyanin (from blue-green algae)
Quinones	disease resistance; in bark, roots fruits and leaves	carbon rings; double and single bonds	juglone (from walnuts)
Tannins	absorb oxygen from air to become brown or black; granular, in cell sap, cell walls or cytoplasm	large complex molecules; carbon rings; double and single bonds	pyrogallol tannin containing ellagic acid (=R in structure) (from oaks)
Photo-morphogenic pigments	plant growth and development; energized by light to active form	carbon rings; double and single bonds; combined with protein	phytochrome
Indigo	found in many parts of some plant species; used as dye	derivative of the glucoside indican; carbon rings	indigo (from indigoferas)
Alizarin	found in roots of madder plants; used as dye	glucoside derivative	alizarin (from roots of madder)

CHAPTER 7

COLOUR OF FLOWERS AND FRUITS

PL. 7.15 The pigment that causes the orange-red colour of geraniums is the anthocyanin pigment pelargonidin. *Photo: W. Farrant*

Unlike animals, plants are stationary and cannot seek out potential mates so their flowers are pollinated and their seeds dispersed by animals and other moving things (such as wind and water). This is why flowers and fruits are the most colourful parts of many plants: to attract the animals that are going to carry their pollen, eat their fruit and drop their seeds.

EVOLUTION OF FLOWER COLOUR

Flowers are the reproductive parts of the most advanced group of plants, the flowering plants (see BOX 1) and are believed to have evolved from leaves. The simplest flowers are usually radially symmetrical, cup shaped and a single colour. The most advanced flowers are structurally more complex: usually bilaterally symmetrical with highly modified parts and more than one colour. Contrasting colours within a flower, as lines, spots and patches, make the flower more noticeable to animals (pl. 7.1).

PL. 7.2 Above: In terms of genetics and evolution, plants with blue, purple or multicoloured flowers are more advanced. *Photo: R.J. King*

PL. 7.1 Above: Flowers that hang downward are usually more brilliantly coloured on the outside than the inside. *Photo: R.J. King*

Different colours are related to the pigments present and their relative amounts in various parts of the flower. Flower colours are produced by many of the same pigments that occur in leaves; in leaves, however, chlorophyll masks them. The most primitive flowers with the simplest structure are often yellow, whereas slightly more complex flowers tend to be white, and more advanced flowers are generally red, pink or purple. The most advanced flowers are those that are blue or a mixture of colours (pl. 7.2).

Colours become increasingly advanced and complex as more genes are involved. Whereas an advanced blue-flowered species has the genes for yellowness, whiteness and redness, the more primitive species only has the genes for yellowness. Thus if there is a mistake in the inheritance of blue coloration, a normally blue-flowered plant might produce pink or even white flowers. Peculiar flower colours that appear from time to time in some species therefore depend upon the coloration of the parent flowers and there is a tendency to revert to a less advanced colour. White-flowered plants tend to revert to yellow and pink and red-flowered species revert to white (pl. 7.3).

Reversion to the green of the ancestral leaf seems to occur from time to time regardless of the normal colour of the species. These individuals are the result of chance mutations, events that can lead eventually to the formation of new species, e.g. aquatic and other plants believed to have descended from more colourful ancestors. Mutations in the opposite direction, especially to produce blue coloration in flowers, are much less likely because new genes need to be introduced. This is why without genetic engineering it is so difficult to breed a true blue rose: the blue gene does not occur in any plants that are closely related to roses. Few genera contain species with red, white and blue flowers, examples that do being lobelias and delphiniums (pl. 7.4).

PL. 7.3 Far left: Normally Sturts Desert Pea flowers are red and black. Variants like this entirely red-flowered plant occur from time to time. *Photo: R.J. King*

PL. 7.4 Left: The genus *Delphinium* contains species with red, or white, or blue flowers. *Photo: J. Lush*

COLOURFUL PARTS OF FLOWERS

In most cases it is the petals that are the most brightly coloured parts of a flower. In some plants such as buttercups, petals are arranged in a relatively simple whorl to form a shallow, cup-shaped structure around the fertile parts of the flower (pl. 7.5). In other plants such as fuchsias, they are fused together to form a bell, while in orchids, sweet peas and other bilaterally symmetrical flowers, the petals have a quite specialised arrangement and different petals may be different shapes and colours. The petals are not always the most colourful parts of the flower. In tulips, both sepals and petals are showy, and usually similar in colour. The sepals and petals of fuchsias are showy too, but they have different colours (pl. 7.6).

Sometimes the flower's colour is due to the fertile parts. The female parts of a flower are seldom the most colourful because the ovary is hidden from animals that might damage the tissue that will protect developing seeds. On the other hand, many flowers have exposed, colourful stamens from which animals collect pollen; animals usually do this inadvertently while searching for nectar. Australian wattles and bottlebrushes are good examples of plants with flowers in which stamens provide the colour that attracts pollinating insects (pl. 7.7).

The vivid colours of bougainvillea flowers are due to bracts, specially modified leaves that surround the flowers and look like petals (pl. 7.8). Parts of some bromeliad leaves become vividly coloured or even white in the regions near maturing flowers and these colours probably attract pollinators.

Inflorescences

Flowers are usually clustered on a plant to provide a mass of colour that can be seen more easily by an insect, bird or mammal at some distance. Many of the flowers we are familiar with, such as daisies (pl. 7.9), bottlebrushes and proteas (pl. 7.10), are actually groups of flowers arranged on a single stem, and they are known more correctly as inflorescences. Like some single flowers, many inflorescences, including those of poinsettias and flamingo flowers are attractive because of brightly coloured bracts around them (pl. 7.11). The attractiveness of flowers clustered into inflorescences is further enhanced if plants of the same species, or even many different species, all flower at once in the same area (pl. 7.12).

PL. 7.5 Buttercups: yellow petals form a shallow cup-shaped structure around the outside of the fertile parts of the flower. *Photo: R.J. King*

Variable and changing colours

The most vivid colours are generally shown by flowers when they are mature, when the fertile male and female parts are ripe and ready for pollination and fertilisation. Flowers often change colour as they mature and this usually involves changing from an inconspicuous colour to one or more that stand out against background browns and greens, so they become easily visible to pollinating animals (pl. 7.13).

PL. 7.6 Above: Fuchsia flowers have colourful sepals and petals, usually of different colours. *Photo: P. Farrant*

PL. 7.7 Left: In wattles, stamens are abundant and bright yellow while the petals and sepals are small and inconspicuous. *Photo: P. Farrant*

PL. 7.8 Bougainvillea flowers are surrounded by colourful bracts. *Photo: R. Berthold*

PL. 7.9 Above: A daisy is not a single flower but an inflorescence, a group of flowers arranged on a (very short) stem. The spirally arranged individual flowers can be seen in this photo. *Photo: R.J. King.*

PL. 7.10 Right: Proteas and their relatives have small flowers grouped into conspicuous inflorescences. *Photo: P. Farrant*

PL. 7.13 The greyish sepals and petals of these eucalypt flowers separate to reveal red and yellow stamens. *Photo: R.J. King*

At the same time, the flower's attractants for animals must be ready. When flower colours are brightest, pollen grains are ripe and ready for release from the anthers, the stigma is moist, turgid and receptive, and nectar supplies or other attractants are at their best. At this time the flower may also produce an odour to make it even more attractive to animals with a good sense of smell.

As the individual flowers of a red hot poker change colour with age, perhaps induced by pollination and fertilisation, the flowers that are different ages change

PL. 7.11 Above: The colourful red structure around this flamingo flower is a bract, or specialised leaf. *Photo: R. Berthold*

PL. 7.12 Right: Heather in Scotland: mass flowering helps to attract pollinating animals and to ensure cross pollination. *Photo: R.J. King*

colour. Young flowers form the red tip of a red hot poker, while older flowers beneath are yellow: the contrasting colours within the inflorescence may attract the African sunbirds that pollinate them.

Following the flower's peak in maturation, and often associated with fertilisation, flower colour changes again: usually it fades or blackens, the flower stops producing perfume, the stigma loses its receptivity and no pollen is left in the anthers. These changes are all associated with seed set if pollination and fertilisation have been successful: the ovule starts to swell as the seed inside develops. Around the seed the ovary begins to develop into the fruit and the sterile parts of the flower may then fall off. Alternatively they may change colour and remain attached to provide colour contrast to an inflorescence or a mass of flowers, or they may wither but remain attached to the developing fruit and play no further role.

A change in colour with age or with pollination is beneficial to plants: time and energy are no longer used in providing attractants for animals (pl. 7.14).

The night-flowering honeysuckle has flowers that change from yellow to white in around 24 hours, and it is thought that this is caused by pollination of the flower. The flowers of the day-flowering morning glory can change from blue to pink during a single day, probably for the same reason.

ATTRACTIVE COLOURS

The colours of flowers can be caused by pigments or by the surface structure of the flower, or by a combination of both. The most important pigments that give flowers their bright colours are flavonoids and carotenoids. Of the flavonoids, anthocyanins and anthoxanthins, the former are by far the most important: these cause the blue we see in many flowers such as delphiniums, the bluish red we see in red roses, and the orange-red we see in geraniums (pl. 7.15). Anthoxanthins are less widespread and provide less vivid colours, e.g. the yellows and creamy whites of primroses and clover. Carotenoid pigments (see p. 74) are often responsible for yellows and oranges (pl. 7.16), e.g. red hot poker flowers derive their colour from red carotenoids (pl. 7.17) and some orchids are coloured by brown carotenoids. Yellow coloration in flowers can also be caused by a combination of carotenoids and anthoxanthins, and orange coloration, as in nasturtiums, by a combination of a yellow carotenoid and a red anthocyanin.

FLAVONOIDS

Anthocyanins and anthoxanthins are plant pigments that do not gather light energy for photosynthesis or for photomorphogenic processes; they provide plants with attractive colours.

There is an enormous variety of anthocyanin pigments found in plants, especially in flowers. Mostly they are related to the red pigment from geraniums (pelargonidin), the blue pigment from delphiniums (delphinidin) and the red pigment from roses (cyanidin). These chemical compounds are soluble in water, so they are found dissolved in the

cell sap of flowers, fruits, stems and leaves. They are not leached out by water unless cells are damaged.

Unlike carotenoids and chlorophyll, which are isolated in compartments (plastids) within plant cells, anthocyanins, being dissolved in cell sap, tend to be affected much more by the chemical environment of the cell. Their colour can vary with different conditions of acidity, temperature and other metabolic reactions within the cell sap because of small changes in the structure of pigment molecules and the resulting change in the excitation energy of their electrons. Blue pigments usually change to pink when the cell environment becomes more acidic: e.g. delphinidin varies in colour between blue and magenta, and pelargonidin varies in colour between scarlet and violet-blue (fig. 7.1).

Co-pigmentation

Co-pigmentation is the loose combination of anthocyanins with other pigments in cell sap, e.g. the colours of fuchsias and black grapes are caused by anthocyanins in combination with tannins (see p. 98. Mostly, however, anthocyanins are co-pigmented with other flavonoids, especially anthoxanthins. When anthocyanins like cyanidin and pelargonidin are co-pigmented with anthoxanthins they tend to become more stable and provide flowers with a less variable colour than they would if present on their

PL. 7.14 Above: The beetle-pollinated flowers of the giant water lily are white when they first open. They close up and trap the pollinating beetles, releasing them after about 18 hours: at this time the colour of the flowers changes to dark purplish red; they sink beneath the surface of the water where the seeds develop.
Photo: R.J. King

PL. 7.16 Below: The colours of daffodils are due to carotenoids.
Photo: R. Berthold

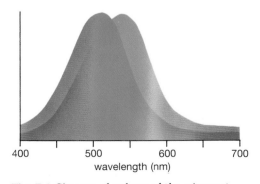

Fig. 7.1 Change of colour of the pigment delphinidin from strongly acidic conditions (left peak) to moderately acidic conditions (right peak).

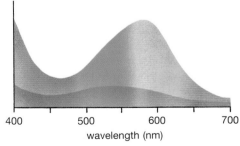

Fig. 7.2 The pigment malvidin (lower curve) is changed in both colour and intensity when it is co-pigmented with quercetin (top curve).

PL. 7.17 Flowers at the tip of a red hot poker contain red carotenoids. *Photo: W. Farrant.*

PL. 7.18 Red flowering gum, Western Australia. *Photo: W. Farrant*

own. The co-pigments may also intensify pigment colours, even if they are not coloured themselves (fig. 7.2). This is the because colourless molecules affect the distribution of electrons in the coloured pigment molecules. The brown coloration of some orchids is probably due to co-pigmentation of anthocyanins and anthoxanthins in the cell sap of these flowers.

Like all other pigments found in plants, anthocyanin molecules have a definite lifespan and eventually break down. They become brown through oxidation (a chemical reaction with oxygen) and are then no longer soluble in the sap. If they are not removed and the plant does not produce any more fresh molecules of anthocyanin to replace them, the flower (or other organ) will become increasingly brown and eventually die. This is why a dying flower goes brown gradually. Oxidation also accounts for the browning of damaged plant tissues: when we handle gardenias or cut an apple, oxygen enters damaged plant tissue and reacts to form brown insoluble particles.

Environment and Colour

Whether or not a plant produces anthocyanins depends on both genetic and environmental factors. A plant's genes determine when and where it produces anthocyanins, e.g. these pigments are particularly common in the young foliage of plants that are otherwise anthocyanin-free, and in mature flowers and fruits, whose changing colours advertise their receptivity or ripeness to potential pollinators or dispersers. Yet all plants seem to have the genes necessary for producing anthocyanins, and even if they do not normally produce these pigments many appear capable of doing so under certain conditions of temperature, nutrient supply, water supply and light. This ability may help plants to survive under extremes they do not usually encounter, so the pigments probably have a protective function.

It is well known that hydrangeas produce pink or blue flowers depending on soil acidity, and this is due to co-pigmentation of the pigments with aluminium (or iron) from the soil. These transition metals affect the electron orbits of the pigment molecules and cause them to absorb different wavelengths of light. The plants can take up aluminium when it is in soluble form only, and this occurs in acidic soils, to produce blue flowers. In contrast, acidic sap causes cornflowers and forget-me-nots to become pink.

Apples can be redder on one side of a tree than the other because light is important in promoting the production of anthocyanins in some plant organs. A few plants, such as red cabbage, are capable of synthesising anthocyanin in the dark, though it is not known why. High light intensity (especially ultraviolet) can also induce the production of anthocyanins in roses, causing reds and pinks to become bluer, or to fade or blacken, while yellows become green. The rose 'Peace' produces different coloured blooms in different seasons, from pinkish in summer to orange in autumn and yellow in winter.

While genetics is often the most important cause of differently coloured flowers on different plants (e.g. the flowers of one of the red flowering gums, *Eucalyptus ficifolia* (pl. 7.18), which range from brilliant scarlet to almost white), in other cases the colours depend mainly on environmental factors such as the amount of sunlight, soil type, prevailing winds, and the amount and timing of rainfall (e.g. the Madagascan poinciana, which has flowers anywhere between pale orange and deep red, pl. 7.19).

PHYSICAL COLOUR

Pure white is usually formed in flowers by physical effects rather than pigments. Although the white petals of mayweed contain white pigments, the white

PL. 7.19 Madagascan poinciana. *Photo: R.J. King*

PL. 7.20 The colour of most white petals is due to air within their structure rather than to white pigments. *Photo: R.J. King*

petals of most flowers, such as water lilies and chrysanthemums, are actually colourless - the petal tissue contains air spaces that reflect and refract light and the petals appear white because none of the wavelengths is absorbed. As all wavelengths of sunlight are reflected, structural white coloration can be very intense (pl. 7.20).

If petals contain coloured pigments, then air spaces in the tissue can lessen the colour intensity. However, pale colours may also be due to cells having fewer pigment molecules or only some cells being pigmented. Flowers which are basically white but have coloured tips, stripes or spots (such as many lilies), or flowers which have bright colours with small areas of white (such as some petunias), have pigmented cells in the coloured areas and either pigment-free cells in white areas, or cells containing whitish pigments such as anthoxanthins. When we take into account all the possible combinations of different pigments (in the same cells or in different cells) and flower structures, it is easy to see why flowers show so much variation in colour.

Other physical features of a flower's surface can also cause whitish coloration and in nature these are probably important in protecting the flowers against ultraviolet radiation and excessive water loss. This may explain why there are more pale flowers at high latitudes and on mountains. Hairs on the surface of petals cause them appear velvety or silky: e.g. gloxinia petals, which are covered by small projections, and the petal-like hairy bracts of edelweiss which reflect and refract sunlight and appear a diffuse white colour. The oily sheen of buttercup petals is caused by an outer layer of yellow, oil-filled cells with an underlying layer of white, starch-containing cells; the underlying cells reflect a large amount of light back through the outer layer. Very smooth surfaces can also be responsible for the gloss of other flowers such as tulips and hyacinths.

POLLINATOR PREFERENCES

The colours of flowers are related to their method of pollination. The pollen of sea grasses and other aquatic plants that produce their flowers underwater, is distributed by moving water, so colour is not important for pollination. Grass flowers are wind-pollinated and likewise not usually colourful (pl.

7.21). These plants usually have flowers that are green and inconspicuous, although some jungle grasses have colourful flowers because there is little wind in their habitat and they are pollinated by insects. Aquatic plants such as water lilies have showy flowers that are held above the surface of the water to attract flying insects (pl. 7.22).

When animals are involved in pollination, flower colours must match the spectrum of colours the animal can detect. As well, the flower must provide an attractant for the animal, such as nectar or pollen, and the quantity must be just enough to whet the animal's appetite and therefore ensure that it visits another flower and transfers pollen from one to the other in the process.

Bee purple and other insect colours

Insects have different colour vision from ours: most can detect ultraviolet as a separate colour, whereas few other than butterflies can detect red at all, i.e. they cannot distinguish it from grey. Insect-pollinated flowers therefore tend to be yellow, orange, white or blue; when they have been pollinated

PL. 7.21 Left: Grass flowers are pollinated by wind and are usually not colourful. *Photo: R.J. King*

PL. 7.22 Below: Water lily flowers are held above the surface of the water and pollinated by flying insects. *Photo: R. Berthold*

PL. 7.23 Above: Lines and markings on flowers like crocuses attract and guide pollinating insects to nectar and pollen. *Photo: R.J. King*

PL. 7.24 Right: The yellow filaments and anthers of eucalypt stamens provide the splash of colour that attracts insects. *Photo: W. Farrant*

PL. 7.25 Below: Both butterflies and moths have long tongues that can reach into tubular and bell-shaped flowers. *Photo: J. Landy*

attract insects from a distance, then the petal markings guide them towards nectar and pollen supplies when they land. This is why lines and markings on flower petals are called honeyguides (pl. 7.23).

Flowers that are pollinated by insects tend to be colourful, but their attractiveness is usually reinforced by perfume. Though wasps sometimes pollinate dark brownish red flowers, and some ants pollinate inconspicuous greenish flowers, the most important insect pollinators are bees, butterflies, moths, flies and beetles.

Bees are attracted to yellow and white flowers such as clover, gorse, daisies, apple flowers and primroses, especially if they have large quantities of pollen (pl. 7.24). The colour known as bee purple is a mixture of the ultraviolet and yellow wavelengths at the opposite ends of the bee's spectrum: it is thought that bees see this as a separate colour in the same way that we see purple as a separate colour.

Butterflies are practically the only insects that can detect red, though they also feed upon other colourful flowers open during the day. Moths, which are mostly nocturnal, are attracted to whitish or mauve flowers because they stand out at night (pl. 7.25).

Colour vision of beetles and flies is not as good as that of bees and butterflies: both are attracted by the odour of a flower more than its colour (pl. 7.26). Fly-pollinated flowers tend to be green, white and reddish brown and are relatively inconspicuous apart from their odour. Both colours and odours tend to become stronger towards the middle of the flowers where the fertile parts are.

Beetles are attracted by the odour of a flower, and they often pollinate white or dull-coloured flowers that have nectar or special edible bodies. Beetles are quite destructive, so the flowers they pollinate tend to have the delicate parts of the ovary well hidden below the level of the rest of the flower.

Bird-pollinated flowers

Birds have excellent colour vision, though they are often less sensitive to blue than the other colours because of colouring substances in their eyes that cut out blue wavelengths to reduce the glare from the sky. Birds are particularly attracted to red, but also to orange, yellow and blue flowers: red flowers tend to be pollinated by birds rather than insects,

successfully or have run out of attractants, the colour may change and no longer be attractive to insects. Changes in the colour of petals can occur over a single day or night or may take up to a month.

Insect-pollinated flowers often have markings that are invisible to us, but which reflect ultraviolet light and are therefore visible to insects. Flower colours

PL. 7.26 Above: Beetles have poor colour vision and usually are more attracted to a flower's scent than its colour. *Photo: P. Farrant*

few of which can detect this colour (pls 7.27, 7.28).

Flowers of many colours

Some species of bird-pollinated plants are polymorphic for colour, i.e. different populations of plants produce flowers of different colours (pls 7.29, 7.30). One South African species of heath can be any of eight different colours: red, orange, yellow, brown, green, pink, yellow-green, yellow and purple-brown. Usually, however, any one population contains plants that are all the same colour. A range of different flower colours may be useful for attracting pollinators when the species is distributed over a wider area than any one pollinator or when any one pollinator is not present for the whole flowering period. The differently coloured populations of heath plants are probably pollinated by birds rather than insects because birds are present and active year-round and cover greater distances in flight than insects. Many insects feed on a single species while it is in flower and will not venture to feed on flowers of other colours until that source has run out.

Mammal-pollinated flowers

Most mammals do not have very good colour vision, and many are nocturnal, so mammal-pollinated flowers are not particularly colourful. Some more colourful flowers attract a range of animals, such as insects and birds, as well as mammals, e.g. red bottlebrushes can be pollinated by possums and honeyeaters. Mammals in general are attracted to the scents and nectar supplies of flowers. Nectar-eating bats are particularly attracted to whitish flowers that stand out in the dark, whereas small nocturnal marsupials usually pollinate dark-coloured, scented flowers.

COLOUR OF FRUITS

Like flowers, fruits are often brightly coloured. Animals such as birds and mammals are attracted to fruits just as we are attracted to apples, apricots and oranges. Plants form fruits after their flowers have been fertilised. Seeds develop and as they harden, the ovary wall becomes the protective wall of the fruit and the ovary tissue itself may develop into edible fruit tissue.

The fruits most attractive to animals are fleshy and edible. Tropical rainforest plants often have fleshy fruits because there is insufficient air movement for dry fruits or seeds to be dispersed by the wind: myrtles, figs, and plants in the arum and nightshade families are examples. Most fleshy fruits are eaten by birds or mammals because they are too large for insects to carry away, and as with flowers, the colours of fruits are generally well suited to the type of vision of the animals that eat them.

Colours to attract birds

Birds are most attracted to fruits that are red, orange, yellow or black (pls 7.31, 7.32), though other colours such as white, blue, purple and pink may be attractive to some species (pl. 7.33). Many plants, e.g. rowan and hawthorn, produce red berries that are easily seen by birds, but which are not as conspicuous to

insects. Bird-dispersed fruits such as these, and also cultivated fruits such as cherries and apples, are usually clustered on top of the tree or at the ends of branches so they are easily visible as birds fly by. Fruits also tend to stay on the tree for a relatively long time when they are ripe rather than fall to the ground straight away. Birds such as cassowaries, pigeons, hornbills and toucans play an important part in the dispersal of fruits in tropical rainforests, while birds such as thrushes, broadbills and blackbirds do the same in temperate areas.

Fruit bats are well known for their night-time raids into fruit plantations. They are attracted to many cultivated fruits, as well as to fruits of native trees such as figs. Like birds, and mammals such as monkeys, bats eat fruit directly from the tree. However, other mammals such as elephants and gorillas, eat fruit from the ground. Since most mammals other than monkeys and apes are virtually colour-blind and many are nocturnal, colour does not play such an important part in attracting them. In fact, many of the brightly coloured fruits attractive to birds are poisonous to mammals, e.g. nightshades.

PL. 7.27 Flowers or inflorescences (e.g. banksias) that are pollinated by birds are often red, orange or yellow. *Photo: W.H. King*

PL. 7.28 Above left: Some kangaroo paw flowers are green when they are mature and therefore attract only particular birds. *Photo: W. Farrant*

PL. 7.29 Above: Different populations of copper cups produce flowers of different colours. *Photo: R.J. King*

PL. 7.30 While this population of copper cups produces red flowers, others produce orange flowers. *Photo: R.J. King*

PL. 7.31 These aroid fruits change from green to red as they mature. *Photo: R.J. King*

Other features such as scent are more important in attracting mammals, though pale colours can be attractive in the dark of night or on the dim rainforest floor.

Some fruits, such as gumnuts, walnuts and almonds, are dry and woody (pl. 7.34). Dry fruits, as well as the fleshy fruits dispersed by wind or water or by sticking to animals, are not usually brightly coloured. Dry fruits often change colour as they mature, usually from green to brown (pl. 7.35). This colour change occurs because the mature fruit no longer photosynthesises, so tissues become woody and eventually become completely dry, e.g. the seed pod of the lotus changes from green to brown, then bends over so seeds drop into the water for dispersal.

Ripening fruits

As seeds become mature, the fruits containing them ripen and become attractive to animals. The fruit undergoes changes that make it ripe: bitter flesh becomes sweet and palatable, it develops a pleasant odour and softens. These changes are usually accompanied by changes in colour and glossiness. Whereas ripening fruits need to be inconspicuous and are therefore probably green, ripe fruits are often vividly coloured so that they are conspicuous to the animals that eat them.

The green of unripe fruit is due to chlorophyll in fruit tissue. Later, ripe fruits are coloured by anthocyanins, carotenoids and other pigments (pl. 7.36). Red carotenoids are relatively rare in plants, but they are responsible for the colour of ripe tomatoes and rose hips. In red peppers two carotenoids account for 60% of pigment in the ripe fruit. Carotenoids mostly provide yellows and oranges, though the situation is not always simple, e.g. orange peel contains carotenoids, but also yellow oil cells, cells with red sap and a yellow outer coat of wax. The brown colours that appear in fruits when they are cut open or bruised are caused by the oxidation of substances in the walls of cells within the fruit tissue.

Anthocyanins, which cause the purplish red in autumn leaves, and the red colours of new shoots and leaves, are the most important pigments in fruit coloration, providing most of the reds, purples, pinks

PL. 7.32 Red fruits are particularly attractive to birds. *Photo: P. Farrant*

PL. 7.33 Purple fruits like geebungs, are coloured by anthocyanins, and probably attract birds. *Photo: P. Farrant*

and blues of ripe fruits, e.g. red grapes, many berries such as blackberries and raspberries, and apples, pears, apricots, black currants, tamarillos and aubergines. Anthocyanins are located in cell sap, in skin or flesh, or in all parts of the fruit.

The commonest colours of ripe fruit are red, black and orange; these are most conspicuous to birds, which form the biggest group of fruit-eaters. The berries of herbaceous plants are most often red or orange, whereas the fruits of woody plants are more

PL. 7.34 Banksia fruits are woody and stay closed until the heat of a bushfire opens them and releases the seeds. *Photo: P. Farrant*

PL. 7.35 Woody fruits like these wattle pods change from green to brown as they mature. *Photo: P. Farrant*

PL. 7.36 Anthocyanins gradually increase in ripening fruits, making them attractive to animals. *Photo: P. Farrant*

likely to be black. The attractiveness of black fruits probably has more to do with gloss than colour. Black colour in a fruit can be caused by a dense concentration of dark anthocyanins or by anthocyanins in the fruit tissue combined with an outer skin of green chlorophyll-containing cells.

COLOUR OF SEEDS

Colourful fruits contain the plant's seeds. Each seed contains a developing embryo and its initial food reserve. Seeds are usually covered with a hard outer coating that protects the embryo and allows a dormant period, so that they germinate only when conditions are suitable for growth. Seeds are therefore usually indigestible and relatively unattractive to animals as a source of food and they are often protected by an attractively coloured and edible package, the fruit. If an animal eats the fruit,

the seeds will probably pass through its digestive system intact; this is how plants such as blackberries become widely distributed.

Though most seeds are not particularly attractive by themselves, some are coloured in such a way that they contrast with the colour of the fruit when it opens. The seeds of woody fruits are often red, while many are shiny and black, and so contrast with white or yellow inside the fruit or with a coloured aril. Arils are edible fleshy outgrowths of the seeds (of both fleshy and dry fruits), e.g. nutmeg fruits have a red aril, which when dried is known as the spice mace; the seed itself is the spice we know as nutmeg.

Flowers and fruits are particularly well adapted to the degree and type of colour vision that their animal pollinators and dispersers possess: the next chapter investigates the eyes and colour vision of these and other animals.

BOX 1

STRUCTURE OF FLOWERING PLANTS

The vegetative parts

Flowering plants have an aerial portion, the stem, which bears the leaves, flowers and fruits, and an underground portion, comprising the roots. The stem or stems support the leaves so that they intercept sunlight for photosynthesis, whereas the roots absorb water and mineral nutrients from the soil, and anchor the plant in the ground. The stems, roots and leaves comprise the vegetative parts of a plant. The flowers and fruits are the reproductive parts of the plant (see below).

Leaves

Many leaves are flat and present a large surface area to the sun's light. Most of an individual leaf is made up of mesophyll, green photosynthetic tissue. The mesophyll is protected by an epidermis, or outer layer.

Stems

A plant may have one or more stems. Trunks and branches are stems, and those of woody plants are protected from the weather and micro-organisms by an outer covering, the bark. Green stems owe their colour to chlorophyll, and this means that they function as photosynthetic organs in some plants: in fact some plants, such as cacti, have their leaves reduced to spines and they rely on the stems to manufacture all their food. The main part of a stem, underneath the protective epidermis and any green tissue, is usually fairly colourless in herbaceous plants, but in woody plants may be coloured by various chemical compounds, such as tannins and quinones (pl. 7.37).

Bark

The colours of barks vary enormously: green, brown, grey, orange, red, pink, purple, cream, white, yellow, black and probably more, and they show great variety of patterns and mottling (pls 7.38, 7.39). Barks often contain tannins (which are also found in leaves and fruits), substances that are used by humans for tanning leather and which are usually yellow or brown. White coloration of bark may be caused by pigments or by air spaces in the outer bark, as is the case for aspens, while other colours such as yellow, orange or purple, are often caused by quinones. If the bark layer is broken so that oxygen or micro-organisms (e.g. bacteria and fungi) can enter, then the plant may produce more protective substances in the damaged area; these will colour the bark and to some extent the wood beneath it. Damage by micro-organisms usually causes a darkening of wood.

PL. 7.37 The heartwood in the middle of a tree trunk is darker than the living outer sapwood because it contains tannins and oxidised substances. Wet wood is attacked by fungi and bacteria and the tannins react with iron to form insoluble dark compounds, though if there is plenty of sunlight wood usually turns grey because the dark substances are leached and bleached. In coastal localities, where salt inhibits the growth of micro-organisms, driftwood weathers to an attractive silvery grey. *Photo: P. Farrant*

PL. 7.38 The colours of barks are due mainly to tannins and quinones. Scribbly gum. *Photo: P. Farrant*

Roots

Most plants' roots are brown because of substances such as tannins and quinones. Sometimes a brownish red coloration can indicate the presence of iron rust around the outside of the roots: this is especially likely in wet soils. Beetroot owes its colour to red betacyanins which are pigments that are not flavonoids but which belong to a different, more complex group of substances; these pigments are located in the sap of cells throughout the root, whereas the anthocyanins in red radishes occur only in the outer layer of root cells. The reason for bright colours in underground roots is unknown.

Some plant roots that are popular foods also owe their colours to anthocyanins, though once again the function of the colours in the plant is unknown: included in this group are various species of sweet potato as well as red radishes.

The reproductive parts: flowers and fruits

A flowering plant reproduces by producing flowers. Flowers, like leaves, occur on the stems of plants, either singly or in groups. Each flower usually has both sterile and fertile parts. The outermost sterile layer consists of a number of sepals which surround the petals. The sepals and the petals form two sterile layers that surround the innermost, fertile parts. Sepals protect the flower, especially while it is developing, and petals provide a showy display to attract pollinating animals once the flower opens (fig. 7.3).

The innermost parts of a flower are the fertile parts, containing male pollen grains and female ovules, or unfertilised seeds. Pollen

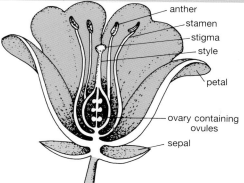

Fig. 7.3 The sterile and fertile parts of a flower.

grains are produced in anthers which normally sit on top of a stalk or filament - each anther and its filament are known collectively as a stamen. The ovules are enclosed in the ovary right in the middle of the flower. The ovary is normally at the bottom of the female part, and there is a filament, or style, above the ovary. The style has a swollen tip, or stigma, for receiving pollen grains. For the ovule to be fertilised by a male cell from a pollen grain, the pollen first has to arrive at the stigma, and this process is known as pollination (fig. 7.4).

After pollination

When a pollen grain has been deposited, by an animal onto the stigma of another flower, the flower is said to have been pollinated. The pollen grain germinates by growing a long tube, called a pollen tube, down through the style towards the ovule in the ovary of the flower. Upon reaching an ovule, the male cell leaves the pollen tube and enters the ovule to join up with the female egg cell. The amalgamation of the male and female cells is called fertilisation. After fertilisation, the ovule develops into a

PL. 7.39 Plant gums and resins are usually produced after damage or trauma.
Photo: P. Farrant

seed, and the surrounding ovary wall (or one or more of the other parts of the flower) develops into a fruit that encloses the seed or seeds (fig. 7.4). Though each ovule must be fertilised by a different pollen grain, and therefore develops into a separate seed, in some species a number of seeds can be enclosed in the same fruit.

Cross pollination is important for introducing new genetic material. Therefore it is best if one flower is fertilised by pollen from a different flower, and even better if the pollen comes from a different plant.

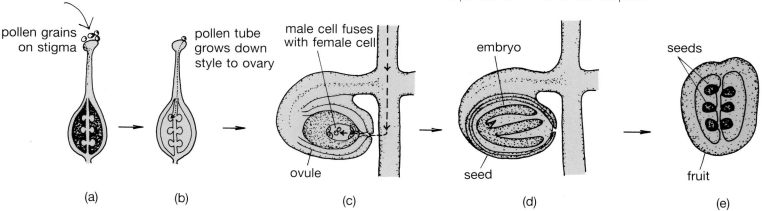

pollen grains on stigma (a)

pollen tube grows down style to ovary (b)

male cell fuses with female cell ovule (c)

embryo seed (d)

seeds fruit (e)

Fig. 7.4 Pollination occurs when a pollen grain arrives at a flower's stigma (a). The pollen grain germinates and grows down into an ovule within the flower's ovary (b). When it enters the ovule, fertilisation occurs as male and female cells unite (c). The fertilised female cell develops into an embryo within the fertilised ovule or seed (d). The ovary wall develops into a fruit around the developing seeds (e)..

CHAPTER 8

SEEING IN COLOUR

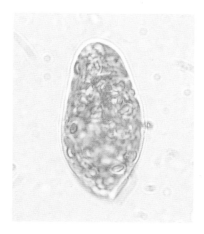

PL. 8.1 Above: This single-celled organism has an ocellus (called an eyespot) containing pigments that sense light and dark. *Photo: P. Farrant*

PL. 8.2 Right: Corals have ocelli distributed over the body surface for detecting light and dark and sometimes colour. *Photo: P. Farrant*

PL. 8.31 Left: Owls have better binocular vision than most other birds because of the amount of overlap of the fields of view of the two eyes. However, their field of view is not great and they need to swivel their necks to look around. Owls see especially well in the dark because their eyes have large openings, spherical lenses and retinas with a large number of rods; being nocturnal they do not need to see in colour. *Photo: W. Farrant*

All animals see by detecting light that is emitted or reflected from objects, other organisms and their surroundings. Even very primitive organisms are able to detect different wavelengths of light through light-sensitive cells on their body surfaces. More advanced animals can also detect the direction of this light by means of cup-shaped eyes. Still more advanced animals have eyes with lenses for focusing light rays onto light-sensitive cells; different types of light-sensitive cells contain different light-sensitive pigments for absorbing specific wavelengths or colours of light. The most advanced animals are not necessarily those with the best vision, but those that have good vision and well-developed brains for processing and interpreting the information received by the eyes. Despite the wide range of eyes and varying degree of colour vision in the animal world, all animals have eyes and vision suitable for their particular way of life (see BOX 1).

OCELLI

The simplest types of light receptors are known as ocelli, and these are so simple that they cannot even be called eyes. Ocelli are light-sensitive regions in single-celled organisms (pl. 8.1), or light-sensitive cells in simple multi-celled organisms. They usually detect whether the animal's surroundings are light or dark, although some more advanced types can detect the direction of a light source. The amoeba, a simple single-celled organism, is sensitive to light: it moves away from light to prevent its relatively unprotected body from the risk of drying out.

Simple multicellular animals such as corals (pl. 8.2) and sea anemones (pl. 8.3) have simple ocelli, usually of alternating pigment and sensory cells (fig. 8.1). These are scattered over the animals' whole body surfaces. The light-sensitivity of these animals is rather poorly developed; they are fixed in position and only need to gather information about the intensity and quality of light. Some corals and sea anemones cannot perceive colour, but others have ocelli containing pigments that specifically absorb certain wavelengths of light. These are usually the blue-green wavelengths that penetrate furthest through water, so the animals are ensured of capturing the maximum light available.

Some jellyfish, which have an active swimming life, have pigmented ocelli (fig. 8.2). Each ocellus is

BOX 1

ANIMAL CLASSIFICATION

KINGDOM ANIMALIA

Phylum	Class	Example(s)
Single-celled organisms:		
Protozoa		foraminiferans
		euglenoids
		amoebae
Multicellular invertebrates:		
Porifera		sponges
Coelenterata (Cnidaria)	Hydrozoa	hydroids
	Scyphozoa	jellyfish
	Anthozoa	anemones, corals
	Ctenophora	comb jellies
Platyhelminthes		flatworms
Aschelminthes		rotifers (wheel animals)
		nematodes (round worms)
Annelida	Polychaeta	bristleworms
	Oligochaeta	earthworms
	Hirudinea	leeches
Arthropoda	Crustacea	shrimps, crabs, lobsters
	Insecta	butterflies, beetles, bugs
	Myriapoda	millipedes, centipedes
	Arachnida	spiders
Mollusca	Amphineura	chitins
	Gastropoda	snails, slugs
	Bivalvia	oysters, mussels
	Cephalopoda	squid, octopus, cuttlefish
Echinodermata	Asteroidea	sea stars
	Ophiuroidea	brittle stars
	Echinoidea	sea urchins
	Holothuroidea	sea cucumbers
	Crinoidea	feather stars
Chordata	sub-phylum Protochordata	sea squirts, salps
Vertebrates:		
Chordata		
sub-Phylum Vertebrata	Pisces	fish
	Amphibia	salamanders, newts, frogs
	Reptilia	snakes, lizards, crocodiles
	Aves	birds
	Mammalia	mammals

The classification of the koala (*Phascolarctos cinereus*) is as follows:

Kingdom .... Animalia
    Phylum .... Chordata
        Sub-phylum .... Vertebrata
            Class .... Mammalia
                Sub-class .... Marsupialia
                    Order .... Diprotodonta
                        Family .... Phascolarctidae
                            Genus .... *Phascolarctos*
                                Species .... *cinereus*

PL. 8.3 Above: Sea anemones are sedentary and have simple ocelli distributed over the body surface. *Photo: P. Farrant*

PL. 8.4 Right: Seastars have simple ocelli on the dorsal surface and pigmented ocelli at the tips of the arms. *Photo: P. Farrant*

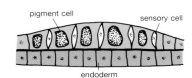

Fig. 8.1 Simple ocellus of jellyfish, in which pigment cells alternate with sensory cells.

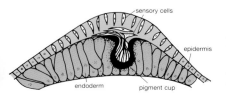

Fig. 8.2 Pigment cup ocellus of jellyfish.

multi-cellular and contains two different types of pigmented cells: cells that shade and cells that are light-sensitive. This type of ocellus not only allows an animal to tell the direction of a light source, but its multicellular nature allows it to detect an object moving past it, because the shadow is detected by one cell after another as it moves across the ocellus. Being able to detect moving objects gives animals

such as seastars (pl. 8.4) and jellyfish more of a chance to avoid being eaten by predators.

SIMPLE EYES

The transition from the more advanced ocelli to simple eyes is far from clear cut, and simple eyes themselves vary widely in complexity, producing images that range from vague blurs to more distinct shapes (pl. 8.5). The situation is also complicated by the fact that many animals with simple eyes have ocelli as well. Sometimes an ocellus has either a narrow window or a definite lens to bend light rays and concentrate them onto the light-sensitive cells: these are called simple eyes (fig. 8.3).

Whereas primitive jellyfish and corals are radially symmetrical and need ocelli all over their bodies, more advanced animals are bilaterally symmetrical and have true eyes located at the head or brain end of their bodies. Snails, slugs and other gastropod molluscs (pl. 8.6) may have several types of eye, from simple ocelli to eyes with corneas and lenses.

Clams (pl. 8.7), scallops, oysters, other bivalve molluscs (pl. 8.8) and marine segmented worms (pl. 8.9) also have simple eyes of various forms. If there are many light-sensitive cells grouped together in an animal's eye, the light-sensitive area as a whole is called a retina. Spiders often have eight simple eyes (pl. 8.10). Two of the eyes at the front are usually the largest of the eight and are the largest simple eyes of the animal world, reaching a couple of millimetres in diameter. Spiders in general have limited colour vision, though some which change colour to match the flowers they rest on, probably have better than average colour vision.

COMPOUND EYES

More advanced invertebrates, in particular insects and crustaceans, have compound eyes (pl. 8.11, fig. 8.4). These eyes are quite distinct from more primitive simple eyes and are made of a large number of units called ommatidia, each of which is actually a small eye (pl. 8.12). Compound eyes enable animals such as flies and crabs to see objects quite clearly if they are a certain distance away, though the image is

broken up so it is almost as if they were looking through a window with many small panes. Once again, there is a wide range of complexity amongst compound eyes, so that the more advanced animals have compound eyes with the most advanced features (pl. 8.13).

Seeing red

Most insects can distinguish colours and thus discriminate between different objects in their environment, even if the images are unfocused. The number of colours an insect can see depends on how many different types of light-sensitive pigments are in its eyes: each type absorbs a particular wavelength or colour of light. Most insects' eyes contain two or three types of light-sensitive pigments: e.g. bees' eyes can detect blue, green and ultraviolet wavelengths (fig. 8.5). Only some butterflies and fireflies have a fourth type of light-sensitive pigment that allows them to perceive red wavelengths (pl. 8.14). The pigments themselves are opposite in colour to the wavelengths they absorb, in the same way that a green leaf is green because it reflects green but absorbs all other wavelengths. Some insects' eyes have iridescent corneas that accentuate the colours their light-sensitive pigments detect, and many insects' eyes are well camouflaged (pl. 8.15).

Periscopic Vision in Crustaceans

Crustaceans such as crabs, lobsters and prawns, have compound eyes similar to the eyes of insects. Like insects, their eyes can contain various numbers of ommatidia, from several dozen to over 10 000 in the faster moving species. Many of the more active crustaceans such as crabs and prawns, have their eyes on stalks (pl. 8.16). Their bodies are protected by hard shells, so that if their eyes were set into their bodies they could not obtain such a wide field of

PL. 8.5 The simple eyes of flatworms probably see objects only as indistinct blobs. *Photo: P. Farrant*

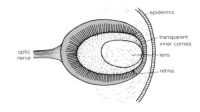

PL. 8.6 Nudibranchs are bilaterally symmetrical and have a pair of simple eyes at the head end. *Photo: W. Farrant*

Fig. 8.3 Simple eye of snail, with cornea, lens and retina.

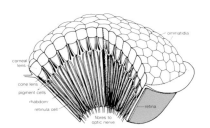

Fig. 8.4 Compound eye, typical of insects and crustaceans, composed of numerous units called ommatidia.

PL. 8.7 Clams' eyes lack lenses but have tapeta that help to form a very crude image by concentrating light rays. *Photo: P. Farrant*

PL. 8.10 Spiders like the huntsman have up to eight simple eyes; the main pair of eyes at the front is able to form a crude image, while the other smaller eyes are used for peripheral vision, detecting movement and judging distances. *Photo: R. Berthold*

PL. 8.8 Above: Scallops have wrap-around vision for detecting approaching predators, with up to 200 eyes in their mantles. *Photo: P. Farrant*

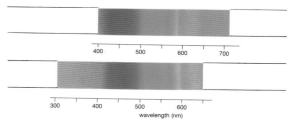

Fig. 8.5 Bees (lower spectrum) can see well into the ultraviolet part of the spectrum, but can hardly detect red at all, whereas humans can see red but not ultraviolet.

PL. 8.9 Right: A 'feather duster' worm lives in a coral and has both simple eyes (one or more pairs) and scattered ocelli. *Photo: P. Farrant*

view (around 200°), nor would they be able to see over obstacles.

Most crustaceans are believed to be able to see colour, because their eyes contain different types of light-sensitive pigments that absorb different wavelengths or colours of light. The mantis shrimp has the most complex colour vision of all animals with compound eyes. Each of its two stalked eyes has two central bands of ommatidia, aligned at right angles to each other, which detect not only colours in the visible part of the spectrum, but also ultraviolet wavelengths and polarised light. This means the animal can gather a great deal of information about its environment: it can detect a wide range of colours and may even be able to use polarised light in some way, e.g. to sense the position of the sun in the sky on a cloudy day.

PL. 8.11 Compound eyes of a fly. *Photo: J. Landy*

Adapting to light or dark

Crustaceans and insects that are active in the day, such as bees, have eyes which are more or less permanently adapted to light and which form an image with reasonably good resolution. There is plenty of light during the day so the eyes only need to use the rays of light that enter the lens at the top of each ommatidium. Pigments in the sides of each ommatidium prevent light entering from neighbouring ommatidia, ensuring that the image is as sharp as possible. In the eyes of animals that are more or less permanently adapted to the dark, such

PL. 8.12 Viewed under a scanning electron microscope a moth's eye is seen to be made up of hundreds of individual units or ommatidia, each of which actually functions as a tiny eye. *Photo: P. Farrant*

as some moths, the shading pigments are located at the base of each ommatidium so that extra light can enter from the sides as well as the top: the image may be rather blurred, but it allows the animals to see where they are going or whether a predator is approaching. Although most insects' and crustaceans' eyes have the shading pigment set in place, either at the base or in the sides of the ommatidia, some are able to adapt to dark and light conditions on a daily basis, either because the shading pigment moves up and down as required, or because the pigment is at the base of some ommatidia and in the sides of the remainder (fig. 8.6).

Eyeshine

Many different animals that are active at night or which live in dark environments (e.g. invertebrates such as spiders, scallops, octopuses and moths, and vertebrates such as fish, possums and cats) have a special light-reflecting surface, a tapetum, in their eyes to trap the maximum amount of light in dim conditions. It acts like a mirror, reflecting light that has passed through the retina without being absorbed (fig. 8.7). This gives the light another chance to trigger a nervous impulse from the light-sensitive cells: the more cells triggered by light, the clearer an image will be. The animals that have tapeta all have large eyes and wide pupils to let in as much light as possible. Their eyes glow when light is shone into them and this is known as eyeshine. The colour of eyeshine depends on the colour of the pigments in the animal's retina, but may be yellow, red or even green (pl. 8.17).

Camera Eyes

Camera eyes are found in all the vertebrate groups of animals and in one group of invertebrates, containing the octopuses, squid and cuttlefish (cephalopod molluscs). The only cephalopod that has simple eyes is the nautilus (pl. 8.18).

A camera eye resembles a camera in its essential elements (fig. 8.8): it is an enclosed sphere (= camera body) connected optically to the external environment by a small opening or pupil (= aperture) in the iris or coloured muscle of the eye (= diaphragm). Light rays from an object enter the eye through the cornea, a tough transparent outer layer at the front of the eye that has a light-absorbing layer on its inside (= protective filter on outside of camera lens). The light rays are focused by means of a lens onto the retina (= film) made up of light-sensitive cells containing light-sensitive pigments (= photographic emulsion). While a camera lens focuses by moving back and forth, the lens of the eye focuses or accommodates by changing shape.

The light-sensitive cells of vertebrates' eyes are known as rods and cones because of their shapes: the rods are used for night vision (= black and white film) and the cones are used for daytime colour vision (= colour film). Just as films of different sensitivities are available for use under different light conditions, the retina can also adapt to different conditions: at night the eye gradually adapts to the dark and by day the eye adapts to bright light.

PL. 8.13 Dragonflies' eyes have a large number of ommatidia; these insects see sharply close up and register movement at a distance. *Photo: J. Landy*

PL. 8.14 Some butterflies, but few other types of insects, can detect the red wavelengths of sunlight. *Photo: W. Farrant*

PL. 8.15 Many insects like this grasshopper have eyes that blend in well with their general body coloration. *Photo: J. Landy*

PL. 8.16 Hermit crab: stalked eyes give a wide field of view (around 200°) and allow it to see over obstacles. *Photo: P. Farrant*

PL. 8.17 Eyeshine, seen in these wallabies, is caused by reflection of unabsorbed light by a tapetum. *Photo: R. Berthold*

An upside-down and back-to-front image occurs on the retina (= film) and the final image is produced either in the eye itself or in the brain (= darkroom). In more primitive vertebrates such as amphibians, analysis of the information detected by the eyes is minimal and so the animals can react rapidly and automatically to visual stimuli.

In more advanced vertebrates, such as humans, complex analysis of visual information occurs in the brain before an image is perceived. The signals received by the light-sensitive cells of the retina are converted to electrical signals that are sent to the

Fig. 8.6 Light-adapted (a) and dark- adapted (b) ommatidia.

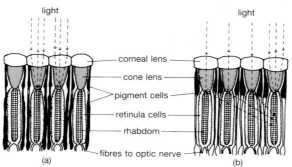

corneal lens
cone lens
pigment cells
retinula cells
rhabdom
fibres to optic nerve

(a)   (b)

light   light

Fig. 8.7 Simple eye of scallop, showing reflective layer or tapetum at the back of the eye.

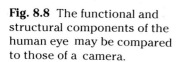

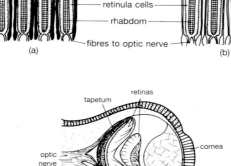

retinas
tapetum
optic nerve
cornea
pigment layer

Fig. 8.8 The functional and structural components of the human eye may be compared to those of a camera.

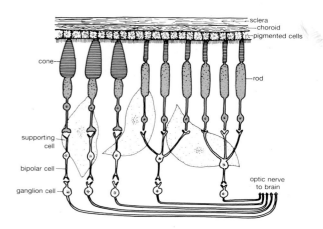

sclera
choroid
pigmented cells
cone
rod
supporting cell
bipolar cell
ganglion cell
optic nerve to brain

Fig. 8.9 Rods and cones, the light- sensitive cells of a vertebrate's retina.

brain via the optic nerve. An image is built up from all the incoming signals and turned the right way up and the right way around. Images formed by the eye are continually processed by the brain, whereas the camera can only produce a series of separate images which must be processed independently in the dark-room. While the camera sees an image quite objectively, however, the brain has a great deal of influence over the way we perceive images.

Like compound eyes, camera eyes occur in pairs. Camera eyes, however, have several advantages over compound eyes: a sharper image is produced, near or distant objects can be brought into focus without the animal having to move, and the eyes can adapt more readily to light and dark conditions, over both short and long periods. Many animals with camera eyes have fields of view that overlap, so they can see a scene in three dimensions: this means that there is a depth of focus, whereby objects at different distances from the animal are all in focus at the same time. Three-dimensional or binocular vision therefore gives

an animal the advantage of being able to judge distances: the majority of animals with compound eyes do not have binocular vision.

Because the pigments in vertebrates' rods and cones are arranged on flat membranes that always lie at right angles to the direction of incoming light, one disadvantage they have, compared to invertebrates, is that their eyes cannot analyse polarised light (fig. 8.9).

Advanced Invertebrates

Octopuses, squid and cuttlefish (cephalopods) have the most highly developed eyes of all invertebrates (pl. 8.19). Cephalopod eyes have the same components as vertebrate eyes: transparent cornea, (spherical) lens, adjustable (rectangular) pupil, coloured movable iris and retina with light-sensitive pigments, but their eyes are structurally less complex and contain light-sensitive cells that are typical of invertebrates.

Cephalopods can change colour almost instantaneously and display extremely complex behaviour patterns. This is made possible by their highly developed vision and complex brains and nervous systems. Surprisingly however, experimental evidence suggests that they do not possess colour vision. Their eyes possess two light-sensitive pigments, but these are very close in colour sensitivity (sensitive to blue and blue-green) and are probably an adaptation for dim underwater light. The arrangement of light-sensitive pigments in their eyes suggests that animals such as octopuses can distinguish polarised light, and this may enable them to spot fish hidden to most predators by reflections from their scales.

Fishes' eyes

Fish have well-developed eyes with transparent protective corneas, opaque irises, large spherical lenses and light-sensitive retinas (pl. 8.20). The cornea is flat and unable to bend light rays travelling through water. Light is mostly bent by a spherical

PL. 8.18 The nautilus is a primitive cephalopod with simple eyes that operate like a pinhole camera. Light enters each eye through a tiny hole that can be opened up. The eyes do not contain lenses, but can form a reasonably sharp image if the hole is very tiny. If the hole is opened wide to let in more light (e.g. deep in the ocean), the rays of light cannot be brought together in focus so the image is blurred. *Photo: R. Berthold*

lens, which protrudes slightly from the iris, allowing light from a wide viewing angle to enter the eye (pl. 8.21).

Fishes' eyes have some important adaptations for their habitat, although they rely less on vision than on other senses. They are protected from glare by shading pigments that can be moved into place when required, and bottom-dwelling fish such as rays and soles also have a special lid that comes down from the top of each eye to protect it from down-glare (pl. 8.22). Fish do not need moveable eyelids or tear glands because the water they live in cleans and moistens their eyes. Most fishes' eyes have tapeta for trapping maximum light under low light conditions, and therefore most fish show eyeshine. Their eyes are normally on each side of the head, so they can see almost back to the tail, as well as forward to the nose, where there is a small area of binocular vision; even predatory fish are preyed upon and need as wide a view as possible. Some fish have grooves along the length of their noses, like the sighting grooves of a gun, so that their noses do not prevent them from seeing what lies directly ahead.

Special adaptations

Fish that feed mainly at dawn and dusk, when light conditions are poor, generally have wider cones than normal, and this allows each cone to capture enough light to create a nervous signal. Fish living at mid-ocean levels, such as the orange roughy, often have very large eyes with wide pupils so that as much light as possible can enter their eyes; their retinas contain mostly rods. Fish living in very deep, dark parts of oceans or in caves, where no light penetrates, often have primitive or non-functional eyes and must depend on their other senses for obtaining food (pl. 8.23).

PL. 8.19 Octopuses have camera eyes, with good depth of focus. *Photo: R. Berthold*

PL. 8.20 Fishes' eyes are well developed, and often reflective, an adaptation for efficient capture of light. *Photo: P. Farrant*

Seeing colour underwater

Colour vision is an important advantage to an animal living in an aquatic environment, where it is more difficult to distinguish objects from their backgrounds on the basis of brightness alone. Most fish have good colour vision, but only as adults: fish larvae lack colour vision. Colour vision is due to cones, so deep-sea fish that only have rod vision do not perceive colour.

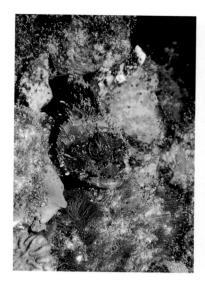

PL. 8.21 Above: The lenses of fishes' eyes protrude from the irises and capture light from a wide angle. *Photo: W. Farrant*

PL. 8.22 Right: Crocodile fish: intricately branched eyelids protect the eyes from down-glare. *Photo: P. Farrant*

PL. 8.23 Cave fish and other animals that live in dark places are often blind or have no eyes at all. *Photo: R. Berthold*

PL. 8.24 Sharks, and sting-rays, probably do not see in colour because their eyes contain few cones. *Photo: P. Farrant.*

Light-sensitive pigments in fishes' eyes vary with habitat: the light-sensitive pigments of fish living in the open ocean are usually most sensitive to blue wavelengths that penetrate best through ocean water, whereas those of fish living in coastal waters are most sensitive to yellow-green wavelengths. The eyes of shallow-water fish are often covered with a yellow filter that absorbs harmful ultraviolet and excess blue wavelengths before they reach the retina; deepwater fish that do not encounter ultraviolet light do not need such filters. Stingrays and most sharks probably do not have colour vision: their eyes have relatively few light-sensitive cells and not many of these are cones (pl. 8.24).

The eyes of some freshwater fish are most sensitive to the infra-red wavelengths of light. Parts of the Amazon River are coloured reddish brown owing to decay of organic matter (see p. 44), and piranhas' eyes are able to use the infra-red light that penetrates the water after the other wavelengths have been absorbed (red) or reflected (other colours) by particles in the water. Piranhas are savage predators and use this ability to prey upon other unsuspecting animals (pl. 8.25). Goldfish, which live under similar conditions in their natural environments, have the greatest known range of colour vision of all animals: they have light-sensitive pigments for detecting both ultraviolet and infra-red wavelengths, as well as colours visible to humans. Fish that live part of their lives in fresh water and part of their lives in the sea, are able to cope with changes in light quality between the two environments by altering the relative proportions of different types of light-sensitive pigments in their eyes.

Amphibians

The eyes of amphibians are similar to those of fish, with a rigid spherical lens that moves backwards and forwards to focus light on the retina. Although salamanders and newts have quite primitive camera eyes, frogs in particular have well-developed eyes. Many amphibians have a 360° view of the world, and binocular vision, which requires overlapping fields of view, is rare. Amphibians' eyes are unusual in not retracting into sockets but rather into the pharynx: here the eyes are used to keep a grip on food in the mouth! The eyes can also be repaired or even grow back. Frogs, toads and other amphibians probably see in colour but to a limited extent: many are active at night and do not need to see in colour (pl. 8.26).

PL. 8.25 Far left: Piranhas' eyes can detect the infra-red wavelengths that penetrate the reddish brown water of their habitat. *Photo: R. Berthold.*

PL. 8.26 Left: Tree frogs: most amphibians have good vision, though their ability to see in colour is usually limited. *Photo: P. Farrant*

Reptiles

Snakes, lizards, turtles and other reptiles can see in colour and their eyes can focus on objects at different distances away to produce good clear images (pl. 8.27). Their retinas have a special area where the cones are very dense and there are no blood vessels or nerves: this is known as a fovea and it is an important development because it creates an extra-clear area within the image, allowing fine detail to be resolved. This is a distinct advantage to reptiles such as tree snakes, which need to recognise potential prey and determine where to strike them most effectively. Reptiles can move their eyes in the sockets, and many therefore have partially overlapping fields of view; binocular vision is best developed in snakes that strike at their prey, as they need to be able to judge exactly how far away the prey is.

Chameleons are well known for their ability to change colour and they have the most fascinating eyes of all reptiles: the eyes are located on turrets on each side of the animal's head and the animal can look backwards and forwards at the same time because the eyes operate independently (pl. 8.28). Chameleons apparently assimilate the views from both eyes simultaneously without any confusion in the brain!

While most reptiles have colour vision, nocturnal and burrowing snakes and lizards, and crocodiles, have eyes with more rods than cones, and are therefore unlikely to see any colour. These animals are well adapted for night vision, with large eyes and tapeta. Some geckos and crocodiles have special pupils that close up during the day to protect the eyes from sunlight, though not completely: small gaps remain open to admit light, giving a clear image and allowing the animals to see by day and by night.

Birds' Eyes

Birds' eyes have reached a very high level of development, giving them the complex colour vision they require for their way of life: flying, soaring, swimming, diving, walking and running. Although many birds have extremely complicated patterns of behaviour, these are mostly instinctive.

Birds' eyes are usually relatively large, with high densities of light-sensitive cells and nerve cells for creating images with excellent resolution (pl. 8.29). The lens is located close to the front of the eye to produce a large image on the retina. The eyes are flattened so that the whole field of view is in focus at any one time, and many birds have eye muscles for changing the shape of both the lens and the cornea, so that the focus can be changed for viewing objects at different distances. Many birds of prey (pl. 8.30) have two foveas in each eye, allowing them to see sharply when they are feeding on the ground, as well as while they are flying at enormous heights above the ground. Many of these birds, such as vultures, even have a type of telephoto arrangement, in which the central part of the field of view is magnified several times. Eagles' eyes have the best resolution of all and they can see many times the detail that we can, although they need good light conditions to achieve this.

Birds that are preyed upon need to see as much of their surroundings as possible, to ensure survival, e.g. starlings have fields of vision that can be moved apart to give a wider picture or brought together to improve the central image. The woodcock's eyes, located centrally on either side of its head, can give 360° vision, enabling the bird to see behind without even moving. The bittern even has rear binocular vision!

Coloured oil droplets

Apart from nocturnal birds such as owls (pl. 8.31), most see in colour. To achieve even better colour vision than is available from having a range of light-sensitive pigments, many birds also have a range of coloured oil droplets in their eyes. These are located within the light-sensitive cells, usually close to the point at which light enters the cell, with each cell containing oil droplets of a single colour (fig. 8.10). These oil droplets function as cut-off filters by blocking the entry of some wavelengths or colours of light while letting others through. The range of light-sensitive pigments in a bird's eye, teamed with

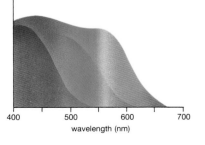

Fig. 8.10 Colours of light absorbed by yellow (left), orange (middle) and red (right) oil droplets from a pigeon's eye.

PL. 8.27 Goanna: most reptiles have binocular vision and foveas, and see in colour. *Photo: M. Porteners*

a range of differently coloured oil droplets, increases the range of different colours that the eye can detect.

Although coloured oil droplets are found in other less advanced animal groups, such as amphibians and reptiles (e.g. turtles' eyes contain red oil droplets which cause the blue light of the sea to be desaturated and other colours brightened), they are best developed in bird's eyes. Seven or so different combinations of light-sensitive pigments and oil droplets have been recorded in birds, giving them a great range of colour vision. Vertebrates without oil droplets are limited to 2-4 different types of light-sensitive cones and one type of rod.

The colours of the oil droplets in birds' eyes are related to their ways of life. Birds that are active during the day, such as eagles, have yellow and orange oil droplets which help to minimise glare and dazzle by cutting out blue light. Surface-feeding sea birds

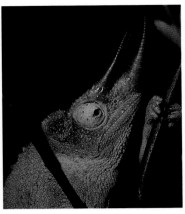

PL. 8.28 Above: Male Jackson's chameleon: these animals can move each eye independently. *Photo: C. Banks*

PL. 8.29 Left: Ostrich: most birds have colour vision, and many have better colour discrimination than we do. *Photo: P. Farrant*

PL. 8.30 Birds of prey like the brown falcon have extra foveal areas in their eyes for magnifying distant objects. *Photo: M. Porteners*

PL. 8.32 Seabirds have red oil drops in their eyes, which filter out blue light and increase contrast in sea haze. *Photo: W. Farrant*

(pl. 8.32) have red oil droplets to help filter out scattered blue light from the sky and improve contrast sensitivity of their eyes so they can see through sea haze. Songbirds have yellow, orange and red oil drops in their eyes, so they are partially blind to blue but see red clearly: for this reason most bird-pollinated flowers are in the red-orange-yellow colour range.

Underwater birds

Some birds can see just as well underwater as above water. Kingfishers' eyes each have two foveas, giving them excellent vision both in and out of the water. Cormorants use their corneas for focusing when they are above water, but for underwater vision they have powerful eye muscles that distort the lenses and force them to bulge out through the iris: in this way the image is focused onto the retina rather than a long way behind it. Although penguins are probably short-sighted out of water, they have excellent focus underwater (pl. 8.33).

Mammals

While most mammals, such as rabbits, dogs and cats, have limited colour vision, their eyes are nonetheless well developed (pl. 8.34). Mammals' eyes have the lenses located close to the corneas to produce large bright images on the retinas; their eyes each have a fovea; and most mammals have binocular vision so that they can see a scene in three dimensions. Rather than containing coloured oil droplets, most mammals' eyes have a single yellow filter in the lens or covering the fovea, and this helps to cut out some of the harmful ultraviolet wavelengths of sunlight.

As in other animal groups, the particular specialisations of mammals' eyes depend upon their way of life. Predatory mammals, e.g. dingoes, polar bears and wolverines, have their eyes placed well forward on the head so they have good binocular vision in front: in conjunction with colour and shade cues, this allows them to judge distances very accurately. The eyes of grassland predators such as cheetahs (pl. 8.35) have a fovea that gives extra sharp vision across the centre of each eye: this enables them to detect prey in a flat landscape. Grazing animals hunted by cheetahs, such as wildebeest, live in the same habitat and have the same sort of adaptation. The eyes of these animals each have a dense band of cones in a strip along the centre of the retina. Elephants, which are large, relatively slow and feed on vegetation, do not need to have eyes so specialised: the density of light-sensitive cells on the fovea of an elephant's eye is relatively low, so their view of the world is a little less clear. Marine mammals have eyes with pigments that are most sensitive to blue wavelengths of light so they can gather as much available underwater light as possible.

Most mammals do not need to see in colour: they are usually not vividly coloured themselves, and colour does not play an important part in their lives. The only mammals to have good colour vision are monkeys, humans and other primates (pl. 8.36).

PL. 8.33 Penguins' eyes are better able to focus underwater than on land. Their eyes contain pigments that are particularly sensitive to the violet, blue and green wavelengths of light that penetrate deepest through seawater. *Photo: A. Leslie.*

PL. 8.34 Mammals, such as this hyrax, have well-developed eyes despite their limited ability to see in colour. *Photo: W. Farrant*

PL. 8.35 A cheetah's eye has a horizontal fovea for seeing clearly along the horizon of a flat landscape. *Photo: P. Farrant*

PL. 8.36 Few mammals other than primates like humans, apes and monkeys, have good colour vision. *Photo: W. Farrant*

Other than primates, the only other mammals with large numbers of cones in their retinas are prairie dogs and squirrels. Cats, which are nocturnal except for the cheetah, probably cannot detect red or green and may have even poorer colour vision in bright light. Dogs have only a small degree of colour vision, and most likely see the world in blues and yellows. Rodents such as mice and rats have little or no colour vision.

Human Eyes

Human eyes are essentially like the eyes of other vertebrates. Our eyes are different colours because of yellow and brown pigments in the iris. Our retinas are well endowed with light-sensitive cells, about 125 000 000 cones and 6 500 000 rods, and these transform light into the nervous impulses that are sent to the visual cortex of the brain, where an image is built up. The eyes of humans are not the most complex in the animal world, and they do not respond to as many colours as those of some other animals: human vision is dependent on interpretation by the brain.

Cones are concentrated on the fovea of the human retina, to provide an area of good resolution in the centre of the image: in fact, the human brain fills in some peripheral information. The so-called blindspot is that part of the retina where the optic nerve connects to the eye, where there are no light-sensitive cells.

Human colour vision

Human eyes have four kinds of light-sensitive cells: rods and three types of cones. Rods contain a reddish purple light-sensitive pigment called rhodopsin (fig. 8.11), which is most sensitive to green light: this is why green leaves appear to be brighter than red berries when the two are seen together at night (fig. 8.12). The three kinds of cones in the human eye contain pigments that are sensitive to blue, green and red wavelengths (fig. 8.13). The cones operate only in relatively bright light conditions to provide us with colour vision. Colour vision depends on the relative absorption of light of different wavelengths by these three types of cones. The different wavelengths of the sun's light must be sampled individually (by different light-sensitive cells) and compared with each other in the brain; therefore not all the incoming light is used. The relative intensities of the signals sent to the brain from these different cones determine the overall colour of the image. Each cone has an almost direct line to the brain, via various nerve cells and the optic nerve, so that cone vision gives images with good resolution.

Rods are located on the periphery of the human retina and provide night-time monochromatic vision as well as assisting in daytime by contributing to vision at the edge of the field of view. Once light has been absorbed by rod pigments, all information about its wavelength is lost. Rods have a higher sensitivity than cones due to the fact that they act in groups to collect light. In this way they can receive light of low intensity but at the expense of resolution: the brain does not know which rod received the stimulus.

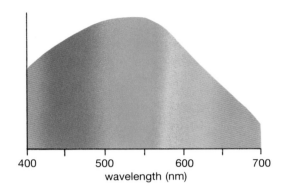

Fig. 8.11 Absorption of light by rhodopsin, the pigment found in human rods.

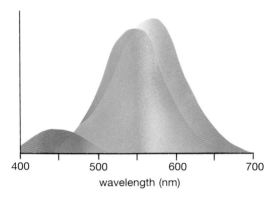

Fig. 8.13 Absorption of light by the three types of cones in human eyes: our eyes are least sensitive to blue wavelengths.

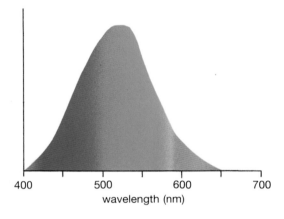

Fig. 8.12 Wavelengths of light absorbed by rods, corresponding with the peak for rhodopsin, and having maximum sensitivity in the bluish green part of the spectrum.

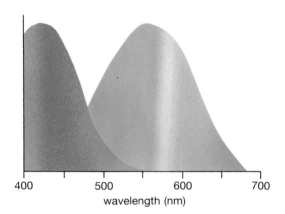

Fig. 8.14 Colours of light absorbed by a person with red-green colour-blindness: only two types of cones are present.

PL. 8.37 The less advanced invertebrate animals, like this spider, have simple eyes.
Photo: A. Leslie

PL. 8.38 Right: Most vertebrate animals, like this parrotfish, have camera eyes and colour vision. *Photo: R. Berthold*

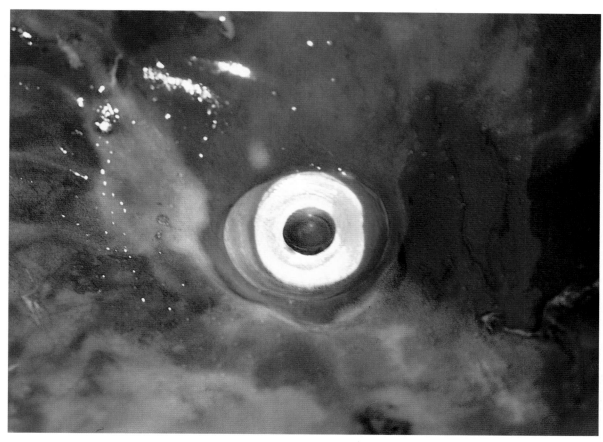

PL. 8.39 Below: Although mammals, like this giraffe, have well-developed eyes, most have limited colour vision. *Photo: W. Farrant*

The light-sensitive pigments of the rods and cones are continually broken down when exposed to light. Resynthesis of rhodopsin is slowest, and this is why our eyes gradually adapt to the dark: full dark adaptation takes about an hour whereas light adaptation takes about seven minutes.

Twilight vision is achieved by the combined action of rods and cones. Since rods are more efficient at absorbing green wavelengths and the cones overall respond best to blue-green wavelengths, these are the colours that we see best just prior to nightfall; thereafter colours become monotone.

Colour-blindness

The term colour-blindness as applied to humans is a misnomer since few people perceive no colour at all; the term refers to a lack of one of the light-sensitive pigments or to the incorrect pigment being present in some cones. Red-green colour-blindness is the commonest form in humans (fig. 8.14), and results from the absence of one of the cone pigments: people confuse red and green and are unable to tell them apart. Men are especially likely to have this colour-blindness because it is a sex-linked trait. Blue colour-blindness is less common and affects both sexes.

An amazing range of eyes and colour vision exists among animals (pls 8.37, 8.38, 8.39). This situation is matched, if not surpassed, by the range of animal coloration, and this will be examined in the following two chapters.

CHAPTER 9

ANIMAL PIGMENTS

Animal colours can be due to pigments or the animal's structure or a combination of both. Structure will be discussed in the next chapter.

Pigment colours are produced by chemical substances in animal tissues. The selective absorption and reflection of different wavelengths of white light give pigments their colour.

Animals have some of the same pigments as plants. Relative occurrence and importance in the two groups, however, differ. Animals cannot manufacture the two most important plant pigments, chlorophyll and carotenoids, and therefore need to take these in as food. Chlorophyll and even its derivatives are found in very few animals; the same is true of the flavonoids, so common in plants. Carotenoids, on the other hand, are very common and occur in almost

all animals (pls 9.1, 9.2).

The most important pigments found in animals include: melanins, carotenoids, respiratory pigments (e.g. haemoglobin), pterins, porphyrins, bilins and quinones (see BOX 1).

WHERE ARE PIGMENTS LOCATED?

Pigments that colour the surfaces of most vertebrate animals are found in special cells called chromatophores (pl. 9.3). These cells are found not in the outermost layer of epidermis that is continually being renewed, but in underlying layers, either the lower part of the epidermis or the dermis, the fibrous layer of skin beneath the epidermis. Some pigments are also found in skin products (hair, fur, scales and feathers), while others are found inside animals (in blood, muscles, bones, central nervous system and other tissues and organs).

The chromatophores of vertebrates are branched cells (fig. 9.1). Their shape is fixed, and an animal changes colour through movement of the pigment within the chromatophores. When pigment in a chromatophore is evenly distributed, a dark colour is achieved. When pigment is contracted into a small region of the chromatophore, a light colour results. The movement of pigment within a chromatophore may be controlled by hormones or nerves.

There are several different types of chromatophores, named according to the colour of pigment they contain. Melanophores are chromatophores that contain black or brown melanin: the pigment is in the form of granules called melanosomes. Xanthophores and erythrophores are yellow and red chromatophores respectively, which contain carotenoids or pterins.

In addition to pigment-containing chromatophores, other types of cells which do not contain any pigments are found in the skin of fish, amphibians and some reptiles (pl. 9.4). These non-pigmented cells are known variously as guanophores, leukophores, iridophores or iridocytes, and they contain crystals of guanine (a white excretory product of animals) or similar substances that reflect light.

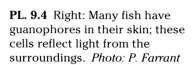

Fig. 9.1 Typical animal chromatophores, the branched pigment-containing cells of reptiles, amphibians, fish and most invertebrates.

BOX 1

ANIMAL PIGMENTS

ANIMAL PIGMENTS

Group	Function/location	Colour-producing & chemical features	Example	Structure
Melanins	granular; in hair, feathers, cuticles; usually in chromatophores; dark brown or black (eumelanin) or yellow brown (phaeomelanin)	very large molecules (polymers); carbon rings; often linked to proteins	most forms of melanin are large molecules made up of many molecules of endoquinone (shown)	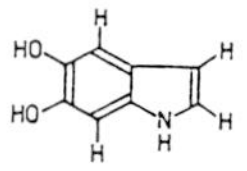
Ommochromes	granular; first discovered as shielding pigment in insects' eyes	related to melanins; often attached to proteins	xanthommatin (butterfly)	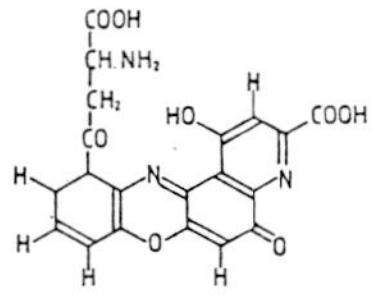
Tyrian purple	colour develops outside the animal as secretion; only in some marine gastropods	related to ommachromes and melanin; contains bromine	tyrian purple (some gastropods)	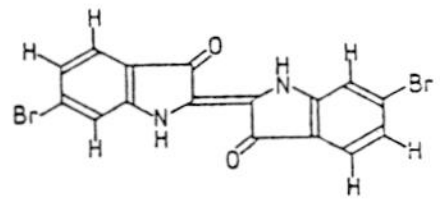
Carotenoids (Lipochromes)	derived from plants in food; animals unable to make these pigments	carbon chain; carbon rings; double and single bonds	beta-carotene (carotene in some crustaceans)	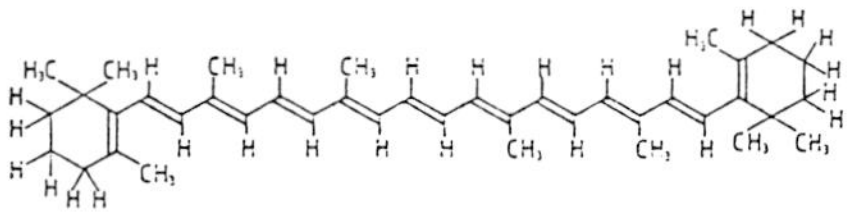
			astaxanthin (xanthophyll in lobsters)	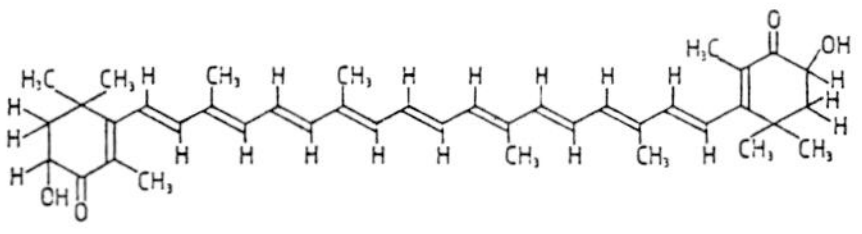
Visual pigments	derived from carotenoids; in rods of vertebrates' eyes	made from vitamin A; double and single bonds	rhodopsin (human eyes), chrysopsin (deep-sea fish), porphryopsin (tadpoles) are all based on cis-retinene (shown)	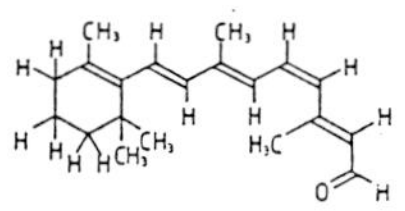
Porphyrins	excretory products; tend to accumulate in calcareous parts of animals	related to haemoglobin and cytochrome; carbon rings	uroporphyrin (many animals, including human urine)	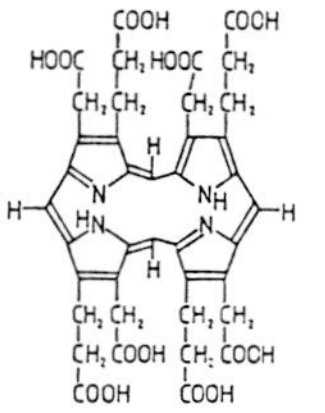
			coproporphyrin (human faeces)	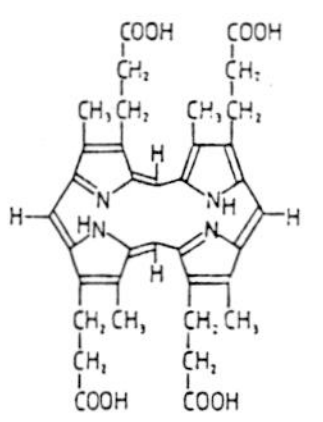

Bilins	breakdown products of porphyrins; found in bile; often in calcareous parts of animals	carbon rings; not combined with metals or proteins bilirubin	**bilverdin** (birds' eggs)	
			bilirubin (human bile)	
			urobilin (mammals' intestines)	
Phycobilins	derived in food from plants	carbon rings; double and single bonds	phycocyanin (fish bones)	
			phycoerythrin (some fish)	
Cytochrome	physiological; oxidation of food for energy	haem (iron) and nitrogen; carbon rings; related to chlorophyll	cytochrome (haem part shown only)	
Respiratory pigments	transportation of oxygen in blood	haem (iron); carbon rings; large molecules double and single bonds; attached to protein. Others have metal atoms (e.g. iron in haemerythrin, copper in haemocyanin) but metal not directly attached to protein	haemoglobin (vertebrate red blood corpuscules, haem part shown only)	
			chlorocruorin (blood of some polychaetes)	
Quinones	derived from foods; found in various parts of body, and in eggs, shells and spines of sea urchins	carbon rings; double and single bonds	echinoquinone (sea urchins)	
			spinoquinone (sea urchins)	
			kermesic acid (kermes scale insects)	
			laccaic acid (lac scale insects)	
			carminic acid (cochineal insects)	
			erythroaphin (aphids)	

| Pterins | found in wings of some butterflies | double and single bonds; nitrogen-containing | xanthopterin (some butterflies) | 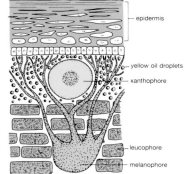 |
| Reflective substances | excretory products of some animals; crystalline | related to pterins; nitrogen containing | uric acid (butterflies)

guanine (fish) | |

PL. 9.5 Left: Cuttlefish: chromatophores at various levels in the skin are continually moving under the control of the animal's nervous system. *Photo: W. Farrant*

Fig. 9.2 Section through a lizard's skin shows yellow layer (oil droplets and yellow xanthophore), branched melanophore and underlying leucophores.

They are usually located below the level of the chromatophores (fig. 9.2). Often the terms guanophore and leukophore are used to refer to cells that are whitish or silvery and reflective but not iridescent, and the terms iridophore or iridocyte are for cells that produce iridescent colours. Sometimes melanophores and iridocytes are closely linked together to form composite structures known as melaniridocytes.

Melanophores

Mammals such as humans have only one type of pigment cell in their skin and hair (see BOX 2). These cells are known as melanocytes, rather than melanophores, because they do not change colour by means of the aggregation and dispersal of pigment (fig. 9.3). Rather, colour change in mammals is relatively slow and depends on changes in the amount of pigment and the rate at which it is produced. This is why mammals do not undergo rapid colour changes. Some reptiles and amphibians also have melanocytes in their epidermal layers, and melanin is the only pigment in reptiles' scales, despite a variety of chromatophores in their skin. Whereas melanophores manufacture their own pigment and cease production when there is sufficient pigment in the cell, melanocytes continually manufacture melanin granules and pass these on to other cells in an animal's skin. A single melanocyte usually supplies pigment to as many as twelve epidermal cells.

Cephalopod chromatophores

Chromatophores also occur in invertebrates such as crustaceans and cephalopods (octopuses, squid and cuttlefish). In cephalopods, however, each chromatophore is a bag-like structure, within a cell (fig. 9.4). The bag contains pigment granules and is held in position by muscle cells: the bag can expand or contract by means of the muscles. The colour changes of octopuses are caused by a change in shape of the cells rather than by the movement of pigments within the cells. Unlike vertebrate chromatophores,

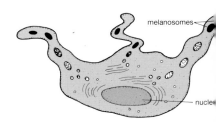

Fig. 9.3 Melanocytes are cells found in mammals. They lie in the base of the animals' skin in the lower epidermis, where they continually manufacture melanin granules (melanosomes) and pass them on to the cells in the outer part of the skin. This is how melanin can increase in our skin when we suntan.

PL. 9.6 Right: Newly hatched baby cephalopods have few chromatophores, of only one colour. *Photo: R. Berthold*

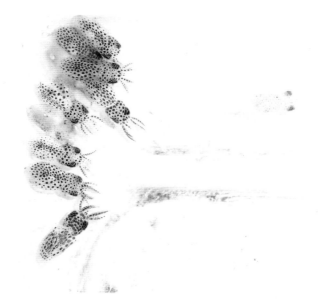

PL. 9.8 Far right: Capybara: red fur is known to contain melanin, but the exact nature of the pigment is still not known. *Photo: P. Farrant*

those of cephalopods are controlled by the nervous system. This means that octopuses, squid and cuttlefish can change colour very rapidly, and their skin appears to shimmer continually when seen close up (pl. 9.5).

Newly hatched baby octopuses have less than 100 chromatophores in their skin, and these contain brownish red pigment granules (pl. 9.6). As the animals age, two groups of differently coloured chromatophores develop: dark ones (black or brownish red) and pale ones (red when contracted or orange-yellow when expanded). An adult octopus may have several million chromatophores. There are layers of iridocytes and guanophores underneath the chromatophores that help to extend the range of the animals' coloration by reflecting local light.

BOX 2

HUMAN SKIN COLOUR

Humans have relatively little hair and so our skin is pigmented with melanins. Minor contributions to our skin colour are also made by structural blues and the haemoglobin in our blood, which shows through in pale-coloured skin (the purple colour of port-wine birthmarks is due to structural blue and underlying blood vessels). Various other factors are also involved, such as age, oiliness and texture of the skin. In mammals generally, a very large number of genes control skin colour, and this is why there is so much variation. In humans, as in other mammals, there is little difference between races with regard to the number of melanocytes present in the lower epidermis. The differences in skin colour are due instead to different levels of activity of the melanocytes. African people for instance, have much more melanin in the outer layers of their skin than do European people (pl. 9.7). While little is known about the causes of freckles in human skin, a surprising fact is that these areas of skin actually have fewer melanocytes than are found in surrounding paler areas of skin.

Large amounts of melanin in human skin protect the underlying tissues from harmful

PL. 9.7 African man. *Photo: P. Farrant*

ultraviolet radiation. Melanin in the outer skin layers absorbs ultraviolet radiation effectively, preventing it from penetrating further to the melanocytes of the lower epidermis and the connective tissue and blood vessels of the dermis. Melanin also provides protection through its chemical properties: the melanin molecules are able to capture charged particles formed by ultraviolet radiation acting on molecules in the epidermis. Dark skin may transmit as little as one-third of the ultraviolet radiation transmitted by light skin.

Light-coloured human skin responds to high levels of sunlight, with sunburn or suntan. In sunburn, ultraviolet radiation causes molecules in the dermis to break down, and this leads to digestion of proteins and expansion of tiny blood vessels. The increased amount of blood through these blood vessels is what gives sunburnt skin its pink and red coloration. Suntanning initially involves the production of small amounts of melanin in the epidermis. This small amount of extra melanin does not persist, but provides a brief darkening of the skin, perhaps helping to prevent sunburn. With further exposure to sunlight, over a relatively long time, more skin cells are produced and melanin is released into these cells from the underlying melanocytes at an increasing rate. A gradual build-up of melanin in the skin reduces the amount of ultraviolet radiation that can penetrate and damage the tissues below the skin surface. The lower the amount of melanin in human skin, the less well it can cope with sunburn, and the higher the likelihood of skin cancer (malignant melanomas are tumours of the melanocytes) and other diseases.

MELANINS

Melanins are the most widespread animal pigments, formed in chromatophores or the melanocytes of mammals. In vertebrates, melanin pigments are linked to proteins, in the form of granules. In invertebrates the situation is generally the same except that in a few invertebrates the melanin is not present as granules but as free pigment, diffusely distributed, e.g. in the outer tissue of some anemones and in the cuticle of black insects.

Two colour forms of melanin are recognised: eumelanin, dark black or brown, and phaeomelanin, light brown or yellow (pl. 9.8). Eumelanin is synthesised in melanophores or melanocytes from the amino acid tyrosine in the presence of the enzyme tyrosinase. In most cases eumelanin is then attached to a protein to form granules. Less is known about the synthesis of phaeomelanin, though this type of melanin is also based on tyrosine and perhaps also cysteine, another amino acid. Many different factors are reported to influence the production of melanin: these include high humidity, low temperatures, high metabolic rate, hormones and daily light periodicity.

Melanins have a very stable structure because the molecules are tightly linked together: melanin has been found in fossils over a million years old. Because of the stability of melanin, structures that contain this pigment, e.g. dark feathers and hair, are usually stronger and more resistant to abrasion than similar structures that contain other, lighter coloured pigments. Melanin absorbs light, especially short wavelength, high energy ultraviolet light potentially harmful to animal tissues, and so is especially important in skin, skin products (pl. 9.9) and eyes (pl. 9.10). Most vertebrates are covered by skin products such as scales, feathers, fur or hair, although this is not the case for amphibians, such as frogs and toads, which spend their time in damp places. An animal's skin is usually not very dark in parts covered by feathers, fur or hair. In some amphibians and reptiles with pigmented body cavity walls, melanin probably protects the reproductive organs from ultraviolet radiation.

Colour abnormalities

Though melanins are usually associated with dark colours - black, dark brown, red brown and some yellows - these colours can be caused by other pigments. Melanins, however, are the commonest pigments in vertebrates. Of all the colour variations in animals, melanism occurs most frequently. A melanistic animal is completely black, e.g. a jaguar. Because of its prevalence amongst animal groups, melanism is thought to be caused by a dominant gene. Other colour abnormalities include albinism (see BOX 3), or absence of melanin, and cyanism, a very rare condition that produces the blue-black of glacier bears and blue arctic foxes.

Melanins are found in various parts of animals' bodies. They are especially common in the hair and fur of mammals (pls 9.11, 9.12), and the feathers of birds: they are also found in bird beaks, frog eggs and fish scales. Amongst invertebrates, melanin occurs in the cuticles of black beetles, the integuments of some snails, the shells of some dark sea urchins, the bristles of polychaete worms and the ink of cuttlefish. Within any one group of animals, the smaller species tend to be melanistic (pl. 9.13). Smaller species are often black, whereas larger species are rarely as dark: this is probably because black surfaces absorb more sunlight than surfaces of other colours, and larger animals have smaller surface areas relative to their volumes for losing heat.

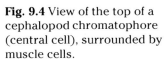

Fig. 9.4 View of the top of a cephalopod chromatophore (central cell), surrounded by muscle cells.

PL. 9.9 Rhino: mammals without hair cover usually have darkly pigmented skin, coloured by melanins. *Photo: W. Farrant*

PL. 9.10 Melanin in the skin and eyes of many animals absorbs potentially harmful ultraviolet light. *Photo: P. Farrant*

PL. 9.11 Only some mammals, such as monkeys, have pigmented skin beneath their fur. *Photo: W. Farrant*

PL. 9.12 Mammals' fur or skin may be coloured by other substances, e.g. mud on hippos' skin, blood on lions' fur.
Photo: W. Farrant.

BOX 3

ALBINISM

Mammals and other animals that are completely lacking in melanin are known as albinos. Albinos are produced occasionally in a variety of species, including whales, peacocks and tigers (pl. 9.14). The absence of melanin in albinos is usually related to a blockage in their production of tyrosinase, the enzyme necessary for converting the amino acid tyrosine into melanin. The melanocytes in which this process takes place are present in the skin, but cannot produce any pigment. The skin and eyes of albinos are colourless but they appear pink because the underlying blood vessels can be seen through the surface (pl. 9.15). Albino animals usually have poor vision because extra light reaches the retina after scattering inside the eye: albinos therefore do not see as clearly nor do they see colours as vividly as normally pigmented animals. In fact, albinos are generally weaker than pigmented animals, and albinism is often associated with other disorders (pl. 9.16).

Albinism is not always complete because incomplete blockages to the chemical pathways can reduce rather than stop pigment formation.

Piebaldism is a rare condition present at birth in humans in which the skin has patches of pigmented areas and patches of unpigmented areas. It is akin to the coloured patches of horses and the roan colours of cattle. In these cases the colours are probably caused by an absence of melanocytes in particular areas of the skin. The white marks at the extremities of horses' bodies represent those areas that were furthest away from melanocyte-producing areas in the foetus.

Albinism should not be confused with leukemism or whiteness, in which an animal has white fur, hair or feathers, while other parts of its body are pigmented. Most white animals, such as snow hares and polar bears, are not albinos and therefore do not have pink eyes. In these animals, the whiteness is generally caused by the microscopic structure of their surface. White pigments are very rare in animals, though they are found in some butterflies.

PL. 9.16 The grey kangaroo in this photo is far less conspicuous than the albino kangaroo.
Photo: P. Farrant

PL. 9.14 Above: This anemone has none of the pigments or symbiotic algae that normally give the species its colour.
Photo: P. Farrant

PL. 9.15 Right: Albino animals' eyes are pink because they have no pigments and the haemoglobin of the blood shows through.
Photo: P. Farrant

OMMOCHROMES AND TYRIAN PURPLE

Not all the dark colours of animals are due to melanins. Ommochromes are dark pigments found only in invertebrates and are usually black or brown, sometimes red, yellow or violet. They are shielding pigments between the ommatidia in the compound eyes of insects and crustaceans (such as dragonflies, shrimps and other crustaceans) (pl. 9.17). Ommochromes occur in cephalopod eyes and in cephalopod and crustacean chromatophores; they also provide the red and brown colours of many insects' integuments and wings.

Tyrian purple is an unusual bromine-containing pigment that provides neither external nor internal coloration to the few marine snails that produce it. The purple colour develops from an initially cream-coloured secretion after it has left the animal's body.

CAROTENOIDS

Most animals contain carotenoids, dissolved in fat globules within chromatophores. Being unable to make these compounds, animals must obtain them from the plants they eat (pl. 9.18). Carnivorous or meat-eating animals obtain their carotenoids from prey animals, but at one time the pigments would have been derived from plants (pl. 9.19). Animals can be selective about what plant carotenoids they take up. While they cannot make their own, some animals are able to alter the colour of the carotenoids they take in as food, e.g. some birds change yellow carotenoids to red ones. Before it was realised that animal carotenoids were the same as plant carotenoids, the animal pigments were known as lipochromes because of their solubility in fat or lipid. We can easily understand this by looking at butter, in which a yellow carotenoid is dissolved in animal fat.

In many animals, carotenoids are linked to proteins and the resulting carotenoproteins may be different in colour to the free carotenoids. Whereas free carotenoids are fat-soluble, carotenoproteins may also be soluble in water. Unlike carotenoids, carotenoproteins often change colour with acidity and this may account for the range of colours in the shells of some sea urchins.

Free carotenoids are generally fairly stable compounds, especially at low light levels and low temperatures. Though excessive light may be responsible for bleaching carotenoids in skin products such as feathers, light more often seems to have the

effect of increasing carotenoid concentration in animals. In this respect, the pigment may protect the animal from ultraviolet radiation, e.g. the dorsal or back surface of crustaceans such as crabs and lobsters is often more highly pigmented than the ventral surface. Sometimes too, animals do not produce carotenoids unless the temperature is higher than a critical level and this may also be a protective mechanism.

Carotenoid colours

Carotenoids provide animals with colours in the yellow-orange-red range, the actual colour depending on the molecular structure and amount of pigment present. On the other hand, carotenoproteins can be almost any colour, and even provide animals with blues and greens (pl. 9.20). The difference between carotenoids and carotenoproteins is well demonstrated by the colour changes that occur when a lobster is cooked. Though some lobsters are

PL. 9.13 Top left: Small species of insects may be melanistic but larger insects have a less favourable surface to volume ratio for heat loss.
Photo: P. Farrant

PL. 9.17 Top: Crayfish: ommochromes are the dark pigments that lie between adjacent ommatidia in the eyes of crustaceans.
Photo: R. Berthold

PL. 9.18 Above: Flamingoes derive their red coloration from their food, either algae or crustaceans that have eaten the algae. *Photo: W. Farrant*

PL. 9.20 Above: The vivid blues of some crustaceans are due to carotenoproteins.
Photo: P. Farrant

PL. 9.19 Right: Ladybirds' colours are usually due to carotenoids derived from the plant-feeding aphids in their diet.
Photo: R. Berthold

naturally orange or red when alive, many have a blackish shell, purplish red epidermis, red antennae, bluish appendages and even green eggs (pl. 9.21). These colours are mostly due to the carotenoprotein astoxanthin. When a lobster is boiled, however, the heat changes the carotenoprotein: protein and pigment separate and in the process the pigment is oxidised. Blue, green, black and purplish red colours all change to the orange-red colour of astacin, the oxidised product of astoxanthin. In this case, the free red pigment is brighter than most of the carotenoprotein colours (pl. 9.22).

Carotenoids, both carotenes and xanthophylls, are widespread amongst animal groups and the species within the groups. Amongst invertebrates, many animals such as sponges have more xanthophylls than carotenes (pl. 9.23). Carotenoids are the main colouring compounds of coelenterates (pl. 9.24). Some of the yellow, red-brown and violet colours of starfish and sea urchins are due to carotenoproteins (pl. 9.25). Carotenoids provide the pinks and oranges of the flesh of a variety of molluscs (pl. 9.26). They are widespread in crustaceans, and the blues and greens of most crabs, prawns and lobsters are due to carotenoproteins, often in conjunction with free carotenoids.

Carotenoids are less important in mammals because all hair and skin colour in this group is caused by melanins. However, carotenoids are common in the skin of amphibians (pl. 9.27) and reptiles (pl. 9.28), and they provide most of the colour of goldfish and the red spots of trout, as well as the colours of some birds' wattles, bills and feathers.

Apart from coloration of the skin and skin products, carotenoids and xanthophylls are also found in a

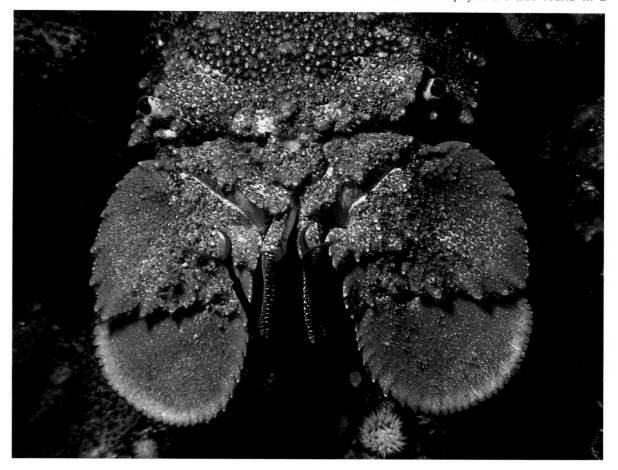

PL. 9.21 Many of the colours of this crayfish are due to carotenoproteins such as astoxanthin. *Photo: P. Farrant*

variety of other animal tissues and organs, including scallops' gonads, red muscles of salmon, birds' egg yolk, fat of cattle and human blood plasma. Carotenoids are also important in the formation of light-sensitive pigments in animals' eyes. Pigments such as rhodopsin or visual purple, chrysopsin, the golden pigment of some deep-sea fish, and porphyropsin, the pigment in tadpoles' and lampreys' eyes, are all based on vitamin A, which is a carotenoid derivative.

CYTOCHROME

Cytochromes are akin to the photomorphogenic pigments of plants in that they are present in such tiny amounts that they rarely provide any noticeable colour to animals, but are extremely important in physiological processes. Cytochrome pigments occur in all living organisms and they are involved in the oxidation of carbohydrate molecules within cells, a process that releases energy for movement, growth and development. Due to their function, cytochromes are concentrated in the most active parts of animals, e.g. wing muscles of insects and birds. However, only in the reddish brown wing muscles of some insects is there enough pigment for the colour to be visible.

RESPIRATORY PIGMENTS

Respiratory pigments are pigments that carry oxygen in an animal's blood. They are usually coloured, sometimes providing colour to the external surfaces of animals, but more usually colouring internal parts. We know that vertebrates such as ourselves have red blood because it contains the red pigment haemoglobin. While some invertebrates have red blood, containing either haemoglobin or another red pigment, haemerythrin, others have a blue, or even a green pigment in their blood. There is only one group of animals known to have two different respiratory pigments in the blood: worms in the genus *Serpula* have both green chlorocruorin and red haemoglobin, and therefore their blood is brownish green. Some snails have the blue pigment haemocyanin in their blood and haemoglobin in their mouth cavities.

Respiratory pigments either carry oxygen in the blood or store oxygen in an animal's muscles. The respiratory pigments are all proteins and contain one or two atoms of a metal that bind reversibly with oxygen, releasing the oxygen when they reach tissues that need to use it for respiration. Thus the respiratory pigments have two different colour phases: that of the oxygenated molecules and that of the deoxygenated molecules.

Haemoglobin

Haemoglobin is the respiratory pigment of all but a very few vertebrates. It also occurs in many groups of invertebrates, though it is not widespread amongst species within the groups. Haemoglobin is even produced by some fungi, in particular yeasts and moulds, and a fungal-plant symbiotic association. However, it does not appear that any plants are able to synthesise it. Chemically, haemoglobin is an iron-containing pigment that binds reversibly with oxygen

PL. 9.22 Above: Cooked spanner crab: when crustaceans are cooked they change colour as the carotenoproteins break down. *Photo: R. Berthold*

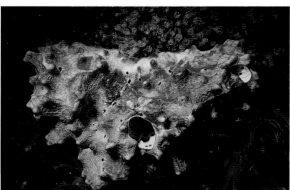

PL. 9.23 Left: Yellow xanthophylls are more common pigments in sponges than orange and red carotenes. *Photos: P. Farrant*

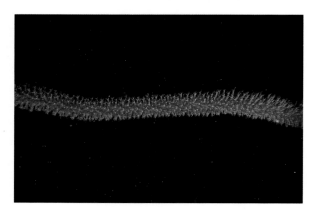

PL. 9.24 Carotenoids provide the yellows, oranges and reds of many coelenterates like this sea whip. *Photo: P. Farrant*

and even more readily with carbon monoxide. There are many different types of haemoglobin in the different animal groups, e.g. in humans, foetal haemoglobin differs from adult haemoglobin.

Haemoglobin owes its colour to its porphyrin molecular structure. Oxygenated pigment is scarlet, deoxygenated is purple, and when combined with carbon monoxide, it becomes bright cherry red. The various haemoglobins of different animal groups vary slightly in colour. Haemoglobin is located within red blood cells in vertebrates' blood, and these cells carry oxygen from the lungs or gills to the animal's tissues. Oxygen can also be stored in an animal's muscles, and the pigment in this case is myoglobin. Red meat, which is muscle, owes its colour to

PL. 9.25 Right: The yellow and reddish brown colours of some starfish and sea urchins are due to carotenoproteins. *Photo: P. Farrant*

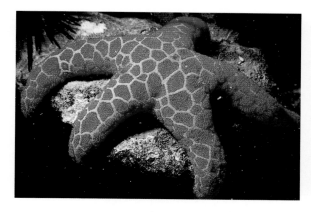

PL. 9.26 Far right: The pinks and oranges of many molluscs, like this nudibranch, are due to carotenoids. *Photo: P. Farrant*

PL. 9.27 Yellow carotenoids help to create green when combined with structural blue: green tree frogs have yellow carotenoids dissolved in fat droplets in the skin, which, when seen against a blue background, makes them appear green; the blue is caused by the animals' surface rather than by pigments. *Photo: M. Porteners*

myoglobin, and the muscles of diving mammals are very dark because of a large amount of stored myoglobin. Haemoglobin is also found in vertebrates' livers and bone marrow, tissues where red blood cells are produced. In humans, red blood cells, and thus molecules of haemoglobin, have a lifespan of around four months, and thousands of millions of red blood cells are manufactured daily.

Haemoglobin does not usually provide colour in the skin of vertebrate animals, unless the skin is exposed (pl. 9.29). When these areas are small, e.g. cocks' combs (pl. 9.30) and monkeys' faces, they are often bright red because of the multitude of blood capillaries just below the skin surface. The pink of albino animals' eyes is due to haemoglobin, visible

because other pigments are absent (see box 3). The only vertebrates that do not possess haemoglobin as their blood pigment are several species of fish.

Among invertebrates, haemoglobin is found in some species of worms, molluscs, nematodes, echinoderms and crustaceans. It is rare in insects, mainly because they do not rely on blood circulation for the supply of oxygen to their body tissues (they have a system of air tubes or tracheae). Haemoglobin occurs in the blood of those invertebrates that possess it, and also (unlike vertebrates) in many other tissues: muscles, eggs, gut wall, fat, tracheae and the nerve cord. Haemoglobin provides skin colour to some crustaceans, worms and the bloodworm, which is really not a worm but the larva of a midge.

Haemerythrin

Haemerythrin is another blood pigment, found only in a few invertebrates, such as some worms and lamp shells. This pigment is an iron-containing protein, like haemoglobin. It is reddish, ranging in colour from pink to purple, red and orange, when oxygenated, and pale yellow when deoxygenated.

Blue blood

The blood of many crustaceans, spiders, scorpions, snails and octopuses is blue due to the respiratory pigment haemocyanin. This is dissolved in blood plasma and so does not impart any colour to the animal as a whole. The pigment is a copper-containing protein. The molecule is blue in its oxygenated form, colourless when deoxygenated. Two copper atoms are needed to pick up each molecule of oxygen, so this pigment is a less efficient oxygen carrier than haemoglobin. Like haemoglobin, there are several different types of haemocyanin in various animal groups. The concentration of haemocyanin varies between species and this also affects blood colour. Haemocyanin is not found in any insects.

Chlorocruorin

Chlorocruorin, an iron-containing green blood pigment, is very like haemoglobin in structure. This pigment is a similar colour in its oxygenated and deoxygenated forms, though the latter is a more yellowish green. Chlorocruorin is found in only a few polychaete worms. It does not usually provide these animals with a green body coloration; they mostly live in tubes and the only exposed body parts are coloured by other pigments.

PORPHYRINS

Porphyrins are related chemically to haemoglobin, chlorophyll and cytochrome. Chlorophyll and haemoglobin are modified porphyrins, with magnesium and iron respectively in their structures. Porphyrins tend to give animals pink and red coloration. These pigments are also closely related to bilins (see below), and like bilins, they tend to be present in calcareous structures: they cause the red patterning on the shells of molluscs (pl. 9.31) and the brownish teeth and bones of the American fox squirrel. In these calcareous structures, pigments usually show red or pink fluorescence under ultraviolet light. Some of these pigments were first found in human urine and faeces, as their names, uroporphyrin and coproporphyrin, suggest.

In invertebrates, free porphyrins are rarely present in the amounts necessary to provide animals with colour. Earthworms have a light-sensitive porphyrin in their integument: when it breaks down in light the blood cells are destroyed and the animals die.

BILINS

In vertebrates, bilins are formed when haemoglobin breaks down. The colour of human bile in the gall bladder is due to the yellow pigment bilirubin. Jaundice is a result of the pigment accumulating in human skin. Bilins in the blood are also responsible for the early blue, green and yellow coloration of

PL. 9.28 Above: Chromatophores located in the skin provide some vivid colours in reptiles; the blue is a structural colour. *Photo: W. Farrant.*

PL. 9.29 Left: Skin not covered by feathers often derives its colour from haemoglobin, or from the structure of the skin. *Photo: W. Farrant*

bruises on human skin. A yellow pigment, urobilinogen, helps produce the yellow of human faeces; this oxidises in air to brown urobilin. A different coloured bilin, the green biliverdin, is found in the gall bladders of frogs and birds.

Amongst fish, some wrasses owe their blue coloration to the bilin pigment phycocyanin, which they probably obtain from red algae in the diet (pl. 9.32). Their blood is greenish blue, probably because of the same or a similar pigment. The red colour of the blood of some other fish may be due to phycoerythrin, another bilin derived from red algae. The different colours of bilins are caused by variations

PL. 9.30 Right: The cockerel's colours are due to a variety of pigments (as well as surface structure). Melanocytes in the feather produce granular melanin pigments. The golden yellow of the feathers is due to carotenoids. The red comb is coloured by the haemoglobin of numerous blood capillaries close to the surface. *Photo: R. Berthold*

PL. 9.31 Below: Pink and red markings on the shells of molluscs, such as this bubble shell, are due to porphyrins. *Photo: R. Berthold*

in acidity: they become yellow, orange or brown in acidic surroundings and blue, violet or red in alkaline surroundings.

Bilins tend to be located in the calcareous parts of many animals. The green bones of garfish contain a green pigment similar to biliverdin. The blues and greens of birds' eggs, and even black in the case of emus' eggs, are caused by biliverdin, too: the pigment is added to the shells as the eggs pass down the oviduct. Sometimes brown or reddish spots and streaks are added too, the former if the eggs remain still for a while, the latter if the eggs keep moving. All these colours arise from the breakdown of haemoglobin pigments from the blood (pl. 9.33).

Bilins also occur in calcareous parts of invertebrates. While most coral skeletons are white when the animal tissue has been removed, some such as *Heliopora coerulea* have permanently blue skeletons that derive their colour from an extremely insoluble biliverdin-like pigment (pl. 9.34). The ink of sea hares (molluscs) is purple due to bilins, and the pigments are probably derived from the phycobilins in the red algae that these animals eat. The green gills of some oysters are coloured by a bluish bilin derived from their algal food, combined with a yellow pigment in the gills. Though the green

integument of some grasshoppers and caterpillars is probably not derived from their food, the colour is thought to be caused by bilins. Bilins are also found in some anemones, corals, butterflies, worms and crustaceans.

Quinones

Quinones are found in plants but are rare in animals. Two quinones, echinochrome and spinochrome, are found in the body cavity, eggs, shell and spines of some sea urchins. They impart brownish purple colours to these creatures. Apart from another echinoderm, these quinone pigments only occur in one other animal, the urchin-eating sea otter, which has purplish bones and teeth.

Anthraquinones, a group of quinones with a slightly different chemical structure, are responsible for the brilliant red of cochineal, kermes and lac dyes produced by certain scale insects. Cochineal for example, occurs in globular form in the eggs and fat bodies of female cochineal insects. There is an Australian feather star that has a deep red anthraquinone pigment in its tissues (pl. 9.35). Another group of quinones includes aphin, a red pigment found in the blood of black aphids and other plant lice. These pigments are usually present in granular form and show greenish yellow or orange-red fluorescence in ultraviolet light. This fluorescence is unusual because it is even visible in daylight.

Pterins

Pterins are colourless, yellow and red pigments that are chemically related to uric acid and guanine (white excretory products of animals) and they are usually present in granular or crystalline form. They occur mainly in insects but also in some crustaceans, cold-blooded vertebrates and bacteria. Pterins provide the yellow colour of wasps, the yellows and reds of some butterflies' wings and probably the sulphur-yellow colour in some crustaceans. Little is known about the colourless pterins that produce blue water-soluble fluorescence found in some insects and crustaceans.

In vertebrates, pterins can be present in melanophores and iridocytes, and they sometimes occur in the same cells as carotenoids, in which case both types of pigments contribute to the yellow, orange and red colours, e.g. goldfish and frogs. In some reptiles these pigments colour internal organs.

PL. 9.32 The blue of some parrotfish and wrasses is due to the phycocyanin, derived from red algae in the diet.
Photo: W. Farrant

PL. 9.33a and b The markings on birds' eggs are due mainly to broken down haemoglobin, added to the shells as the eggs pass down the bird's oviduct.
Photos: A. Leishman

RARE PIGMENTS

There are many more animal pigments confined to only one or several animals and about which little is known. Some of these include: the fluorescent pigments of parrot feathers, the reddish brown to purple pigment of burrowing tube anemones, the deep blue pigment of some nudibranchs, the magenta and brown pigments of some jellyfish, the green pigments of some polychaetes, the purple pigment of planktonic snails and the light green vanadium compound found in the blood of an ascidian. Whereas uroporphyrin provides the reds and pinks, and bilins the greens and blues, of molluscs' shells, there are probably more pigments involved. Iron seems to be responsible for the colour of the red and yellow calcareous spicules of the Mediterranean and north-eastern Atlantic soft coral, and for the red calcareous skeletons of precious coral and organ pipe coral; however, little else is known about the pigments involved. Various colours have been reported for sweat: black, yellowish or reddish, green and blue. However, little is known about the pigments that provide the different colours of sweat. The rose-pink colour of hippopotamus' sweat is known not to be caused by a haem or porphyrin pigment.

There are two possible causes of colour in the surface of an animal: chemically, by means of pigments, and physically, by means of surface structure. The colours of many animals are due to combinations of the two. The next chapter looks at how the structure of an animal's surface can provide it with colour.

PL. 9.34 Above: Some blue corals have pigmented skeletons; when the animal dies, the calcium carbonate remains blue. *Photo: P. Farrant*

PL. 9.35 Right: Some Australian red feather stars contain a deep red anthraquinone pigment in their tissues. *Photo: P. Farrant*

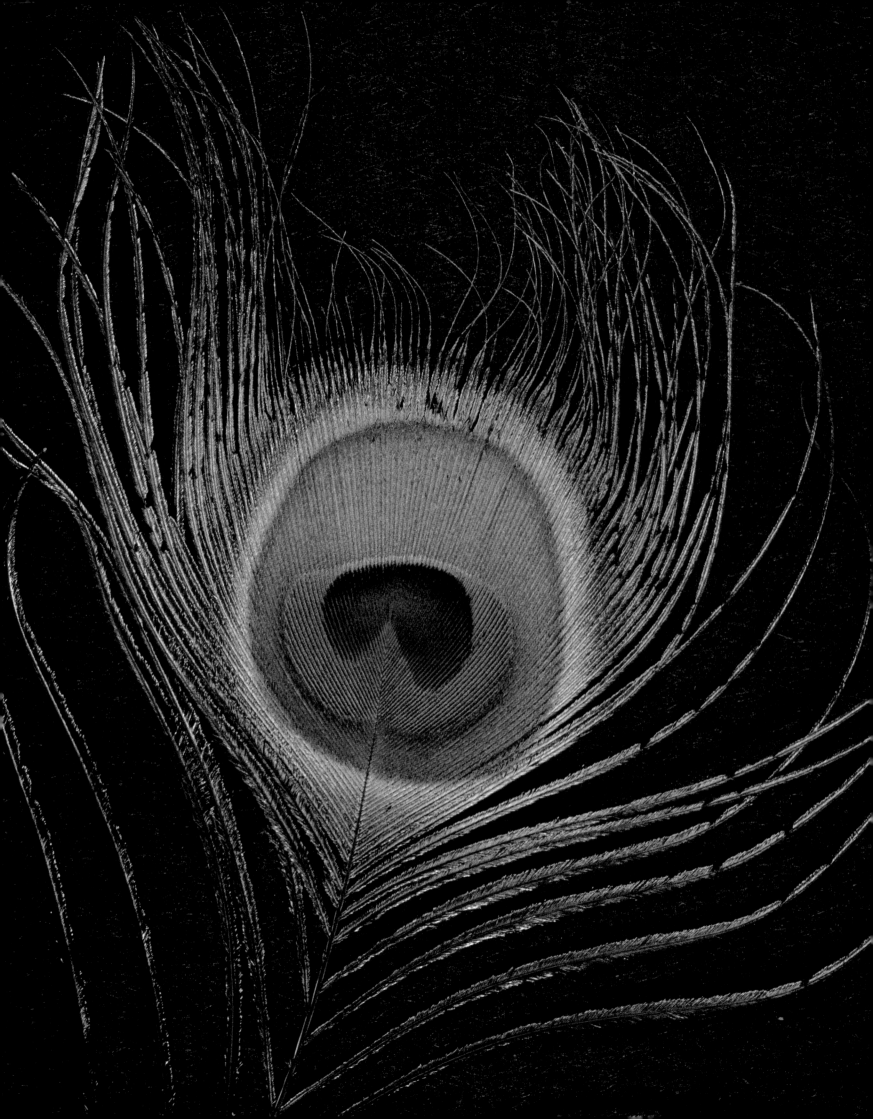

CHAPTER 10

STRUCTURAL COLOUR IN ANIMALS

While pigmentation is the most important source of colour in the animal world, the physical nature of an animal's surface can cause rays of white light to be separated and travel along different optical paths, producing structural colours.

Structural colours are an integral part of the animal's surface, whereas pigments can be separated from the animal by chemical extraction. Structural colours usually disappear when the structures are immersed in water or other liquids, because the liquid fills air spaces within the structures; drying usually restores the colours. After an animal dies its structural colours may or may not remain, depending upon whether or not its structure changes when it dries out.

Structural colours are caused by microscopic features of the surface of an animal: the colour is created without pigments. However, structural colours are only conspicuous when they have an underlying layer of pigment, usually melanin. An animal can exhibit a mixture of many different types of colours, both pigment and structural.

There are several different types of structural colour.

INTERFERENCE: DIFFRACTION AND IRIDESCENCE

Interference colours in animals are commonest in skin products such as feathers, scales and fur: these are all non-living parts of animals and are therefore quite stable. They also occur in softer tissues, but less frequently.

Interference (see p. 10) can be caused by two different types of structure in an animal's skin or skin products. The first type is called a diffraction grating, and usually consists of a series of tiny lines or slits. Light waves falling across the structure are diffracted, and since some wavelengths are diffracted more than others, the light is separated into its spectral colours, e.g. when we look at a light globe through a closely woven piece of cloth, the light is diffracted into its spectral colours. Diffraction colours in animals are rare. They depend upon a unidirectional light source and so are invisible in normal, diffuse light. There are some beetles, however, that show these interference colours if a light beam is directed along the length of their wing cases. These beetles have regularly spaced striations on a dark surface.

Iridescence

The second type of structure contains different substances, often in the form of particles or air pockets, lying in adjacent layers beneath the surface:

iridescence is caused by the interference between light waves reflected from different layers. Iridescent colours are intense and glittering, and change with the angle of view. The iridescent colours visible in a layer of oil on the surface of a puddle of water are due to interference.

In animals, the structures equivalent to oil layers on top of a puddle are usually layers of tiny particles, located either within skin cells or in the keratin or chitin of cuticle, scales, fur, hair or feathers. When light waves enter the skin or skin products, their speed changes, by different amounts for different wavelengths. Some waves of each wavelength reflect off the first layer beneath the surface, some off the second, and so on. If the peaks and troughs of the waves returning from the various levels coincide, then the waves are said to be in phase and the colour of that particular wavelength of light is reinforced. On the other hand, if the waves are completely out of phase when they reach the surface, that colour is cancelled.

Blues and greens are the most widespread iridescent colours in animals. The thickness and spacing of the layers of particles determine which colours of light are reinforced and which are cancelled when viewed from a certain direction. In general, thin layers give blue, blue-green and violet iridescence, whereas thicker layers give gold, orange and red, in the same way that a soap bubble shows different colours as it gradually thickens towards the bottom because of the effects of gravity. As an observer moves, the angle of the incident and reflected light waves, and the length of their paths of travel in and out of the animal's surface, change. Consequently the colour of reflected light changes with the angle of view. From a particular position the angle and length of the path of light will be just right for the blue wavelengths to interfere and reinforce each other, whereas if the observer moves slightly to one side he or she will be in just the right position to see the green wavelengths interfering constructively.

When light waves interfere constructively with each other, the intensity of the resulting wave is not simply doubled but increased fourfold. This is why iridescent colours are so vivid. To compensate for this, the intensity is reduced to zero when waves interfere destructively, and this is why iridescence disappears from view in other directions.

Background colour

Colours caused by interference can be exceptionally pure when there is a dark background of pigment located beneath the scattering layers. This layer

PL. 10.1 Peacock's feather: iridescence is due to interference of light reflected from layers of melanin rods separated by keratin. *Photo: P. Farrant.*

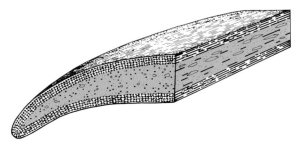

Fig. 10.1 The iridescence-producing structure of peacock feathers comprises evenly spaced melanin rods and air spaces, embedded in keratin.

absorbs all remaining wavelengths of white light that get past the scattering layers: if these were reflected back out to the observer, the colours would be altered or diluted. The interference colours produced by a spider's web and a snail's trail (dried mucous), are rather delicate in comparison to the intense colours seen in a peacock's tail because of dilution of the colours by white light; melanin provides the necessary dark background in the case of a peacock's tail (pl. 10.1, fig. 10.1).

Iridescent or interference colours are found in many animal groups, vertebrates and invertebrates. Mammals show very little iridescence, only in such structures as skin, nails, hair and eyes. The lustrous colours of the coats of the golden mole and various rodents are caused by interference of light as it is reflected by the multitude of scales on the individual hairs. The eyeshine of hoofed mammals, some carnivores and lemurs, is due to interference effects produced by the fibrous structure of their eyes. There is little iridescence among amphibians and reptiles: some boa constrictors and pythons are briefly pearlescent immediately after shedding their skins. Iridescence occurs in many fish, especially in scales and eyes (pl. 10.2) (see below), e.g. tetras, Siamese fighting fish and herrings. However, many colours in fish are caused by pigments, and this is why fish change colour when they die. Birds are by far the most spectacular of the iridescent vertebrates (fig. 10.2), and insects are the most spectacular of the invertebrates (fig. 10.3).

Beautiful birds

Various structural modifications create iridescence in birds' feathers. Usually the surface of feathers is

translucent keratin, and there are layers of melanin granules beneath, their shape and the regularity of their arrangement varying according to species. The barbules of the feathers are usually flattened so that they face an observer directly. Birds display different degrees of iridescence: some such as peacocks, pheasants and birds of paradise have large iridescent areas, whereas others such as sunbirds (pl. 10.3) and riflebirds have small iridescent patches, especially on the head, around the throat and on the breast. Tropical bird species, often with exotic feathers, tend to show the most spectacular iridescence (pl. 10.4).

Many less exotic birds such as starlings, ducks, cockerels and pigeons, also show iridescence. Pigeons have melanin granules that are large, relative to the wavelength of light, but they produce some interference colours, in the form of spectrally coloured points, wherever they meet the outer transparent keratin layer (pl. 10.5).

Iridescent invertebrates

Amongst invertebrates, iridescence is found in the bristles of some worms, the cuticle of earthworms,

PL. 10.5 In pigeons, relatively large granules of melanin produce some interference colours. *Photo: P. Farrant.*

PL. 10.3 Melanin platelets between layers of keratin provide the structural basis of iridescence in sunbirds. *Photo: W. Farrant*

PL. 10.4 The vivid colour of this blue-eared glossy starling is largely due to iridescence, since the intensity changes with the angle of view; however, there is also a component of Tyndall blue, because the bird still appears blue from other viewing angles. *Photo: W. Farrant*

PL. 10.2 Goatfish with iridescent eyes; light is reflected from regular layers of guanine particles. *Photo: P. Farrant.*

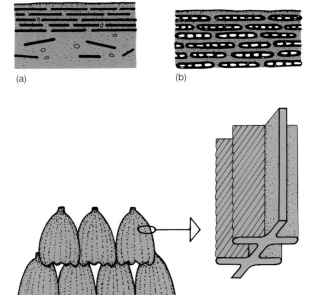

(a)   (b)

Fig. 10.2 The iridescence-producing structure of (a) sunbirds' feathers comprises layers of solid melanin platelets embedded in keratin, whereas that of (b) hummingbirds' consists of hollow melanin-lined flat discs, also embedded in keratin.

Fig. 10.3 Iridescence in morpho butterflies is due to sloping layers within ridges on the wing scales.

PL. 10.6 Iridescence is seen in this cicada's wings, and is common in many other insects, including flies. *Photo: R. Berthold*

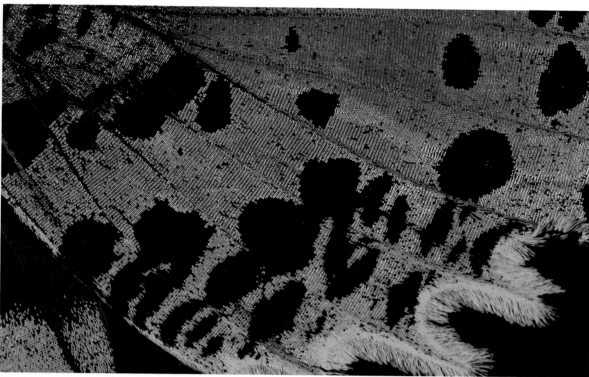

PL. 10.9 Urania moths have iridescent scales containing layers of chitin, air spaces and a backing of melanin. *Photo: P. Farrant*

PL. 10.7 Blue morphos have iridescent scales containing layers of chitin, air spaces and a backing of melanin. *Photo: P. Farrant*

PL. 10.10 Iridescent beetles have multilayered structures within their wing cases and sometimes the layered blocks slant in different directions: this is why their iridescence appears to come from below the surface. A greater spacing between adjacent layers causes red, orange, gold and silver colours rather than the more usual blues and greens. *Photo: A. Leslie*

PL. 10.11 Marchfly with iridescent compound eyes. *Photo: J. Landy*

PL. 10.8 When a blue morpho lands its brown underparts give immediate camouflage. *Photo: P. Farrant*

the integument of cuttlefish, the shells of molluscs, the webs of spiders, and the wings of flies, cicadas (pl. 10.6), butterflies (pls 10.7, 10.8), moths (pl. 10.9), wasps, beetles (pl. 10.10) and dragonflies. Some insects have iridescent compound eyes (pl. 10.11), which may help vision by reinforcing the wavelengths of light to which the cells are most sensitive.

Most insects (other than some beetles and butterflies), do not retain their iridescent colours very long after they die, because their structure changes by stretching or contracting. This is why some animals' colours become pale after death. The iridescent colours of some chrysomelid beetles change colour reversibly even when they are alive, from yellow to green, blue, violet and brown, as their wing cases dry out.

REFLECTIVITY AND IRIDESCENCE

An ordered structure of the scattering particles is achieved in animals that have solid crystalline particles in reflecting cells. Special light-reflecting cells are known as guanophores and iridocytes (the latter are iridescent), and they are particularly common in fish, amphibians and some reptiles. These cells usually contain guanine, or other related compounds, substances that are not pigments but animal waste products.

Guanophores, containing flat platelets of guanine, are responsible for producing the silvery white reflecting undersurfaces of many fish (pl. 10.12). The guanophores are usually backed by melanophores that contain dark pigment. Guanine crystals can be concentrated or dispersed within guanophores,

PL. 10.12 The reflective surfaces of fish scales are due to guanophores, cells that contain flat platelets of guanine. *Photo: W. Farrant*

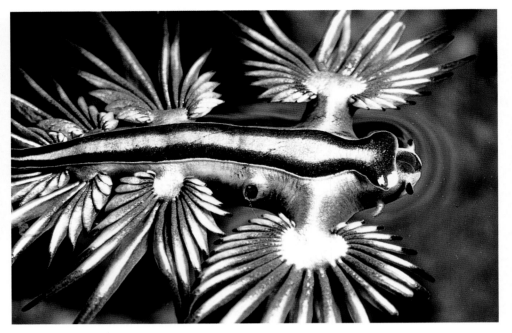

PL. 10.13 Above: Floating sea slug, with silvery reflective surface. *Photo: R. Berthold*

depending on the amount of reflected light that the fish sees in its environment. When the melanin is concentrated in the underlying melanophores, the guanine in the guanophores is dispersed and vice versa, both types of cell being controlled by the same hormone. Other pigments lying above the guanophores can affect the skin colours, e.g. a reddish yellow pigment makes the skin appear golden. Fish that have chromatophores but no guanophores or iridocytes have colour but no lustre.

The iridescent colours of iridocytes (iridescent cells in e.g. fish scales) are caused by interference of light by layers of guanine crystals. Ridges on the scales themselves can also cause iridescence, e.g. in rainbow trout and mackerels.

Iridocytes are also found in the cuticles of earthworms and the skin of snakes. Guanine occurs in the skin of sharks and rays but it is not present in sufficiently ordered structure to produce any lustre. Little guanine occurs in crustaceans or insects, but it may account for the reflectivity of some other invertebrates (pl. 10.13)

PL. 10.14 Left: Cephalopods owe their remarkable cryptic coloration to reflecting cells as well as chromatophores. *Photo: W. Farrant*

Octopuses have two types of reflecting cells: an upper layer of cells that contain ordered platelets of chitinous material and a lower layer of cells that contain an opaque, creamy, guanine-like substance. The upper layer reflects colour from the surrounding environment while the lower layer reflects white light. The reflecting cells, together with the animal's chromatophores, are used to match the surrounding light intensity and background colours, giving the animals remarkable cryptic coloration (pl. 10.14).

PL. 10.15 Below: Tyndall blue is responsible for the flat blue colours of many birds, such as these vulturine guinea fowl. *Photo: W. Farrant*

TYNDALL BLUE

The English physicist John Tyndall (1820-1893) discovered Tyndall blue, also known as diffusion colour. The basis of Tyndall blue coloration in animals is the same as that of Rayleigh scattering in Earth's atmosphere (see p. 11). In the surface layers of some animals there are submicroscopic structures that scatter blue wavelengths of light. An underlying layer of dark melanin pigment may also be present to absorb light waves of other colours: without the melanin backing, transmitted yellow or red light would be reflected back through the scattering layer. The dark background also intensifies the blue

PL. 10.16 Above: Blue-winged kookaburra: the feather barbs contain tiny air spaces that scatter blue light, and melanin for absorbing wavelengths other than blue. *Photo: R. Berthold*
PL. 10.17 Right: Tyndall blue in an angelfish. *Photo: W. Farrant*

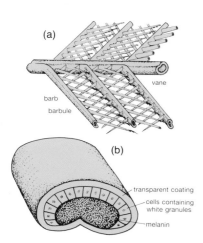

Fig. 10.4 (a) Feather structure of a blue bird.
(b) Section through blue barbule: Tyndall blue is a structural colour caused by scattering of blue wavelengths by microscopic particles in the outer layer of cells. Inside the feather there is a dark melanin backing.

PL. 10.18 The dark background pigment for Tyndall blue in insects like mayflies and dragonflies is ommatin. *Photo: R. Berthold.*

PL. 10.19 Both Tyndall blue and interference account for the electric blue of this orange tailed blue demoiselle. *Photo: R. Berthold*

produced by the animal's structure. As Tyndall blue is caused by scattering, it appears the same no matter what angle it is viewed from, unlike iridescence.

Tyndall blue is commonest in birds (pls 10.15, 10.16), fish, mammals, amphibians and reptiles. Blue colours in fish scales are caused by such small particles of guanine, relative to the wavelength of light, that Tyndall scattering occurs; the blueness is visible because there is a dark background of melanin (pl. 10.17, fig. 10.4). Tyndall blue accounts for most

flat blues in birds' feathers, blue bare skin patches of birds and mammals, and blue eyes of humans and cats (see BOX 1).

This type of structural colour is rather rare amongst invertebrate animals. Some dragonflies owe their blue coloration to Tyndall scattering by tiny colourless granules in their epidermal cells, in combination with a backing of ommatin, a dark brown pigment first discovered in insects' eyes (pl. 10.18). Tyndall blue is also found in some coelenterates and cephalopods, but few other invertebrates. Jellyfish and salps which appear colourless in the sea, often have a distinctive bluish hue when seen out of water. The conspicuous electric blues of some fish are probably due to both interference and scattering (pl. 10.19), and the same explanation probably accounts for the vivid blues of some octopuses. Octopuses alter the intensity of their blue colours through nervous control of the underlying melanophores, e.g. the deadly blue-ringed octopus, which flashes its blue rings when disturbed (pl. 10.20).

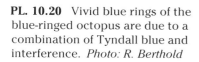

PL. 10.20 Vivid blue rings of the blue-ringed octopus are due to a combination of Tyndall blue and interference. *Photo: R. Berthold*

Greens and purples

Tyndall blue, in combination with pigments, produces greens and purples in animals. Most greens are produced by a structural Tyndall blue in combination with a yellow pigment and a melanin backing. These three variables in different combinations provide an extremely wide range of greens in birds and other animals (pl. 10.21). In birds, e.g. wild budgerigars, the yellow pigment is usually a carotene located in the outer keratin layer of the feather barbs (pl. 10.22). Violet or purple, e.g. in some kingfishers and rollers (pl. 10.23), results from a red or brown melanin backing layer. In some rollers the colour may appear to shift slightly with the viewing angle, indicating some interference colour in addition to the Tyndall blue.

WHITENESS

Whereas black coloration is caused by total absorption of light by pigments such as melanins and ommochromes, white coloration is rarely caused by pigments and is almost always due to a structure that totally reflects light. Even the few animals known to have white pigments, such as cabbage butterflies, that contain white pterins in their wings, also owe their whiteness to structural scattering of light: the animals remain white when the pigment has been dissolved away. The whiteness of butterflies can also be due to uric acid, which acts as a pigment in the wings (pl. 10.24). Some sea anemones also contain crystals of uric acid, in this case in the white tips of their tentacles (pl. 10.25).

In animals, the structures that cause total reflection of light, and thus whiteness, are numerous small particles or air pockets lying within a colourless surface. It is the same physical phenomenon that causes snow to appear white even though the individual ice crystals are colourless. The scattering particles are large relative to the wavelength of light and so all wavelengths are scattered equally (fig. 10.5).

In many cases of white animal coloration, the particles that scatter light are small pockets of air. This is the case for white fur, e.g. the winter coats of polar mammals and albino mammals. In brown fur the individual hairs have long central cells that contain melanin, but in white fur the central part of each hair contains air bubbles separated by solid fragments of keratin. In white birds the barbs of the

feathers contain box-cells with relatively large air pockets that scatter all wavelengths equally, and the barbs do not contain any melanin. Most white butterflies and moths have scales with ribbed and grooved surfaces and sometimes air-filled interior cavities. These structures scatter light in all directions and thus cause their whiteness.

The same principle applies to many animal structures that rely on liquid particles rather than air pockets. These particles often float within other types of liquids, e.g. the fat and protein molecules in milk give it a white colour, and the whiteness of connective tissue, fat, nerves and white muscles has a similar origin.

White of the eye

Inorganic calcareous structures such as the shells of molluscs and foraminiferans, the skeletons of corals, echinoderms and sponges, birds' eggs, ivory, teeth and bones, also derive their whiteness from structures that scatter all wavelengths of light equally (pl. 10.26). The whiteness of some organic substances is caused

PL. 10.21 Green snakes and lizards have a yellow pigment in combination with structural Tyndall blue and a melanin backing. *Photo: P. Farrant*

PL. 10.22 Left: The colour of most green birds is due to a yellow pigment, usually located in the outer keratin layer of the feather barbs, in combination with structural Tyndall blue and a melanin backing. *Photo: P. Farrant*

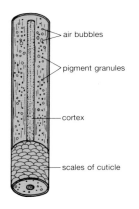

PL. 10.23 Lilac breasted roller: violet and purple are due to Tyndall blue with a red or brown melanin backing. *Photo: W. Farrant*

PL. 10.24 White butterflies' and moths' wings can be caused by the animals' structure, by pigments, or by the waste product uric acid. *Photo: J. Landy*

PL. 10.25 Some sea anemones owe the whiteness of the tips of their tentacles to crystals of uric acid. *Photo: W. Farrant*

Fig. 10.5
Human head hair is often dark because of pigment granules. White hairs have no pigment, and reflection of light by air bubbles causes whiteness.

air bubbles

pigment granules

cortex

scales of cuticle

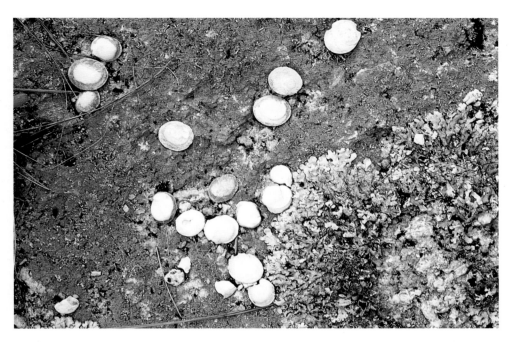

PL. 10.26 Above: Inorganic calcareous structures like these molluscs' opercula owe their whiteness to randomly arranged particles that scatter all wavelengths of light equally.
Photo: R. Berthold

PL. 10.27 Right: Porcupines' quills are white because solid particles in the quills scatter all wavelengths of light equally.
Photo: W. Farrant

PL. 10.28 Below: Spiders' white markings are often due to crystals of guanine inside cells, visible through the body surface.
Photo: W. Farrant

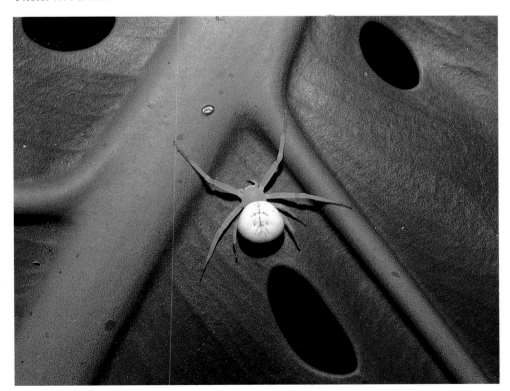

in a similar way, e.g. fibrous keratin in horses' hooves, elastin in the white of the eye, crystalline guanine in invertebrates' leucophores and fishes' scales, and fibres in quills of birds' feathers and porcupines' spines (pl. 10.27). In all these structures, the scattering particles are solids lying within other solid but translucent materials.

If an animal's scattering structures are randomly oriented, a matt whiteness results. The whiteness of most insects is caused by randomly oriented and rather opaque reflecting surfaces. The white markings of spiders are often caused by crystals of guanine that are located within cells inside the animals so they show though the body surface (pl. 10.28). On the other hand, a more regular structure gives a pearly or silvery lustre, bordering on a metallic appearance. The pearlescence of many mollusc shells is caused by an ordered structure: the cuticle is underlain by a thick crystalline layer of calcium carbonate, below which are further layers of calcium carbonate. The layers produce some interference, but the thick layer above tends to diffuse the light over such a wide angle that a pearlescence results. Pearlescence is thus caused by a combination of white scattering and interference. If the layers of calcium carbonate are very thin, then iridescent colours will be formed (see BOX 2). The waste substance guanine is also responsible for pearlescence in some animals.

Greyness

Grey coloration is usually due to a mixture of black and white, e.g. grey hair in mammals is a result of an optical mixture of white and black hairs. Grey birds usually have feathers in which white barbules are interspersed with black ones, though a grey colour may also be caused by powder on the surface of the feathers (see below). Black and white are commonly found in combination when an animal is multicoloured, and related species often have black and white representatives (e.g. swans). Black coloration usually helps an animal to absorb solar radiation and thus regulate its temperature, whereas white helps an animal to reflect unwanted heat.

OTHER STRUCTURAL EFFECTS

Larger surface features can also affect animal coloration. Spiders can appear silvery white because of surface hairs, and the orientation and structure of birds' feathers can affect their colour. Some birds look velvety because the tips of the feathers' barbs and barbules are all at right angles to the birds' body and to an observer, so there is a minimal reflecting surface. On the other hand, a lacquer-like or glistening appearance is caused by flattened feathers that lie side by side with the flat surfaces facing an observer.

While the orientation and shape of feathers has some effect on their colour, a powder on their surface has even more effect. Powdery substances on the feathers usually make the colours paler because the particles prevent incident light from reaching the underlying pigments; these would normally absorb some or all wavelengths. As well, the particles tend to scatter the incident light and produce a degree of greyness. If a powder consists of extremely tiny particles, relative to the wavelength of light, then Tyndall scattering occurs. The resulting colour will depend on the underlying pigments, but in all cases will be delicate: a red background will create violet, a yellow background, yellow-green, and a dark background will produce the grey-blue of some cranes' plumage (pl. 10.29).

TRANSPARENCY

Some animals are relatively transparent. Fish are especially likely to be transparent in their juvenile stages, before their skin pigments develop (pl. 10.30). While most fish lose their transparency as they mature, some adult fish are quite transparent. They tend to be relatively small species, and their chromatophores are only partially developed. Though their skin is transparent, their internal organs are usually darkly pigmented for protection from ultraviolet radiation.

Many crustaceans are almost transparent (pl. 10.31), especially small, deep-sea or freshwater species. These animals owe their transparency to reduced calcification in the cuticle. Like fish, their internal organs may be pigmented, though not if they live in a dark habitat. The colours of these transparent crustaceans therefore depend upon the pigmentation of their internal organs (pl. 10.32). Some of the few examples of chlorophyll providing an animal with colour are caterpillars that have bodies transparent enough for their intestinal contents to show through.

Many coelenterates are translucent because of their relatively simple structure and (usually) lack of internal skeleton. For these reasons, the colours of most coelenterates are delicate.

COLOURED LIGHTS

Bioluminescence is the production of light by living organisms. This light is never white: the colours are usually but not always cool colours such as blues and greens. Most bioluminescent animals are marine, and the commonest colour of marine bioluminescence is blue-green. This makes sense when we consider that the blue wavelengths of sunlight travel furthest through seawater and the eyes of marine animals are usually adapted to perceiving this colour. Blue, green or blue-green bioluminescence in the ocean is shown by squid, various groups of crustaceans and coelenterates, echinoderms, worms and deep-sea fish. An unusual pale blue light is emitted by one bottom-dwelling fish, a rat-tail, which has rows of light organs on the underside of its body. Several genera of deepwater fish produce red and blue light from different light organs. The red light-producing organs of fish are often called 'snooperscopes' because the fish can be seen by others of the same but not of different species which are thus potential prey. The few fish that produce red light have appropriate eyes, with lens filters and red tapeta, for detecting red light.

Bioluminescence is rare in terrestrial animals and occurs in: fireflies, glow-worms, some earthworms, snails, millipedes, centipedes and a single freshwater limpet. Most of these animals produce light that is blue, green or yellow.

PL. 10.29 Above: Delicate bluish grey plumage is due to Tyndall scattering and tiny powdery white particles on the feathers. *Photo: W. Farrant*

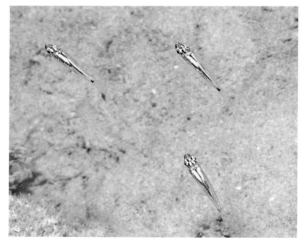

PL. 10.30 Left: The bodies of young fish are often quite transparent until they develop scales. *Photo: W. Farrant*

Animals produce light in special organs known as photophores (fig. 10.6). Photophores have a number of components: light-producing cells or photocytes, a reflecting layer, chromatophores and a transparent outer skin. There are various alternatives to each of these, but the basic chemistry of light production within the organs remains essentially the same in all cases (see p. 83).

The reflecting layer of a photophore is located behind the light-producing cells, and light may even

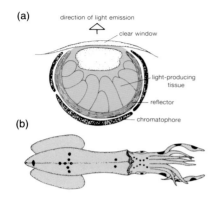

Fig. 10.6
(a) Some features of a photophore, or light-producing organ.
(b) Photophores occur singly, or in often complex patterns on an animal's surface.

be reflected from this layer through a lens, so that it is concentrated into a beam shining in a particular direction through the water. This mechanism resembles a torch beam and is typical of some deep-sea fish.

Bacterial colour

In the mid-depths of the oceans practically all fish produce light, or harbour bacteria that produce the light. The bacteria may be located outside the animal's cells, but they are nonetheless closely associated with the glandular lining of the photophores. The same species of bacteria are found in the surrounding seawater, though here they do not emit light. The bacteria seem to infect young fish, and presumably receive protection and nutrients from them.

Light regulation

The amount of light given out by a photophore can be regulated by chromatophores, located in the

PL. 10.31 Tiny commensal shrimps may be almost transparent except for internal organs and some external markings. *Photo: W. Farrant*

transparent surface of the photophore. Regulation is achieved by expansion and contraction of the pigment inside the chromatophores, or expansion and contraction of the chromatophores themselves in the case of squid.

There are other ways that animals can regulate light. Squid can move the ink from their ink sacs out over photophores and block off light being produced by the symbiotic bacteria. Fireflies and glow-worms can regulate their light by controlling the amount of oxygen that reaches the photophores via their tracheae or breathing tubes: the chemical reaction that produces light cannot proceed when the air supply is closed off. Some animals with bacterial light organs also apparently control light emission by controlling the oxygen supply to their photophores.

Fireflies produce their light in a series of flashes because their light production is under nervous control. In coelenterates, bioluminescence is linked to a nerve net that joins the individual animals in a colony; calcium ions seem to be important in the control of light emission. In some animals where light production is more or less continuous, e.g. some deep-sea fish, light emission is regulated by hormones rather than nerves.

Some animals such as tiny ostracod crustaceans, are able to regulate their light production because of the way they control the chemical reactions: these marine animals secrete two different substances and light is produced only when these mix in the water.

Luminescent lures

Few animals are luminescent over their entire body surface. The exceptions are some coelenterates such as sea pens: these are really colonies of individual animals or polyps that light up sequentially, like a wave passing over the colony as a whole. With most

PL. 10.32 Small transparent shrimps usually have coloured or reflective internal organs. *Photo: P. Farrant*

bioluminescent animals, however, the photophores are restricted in distribution and occur only in specific parts of the body surface. Fish tend to have light organs on their ventral or underneath surfaces. Deep-sea bioluminescent fish, which often have rather exotic names, such as lanternfish, hatchetfish, star eaters, dragonfish, viperfish and anglerfish, often have light organs in front of each eye. Anglerfish have luminescent mouths or luminescent lures (modified fin rays) above their mouths. Deep-sea fish may also have numerous photophores to spread the light over their body surface, though if the light is produced by luminous bacteria, it tends to come from only a few photophores which have diffusing structures to spread it.

In many fish, males and females have different photophore patterns. Other marine organisms have fewer photophores. In the firefly squid, the organs are located at the tips of the arms, while other squid have luminescent mantle cavities and even expel luminescent ink. Marine crustaceans, some fish, a freshwater limpet and some earthworms also expel luminous secretions, e.g. mucus, in the case of the limpet. Most fireflies and glow-worms have single photophores. New Zealand glow-worms have a photophore at the end of the abdomen (pl. 10.33). In bioluminescent beetles, such as fireflies, the distribution of the photophores may be different for larvae and adults.

PL. 10.33 New Zealand glow-worms have a single photophore at the end of their abdomen. The light attracts other insects, which become trapped in the mucous web. *Photo: W. Farrant*

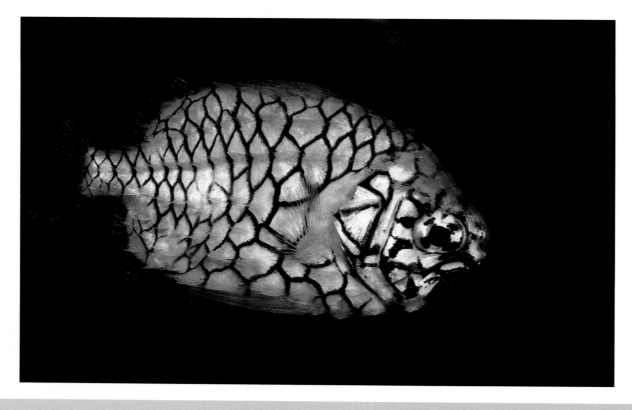

PL. 10.34 Pineapple fish: under each eye there is a single light organ containing bioluminescent bacteria. *Photo: P. Farrant*

BOX I

BLUE EYES

The blue eyes of some mammals, particularly humans and cats, are due to Tyndall blue. Eyes of all colours have a layer of brown melanin at the back of the iris, and this pigment layer is absent only in albinos, whose eyes appear pink because of the haemoglobin in the blood showing through. However, brown eyes also have a layer of melanin on the outer surface of the iris, and sometimes too the stroma or connective tissue of the iris also contains melanins and protein molecules (fig. 10.7). Dark coloured melanin in greater amounts gives dark brown or black eye colour, whereas a fairly even distribution of yellowish melanin in the surface of the iris gives green eye colour.

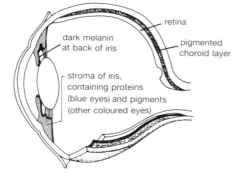

Fig. 10.7 All human eyes except those of albinos, have a layer of melanin at the back of the iris. Brown eyes contain pigment in the stroma of the iris as well; blue eyes do not, but owe their colour to Tyndall blue, preferential scattering of blue light by proteins in the stroma.

There is no melanin in the outer surface of the iris or inside the stroma of blue eyes. Blue eyes, however, do have protein molecules in the stroma, and these particles are tiny enough to scatter blue light. The scattered blue light is visible against the melanin backing, whereas in brown eyes the melanin interspersed with these particles masks the delicate structural blue. The actual colour of blue eyes can vary depending on the quantity of particles in the stroma of the iris. With age, the protein molecules increase gradually in size and this is why a baby's blue eyes change colour. Kittens' eyes gradually develop a layer of yellow carotene and so the eyes of adult cats are often green. In humans, as the scattering particles increase in size, they tend to be less effective at scattering blue light and the eyes tend to become paler with age.

FUNCTIONS OF BIOLUMINESCENCE

The assumed functions of bioluminescence in the animal world are many and varied. Because many bioluminescent animals are nocturnal (fireflies) or live in dark places (glow-worms, deep-sea fish and squid) or in turbid water (some fish) (pl. 10.34), light production may help them to find their way, locate prey, lure prey, scare off predators, find others of the same species for courting and mating or for keeping in a shoal or school. In dark habitats bioluminescence seems to provide camouflage (by counterlighting) in the same way that countershading coloration does for animals living in well-lit habitats (see p. 163).

Many animals change their coloration regularly and many are able to change their colours to suit their habitat. Related species, even individuals of the same species - we need only think of ourselves - may have quite different coloration. The next chapter looks at change and variation in the colours of animals.

BOX 2

MOTHER-OF-PEARL AND PEARLS

Mother-of-pearl or nacreous shell (pl. 10.35), is secreted from the outer skin of molluscs. It contains tablet shaped crystals of calcium carbonate that all face the same way and lie in parallel layers. These uniform layers often produce iridescent colours, providing the outer layers are not too thick or too highly coloured for light to penetrate, e.g. the mother-of-pearl iridescence of green abalone shell shows colours of blue-green, green and pink.

Pearls are similar in structure to mother-of-pearl in most respects. The main difference is that the calcium carbonate structure in a pearl develops around a nucleus, e.g. a foreign particle, and so the layers of pearl are concentric, like the layers of an onion, rather than being more or less flat as they are in mother-of-pearl. Light waves can travel into a pearl because the mollusc tissue is translucent. They are then reflected from the calcium carbonate crystals at various levels. The quality relating to the reflection of light from various depths within a translucent structure is known as the pearl's orient, while the iridescent effect is known as pearlescence. Pearls which have too much colour or very thick layers in their structure, do not have an orient, e.g. Australian pearls and freshwater pearls.

Various factors affect the colours of pearls.

PL. 10.35 Iridescent mother-of-pearl of an abalone shell is due to uniform layers of organic material infilled with crystals of inorganic calcium carbonate. *Photo: P. Farrant*

Chromatophores within the layers of the pearl structure can cause yellow, pink or black coloration. Material lying between the nucleus and the layers of the pearl can cause blue coloration. A high phytoplankton content in the water around the animals can give a green colour to pearls; very salty water will give cream coloured pearls, while various mineral salts in the water, which contain elements such as iron, magnesium and aluminium, may cause pearls to appear brown, blue, grey or cream. The colour of a pearl varies with the species of mollusc that produces it, e.g. clam pearls are usually pink, whereas fan mussel pearls may be a variety of colours, from white to brown, yellow or a reddish brown, and freshwater pearls are usually milky but may contain tints of blue, green, even brown or red.

CHAPTER 11

CHANGING AND VARIABLE COLOURS

The ability of animals such as the chameleon to change colour has been recorded since the time of Aristotle. This ability is extremely widespread and far more common in invertebrates and marine animals than is generally realised.

Fig. 11.1 In most animals darkening of a chromatophore occurs as concentrated pigments become dispersed in the cell.

Fig. 11.2 In cephalopods the chromatophore itself expands and contracts under the control of muscle cells.

Fig. 11.3 Section through mammal's skin showing hair follicle. Pigments are laid down only at the living base of the hair, and so colour change is not possible except by moulting.

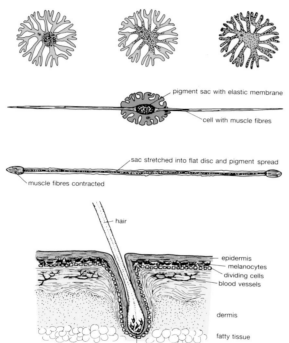

WHERE DO COLOUR CHANGES OCCUR?

Animals with chromatophores (see p. 117) tend to show dramatic colour changes: cephalopods (octopuses, squid and cuttlefish), crustaceans, fish, amphibians (especially tree frogs) and reptiles (especially lizards), as well as some animals in other groups. The dispersal and concentration of fixed amounts of pigments within chromatophores causes most of these animals to change colour, although in cephalopods the chromatophores themselves expand and contract (figs 11.1, 11.2).

Chromatophores containing differently coloured pigments lie at varying depths in an animal's skin, so that dispersed pigment in the uppermost layers effectively shields the colours of underlying layers. When pigment in the uppermost layers is contracted, however, underlying colours become visible (pl. 11.1). With a number of differently coloured pigments, contracted or dispersed to varying degrees, an animal can achieve many colours, as well as black, grey and white. If an animal has iridocytes, its colour range can be further enhanced: these light-reflecting cells are usually situated at an even lower level in the skin, and are exposed when the pigments in overlying chromatophores are concentrated.

The speed at which an animal changes colour depends upon the way its chromatophores are

PL. 11.1 Right: Sponge-dwelling fish: the dark pigment in the chromatophores is contracted so the fish is light in colour. *Photo: P. Farrant*

PL. 11.34 Left: Each zebra has its own individual markings. *Photo: W. Farrant*

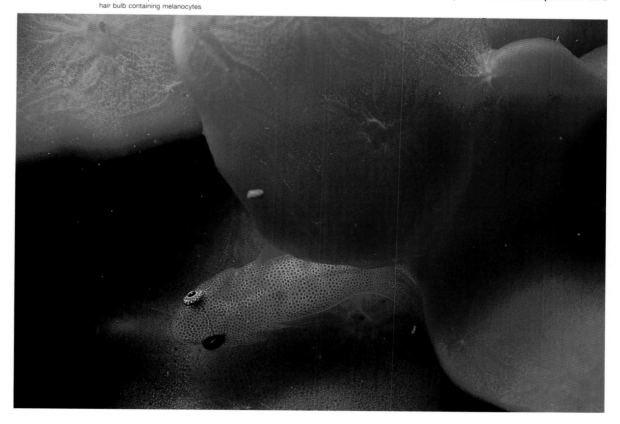

PL. 11.2 Cleaner wrasses are small distinctively coloured fish. They clean the mouths, gills and external surfaces of larger fish, which recognise them and sometimes even change to a lighter colour during cleaning. *Photo: P. Farrant*

controlled. If they are under direct control of the animal's nervous system, the colour change can be very quick, e.g. octopuses, squid and cuttlefish. In most animals, however, colour change is controlled by both nerves and hormones, or hormones alone, so it takes longer: minutes, hours, days or even weeks.

OTHER MEANS OF COLOUR CHANGE

While chromatophores are the most rapid means for an animal to change colour, there are other ways. New pigments may be produced or taken in as food. Mammals and birds may moult, replacing hairs or feathers over several days once or twice a year (fig. 11.3). Movement of hairs, feathers or underlying skin may expose different colours, e.g. the white band of hairs displayed by springbok normally lies in a fold of the animals' skin, and deers' white stars are made up of lower parts of hairs that are exposed only when the hairs stand on edge. Some birds have coloured under-feathers that are exposed when covering feathers stand up, e.g. the Eurasian bustard becomes white by almost turning its brownish plumage inside out during the courting display.

Birds or mammals may change colour quickly by exposing bare skin patches, e.g. yellow sacs on the breast of the male North American sage grouse may inflate. The skin may change colour by the sudden expansion of surface blood vessels, e.g. blushing in humans, and the reddening of the ears of animals such as the Tasmanian devil. Fear or shock causes human skin to pale because blood vessels in the skin contract. In birds, the bare skin patches also tend to occur in the facial and neck regions, e.g. the wattles of some birds which change colour when blood vessels beneath the skin expand and contract.

Animals change colour for a variety of reasons.

IN A COLOURFUL MOOD

Animals that change colour with mood or emotions are usually capable of doing so rapidly. The two best known examples are the octopus and the chameleon (see BOX 1).

Many other animals change colour with emotional state. Fish generally become pale when frightened and dark when angry; they sometimes even change colour to be cleaned (pl. 11.2). Mammals and birds are limited in their ability to change colour quickly, but sometimes, e.g. during the breeding season, change colour when different amounts of blood flow into bare skin patches or when previously hidden coloured areas become exposed.

COLOURS FOR DAY AND NIGHT

Many animals that lighten and darken with emotional state also change colour over a day-night cycle. Crustaceans often turn pale at night as pigments in their dark-coloured chromatophores become concentrated, allowing lighter pigments and reflecting structures to show through: when they are pale or transparent these animals are much less visible to night-time predators (pl. 11.3). Many crustaceans are able to maintain a regular rhythm of colour change for some time without exposure to light, and this is particularly important for burrow-dwelling animals such as fiddler crabs: when these crabs emerge from their holes with the tide, they are light or dark in colour according to the time of day, regardless of the time of the tide. These rhythmic day-night colour changes in crustaceans are controlled by hormones that are released regularly from the animals' eyestalks.

Other invertebrates, e.g. some sea urchins and leeches, also become pale at night; their darker

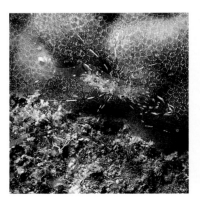

PL. 11.3 Some shrimps become almost transparent at night when the pigment in their chromatophores is contracted. *Photo: P. Farrant*

PL. 11.7 Lizards are darker in the morning for soaking up the sun's heat, but lighten during the day. *Photo: W. Farrant*

daytime colours probably protect them from the light. Most fish that are inactive at night change to a lighter colour; fish that are active at night usually change from their daytime colours and patterns into brighter night-time colours. Night-time patterns and colours (apart from structural colours), may be altogether different from daytime patterns and colours.

Some freshwater fish such as the mosquito fish, have a regular colour rhythm during the day that enables them to change gradually with the changing colour of underwater light. Some cold-blooded terrestrial animals, including many lizards, also change colour in a day-night cycle. These animals are darkest first thing in the morning, so that they can soak up heat from the sun. This heat supplies

BOX I

THE MASTERS OF COLOUR CHANGE

Octopuses can change colour, texture and pattern within seconds, and waves of colour pass over frightened or angry animals (pl. 11.4) Octopuses and other cephalopods use these changes, with jet-propulsion and inkscreens, to confuse predators and flush out prey.

Octopuses, squid and cuttlefish are excellent at blending in with the colours of their surroundings (pl. 11.5). They are usually blotched: e.g. an octopus against a green background has its orange chromatophores contracted, and its yellow and black chromatophores expanded so that the iridocytes show through. Against a grey background the red and yellow chromatophores are contracted and the shade of grey is matched by an appropriate degree of expansion of the black chromatophores. Their ability to match background colours so well is thought to be due to their ability to match the light intensity perceived by their eyes (they have excellent vision), helped by the passive reflection of the surrounding colours by the iridocytes in their skin. Baby octopuses, which do not have as much pigment in their skin, can contract their chromatophores to such an extent that their bodies become almost transparent.

Although chameleons are also famous for their colour changes, they change colour more slowly than octopuses, squid and cuttlefish. Like cephalopods, however, mood and emotions appear to be the main causes of colour change.

An undisturbed chameleon is greenish brown without any distinct pattern. If it is disturbed the animal darkens and develops patterns of stripes, spots and blotches in contrasting colours. The colour change is due to the activity of dark pigment in the animals' melanophores. Yellow pigments in the surface layer of the skin are

PL. 11.4 Left: An excited or aggressive cuttlefish becomes red or brown, and iridescent waves pass rapidly over its body. If it is frightened, waves of iridescence again pass over its body, dark spots appear on its back and its skin becomes prickly in texture. Males show a further colour pattern during the mating season, when they have black and white stripes. *Photo: R. Berthold*

PL. 11.6 Below: Madagascan chameleon. *Photo: S. Wilson.*

PL. 11.5 Below: An undisturbed cuttlefish is usually mottled and blends in with the colours of its surroundings. *Photo: W. Farrant*

underlain by a layer of cells that produce structural Tyndall blue, and beneath is a layer of melanophores whose branches extend up through the layers above. The animals are yellow if the black pigment is fully contracted, and green if the black melanin is dispersed enough to provide a backing for Tyndall blue. As the melanin becomes fully dispersed, the animal becomes darker green and then brown, and sometimes almost black (pl. 11.6).

their energy needs for the day, so they gradually become paler and more active as they warm up (pl. 11.7). Colour changes over a day-night cycle always seem to be controlled by pairs of antagonistic hormones.

COLOURS TO MATCH

One of the commonest reasons for colour change is to match the changing colours of the background or habitat. If an animal moves quickly from one background to another, then it needs to change colour quickly. Some surgeonfish and wrasses change from a yellow or black seabed coloration to a silvery blue surface coloration as they swim upward through the water (pl. 11.8), while gropers can change quickly between several differently coloured patterns in as many seconds (pl. 11.9). Seahorses (pl. 11.10) and flatfish (pl. 11.11), too, can change colour fairly quickly, to match the colours of the seaweed or sand around them.

Animals that are slow moving, or whose background changes colour only gradually, tend to change colour more slowly. These changes are caused by hormonal activity or a change in the colour of food, e.g. sea hares gradually change colour as the seaweeds they eat vary through the year (pl. 11.12). Some crustaceans, insects and spiders change their general coloration over a period of days or weeks so they become difficult to detect against their backgrounds. In the case of blossom spiders, the change from white to yellow is due to a transfer of yellow pigment from the animal's gut, where it is stored, to its skin (pl. 11.13).

Some animals change colour only when necessary: immature locusts can match their background when they are on their own; as part of a large group, their black and orange coloration does not pose as much risk from predators (pl. 11.14).

Environmental factors

Specific environmental factors, such as light, heat and humidity, can also cause some animals to change colour. In some cases light promotes the production of melanin in an animal's skin, e.g. many humans develop a suntan in response to increased ultraviolet radiation. Many animals that live in caves are normally pale, but begin to produce pigment if they are exposed to the light. On the other hand, some African frogs lose their bright red colours if exposed to bright light.

Temperature can affect an animal's colour. The colour of some species of moths depends on the temperature experienced during their pupal stage. Crabs subjected to increasing temperatures tend to lighten: their dark pigments become concentrated, the white pigments disperse and the resulting pale coloration prevents them from absorbing too much heat. Although the light daytime colours of many desert and high altitude lizards and terrestrial invertebrates mean that they blend in well with their surroundings, the primary function of colour change in these animals is probably temperature regulation. The pigments in the animals' chromatophores are dispersed in the morning because dark skin can more efficiently absorb heat from the sun; then as the

PL. 11.8 Some fish are yellow when close to the seabed, but become blue as they swim up into the water. *Photo: W. Farrant*

PL. 11.9 Gropers can change their colours and patterns within seconds, although their repertoire is limited. *Photo: P. Farrant*

PL. 11.10 Left: Seahorses can change colour by movement of pigments in their chromatophores, to match seaweeds they cling to. *Photo: P. Farrant*

PL. 11.11 Below: Flatfishes like soles and flounders that live on the sea floor generally change colour quite quickly and their ability to match their background colours (grey, black, orange, yellow, blue, green and pink) and patterns is quite remarkable. *Photo: W. Farrant*

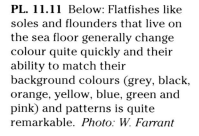

PL. 11.14 Locusts often match background colours unless they are part of a large group. *Photo: R. Berthold*

PL. 11.13 Blossom spiders change colour slowly by moving pigment from the gut to the skin, to match flower colours. *Photo: R. Berthold*

stimuli by means of their pineal gland or third eye, an organ on the top of the head that secretes melatonin, a substance that acts on the animal's chromatophores. As the animals mature, their eyes take over the function of perceiving stimuli. Caterpillars are thought to detect background colours through their eyes, information that each animal's brain uses in controlling the colour of pigments laid down in the skin prior to the pupal stage (pl. 11.15).

In some cases, external stimuli may directly affect the expansion and contraction of pigments within chromatophores. Geckos change colour in response to moisture, while other lizards respond to temperature, and many amphibians respond to touch. Usually however, stimuli received through the eyes or other senses affect internal controls, namely hormones and other glandular secretions, and the animal's nervous system. These in turn control the expansion and concentration of pigment in the chromatophores.

SEASONAL COLOUR CHANGES

Many animals change colour at regular intervals with changing seasons or when the environment changes from wet to dry. The direct causes of such changes vary but are usually linked to climatic changes in the animal's environment. Possible direct causes include changes in the relative lengths of day and night and the amount of rainfall. Seasonal changes in colour are often also related to changes in the sexual cycles of animals.

Seasonal changes in coloration are most noticeable in some, but not all, mammals, birds and insects. In temperate parts of the world, the pupae of cabbage white butterflies may be differently coloured in different seasons: the pupae are green or brown, sometimes even a mixture, and they match the background vegetation in different seasons. The caterpillars of geometrid moths in Arizona also vary in colour depending on the season: the spring generation resembles the yellow and brown oak catkins they eat, whereas the summer generation is greyish green and resembles the twigs that remain on the tree at this time of the year.

While some insects, e.g. stick insects and mountain grasshoppers, are able to change colour during the day, most insects, like mammals and birds, are

animal warms up and no longer needs to trap this heat, its pigments become more concentrated and its colour lightens.

Changes in humidity can also cause an animal's colour to alter, either by long-term darkening or lightening, e.g. some frogs, or in the short-term through wetting and drying of an animal's surface structure. Hercules beetles are black when conditions are moist but turn yellow when conditions are dry: when the outer yellow part of their skin moistens it becomes spongy and translucent, no longer reflecting yellow wavelengths but instead allowing the underlying black pigment to show through.

Visual stimuli

While emotional state and environmental factors can stimulate colour change in some animals, visual stimuli are probably more important. In many cases blind animals become unable to change colour. Larval vertebrates, whose eyes have yet to form, often have different colour responses from adults of the same species. Amphibian larvae, for instance, detect generally limited in their ability to change colour quickly, and colour changes usually occur as the animals change from one stage of the life cycle to the next (pl. 11.16).

Moulting

In mammals and birds, the moult is the only time that hair and feathers can change to an altogether different colour. The change in mammals is most noticeable where environmental colours change dramatically, especially at high latitudes or altitudes where summer greens and browns give way to a white snow-covered winter landscape. In these areas, when there is little plant material and few insects, some mammals such as snow hares, polar foxes and stoats, and some birds such as ptarmigan, change to a white covering for winter. In some cases, animals of the same species living at lower latitudes do not change in this way, which supports the notion that white winter colours are for camouflage. Some ptarmigans actually change their plumage several times during the year: they are variegated in spring and autumn, white in winter and brownish in summer.

While some arctic mammals become white for winter, there are many animals which either do not change colour or become darker. This is especially true of animals protected by living in herds or flocks: in most habitats they can afford to be conspicuous. In warmer areas, where seasons are not so pronounced, fewer animals change colour and those that do, show gradual changes, e.g. from a warm brown to a cooler brown. Some colour changes related to the sexual cycle are caused by secretions that colour the male's fur for a short time. These colours can be quite vivid, often turning brown or yellow-brown fur to pink or red. The apparent colour change of sloths, from green to brown, as the animals go from wet to dry conditions, is caused by the drying out of symbiotic algae in their fur (pl. 11.17).

Like mammals, birds can change colour completely when they moult. Moulting involves the production of feathers within the dermal quills of the old ones, which gradually fall out. Often the colour change is noticeable but not striking, e.g. new feathers of starlings have white tips that gradually wear down through the year, causing the birds to become gradually blacker (pls 11.18, 11.19). The spectacular colours of male ducks and some male blue wrens are seasonal changes related to the animals' sexual cycles.

SEXUAL COLOURS

In many species of animals, males and females are differently coloured. This sexual dimorphism is important as it provides a means of recognising potential mating partners amongst individuals within a species (pl. 11.20). Colour often also indicates which members of the species are sexually mature. This saves time and energy during courtship. In most cases, it is the male of the species that is brightly coloured (pl. 11.21). Females are usually dull in colour and are therefore well camouflaged when they look after the young (pl. 11.22). There are exceptions to this, however: males that incubate eggs or look

after young tend to have camouflage coloration, e.g. male tinamous, emus, dotterels and phalaropes.

The most striking differences between the sexes are found amongst fish, birds and insects. The colour differences between many male and female fish (pl. 11.23) and birds (e.g. ducks, weaver birds and peacocks) are so great that in both groups many were originally described as two separate species, the male as one and the female as another.

Some mammals, including species of monkeys, antelopes, bushbuck and kangaroos, show marked

PL. 11.15 Caterpillars are thought to detect background colours through their eyes, and so control the colour of pigments laid down in their skin before they pupate.
Photo: R.J. King

PL. 11.16 Insect larvae often have colours that are different from adults of the same species, especially when the two live in differently coloured habitats. Cicada nymphs, for example, are brown and live underground, but when they pass through their final larval stage they climb up a nearby tree and emerge with green or black adult coloration.
Photo: R. Berthold

PL. 11.17 Sloths change from green to brown in dry conditions because of symbiotic algae in their fur. *Photo: W. Farrant*

PL. 11.18 Cygnets are quite different in colour from adult swans; colour changes in birds occur when they moult. *Photo: P. Farrant*

PL. 11.19 This 11-day old yellow-eyed penguin chick does not yet have any of the light markings of the adult. *Photo: A. Leslie*

PL. 11.20 Male ostriches are darker than females. *Photo: W. Farrant.*

PL. 11.21 Some species of fish live in large groups where there is one dominant, colourful male and many less colourful females. The females retain the ability to change sex, so when something happens to the dominant male, one of the females takes on male coloration. *Photo: P. Farrant*

but not striking differences in coloration between
the sexes (pl. 11.24). Some amphibians, and rather
more reptiles, especially lizards, show sexual
dimorphism.

Male animals often become even more colourful
during the mating season. Seasonal environmental
factors, such as temperature and light, trigger a rise
in the level of the animals' sex hormones and cause
colour changes. Castrated males revert to female
coloration as their hormone levels decline, in the
same way that males of some species revert to colours
similar to those of the females when the breeding
season finishes.

Although some sexually dimorphic species may
have relatively permanent colour differences, in many
other species the sexual coloration is only temporary.
Birds can accomplish this by growing differently
coloured feathers after a moult. Animals with
chromatophores achieve a temporary colour change
during the breeding period through a change in the
relative dominance of their variously coloured
pigments. Exposure of coloured areas may also be
used during courtship displays, e.g. male lyrebirds,
pheasants, peacocks and birds of paradise.

COLOUR CHANGES WITH AGE

Unlike seasonal and sexual colour changes, each
colour change concerned with age usually occurs
only once in an animal's lifetime. The greatest
changes usually occur in the early part of an animal's
life. Often the young of a species are altogether
different in colour from their parents. Drastic colour
changes can occur if the animal passes through
different stages in its life cycle or if it moults. Other
more subtle changes happen more or less
continuously. In general terms, as animals grow
older, their colours become gradually duller, vivid
colours darken, patterns become less clear and in

the case of some mammals, some of the hair cover is lost, while the rest may turn grey, e.g. humans, dogs and gorillas.

If young animals have the same coloration as a parent, then it is usually the female they resemble. Young males change to adult coloration with sexual maturity. While they may be essentially similar in colour to their mothers, young animals frequently have one or two different features, e.g. young stoats, otherwise similar to their mothers, have white ear rims (pl. 11.25). If young animals differ substantially in colour and pattern from their parents, the coloration is usually protective, i.e. matches colours and patterns of their immediate surroundings (pl. 11.26). The young of ground-nesting birds such as pipits and emus have excellent camouflage coloration, and species of young seals born on the Arctic or Antarctic ice, are white before they change to the darker adult coloration at the first moult. With age, young animals' colours change, in one or several steps, to adult coloration. In the case of birds especially, the young may go through several moults before they achieve full adult coloration (pl. 11.27).

Among reptiles, there are fewer examples of colour changes with age, and the changes are rarely dramatic. Some young lizards have bright blue tails which change colour before they reach adulthood. With most reptiles, colour changes with age are subtle and occur because their skin is replaced at intervals

PL. 11.25 Many young mammals that are similar in colour to their parents have small distinguishing features, e.g. lion cubs have spots and rings on the tails. *Photo: W. Farrant*

PL. 11.26 Young terrestrial animals tend to have colours that help them to blend in with their surroundings: young deer are difficult to see in a forest. *Photo: P. Farrant*

PL. 11.27 Below: Young flamingoes are grey and must obtain sufficient pigment in their diet, before they moult, to become pink. *Photo: W. Farrant*

PL. 11.28 Above: Some adult fish that live in burrows lose their pigmentation as they adopt a life under the sea floor.
Photo: W. Farrant

PL. 11.29 Right: The larva of the yellow spot jewel butterfly.
Photo: J. Landy

PL. 11.30 The pupa of the yellow spot jewel butterfly.
Photo: J. Landy

throughout their lives. As with birds' feathers and mammals' fur, reptiles' scales become gradually duller as the animals age. Amphibians may show dramatic colour changes when they pass from larvae to adults, e.g. some adult salamanders have vivid contrasting colours.

Some young fish develop their adult pigmentation during a prolonged time in the egg, whereas others, such as eels, hatch out quickly at a stage when they have little or no pigment. The first parts of young fish to develop pigment are the eyes, then the pigment is gradually deposited in the rest of the skin (pl. 11.28).

Colour changes with age also occur in many invertebrates. The pigments in the chromatophores of young crustaceans and cephalopods often develop slowly like those of some young fish. Most larval marine invertebrates are more or less colourless, and only develop their adult coloration when they settle out of the plankton. Like fish, invertebrates that spend a long time in the egg are usually more highly developed, in terms of coloration and pattern, at the time of hatching. Young spiders are almost always light in colour, acquiring their darker colours gradually with age, and their full adult colours and patterns when they are old enough to make their own webs. Insects often change colour dramatically as they pass from stage to stage through their life cycles: it is well known that many caterpillars and grubs, which are often dull in colour, turn into beautifully coloured butterflies and moths (pls 11.29-11.31).

Animals change colour for the final time when they die. These colour changes are due to the breakdown of pigments and of the hormonal and nervous systems that control colour. While some structural colours may remain unaffected by death, even these colours are usually lost as the animals dry out and the structures that cause the colours are altered irreversibly. Exceptions are scarab beetles, which retain colour after death and have been used for ornaments and jewellery since ancient times.

COLOUR AND GENES: VARIATION

The colours of individual animals often vary considerably over their surfaces: even birds' feathers and mammals' hairs are usually different at the base and the tip (pl. 11.32). Variability of colour within any one animal species may be due to differences in the age and sex of individuals, but it is ultimately caused by genetic differences, of individuals or even of whole populations (pl. 11.33).

The colours of animals (and plants) are often affected by several genes, so considerable variety may exist in a species, even before considering environmental and other influences. In the simplest case of colour variation, where colour is determined by a single gene with two different forms or alleles, an animal with two different alleles (one on the chromosome it received from its mother, the other on the chromosome from its father) will be the colour of the dominant allele. If the two chromosomes both carry dominant alleles, the animal is the colour of the dominant allele. The two chromosomes must both carry the recessive allele for the animal to have the recessive colour (fig. 11.4). Occasionally neither allele is dominant, the alleles are said to be co-dominant, and the animal is an intermediate colour. The most famous examples of this co-dominance are roan cattle and pink snapdragons, both of which are the result of a cross between one red and one white parent (fig. 11.5).

White and albino alleles are usually recessive to other colours and this is why blue or green budgerigars, and purple, red, pink or blue flowered plants, sometimes produce white offspring. These white individuals do not have any dominant alleles of the colour genes, so they are unable to produce the normal pigments. More or less continuous variation in the colour of individuals in a population is caused by a larger number of genes.

The different alleles that cause the variety of colours in both animals and plants originate as mutations, or physical changes of chromosomes. These chance events provide the raw material for natural selection. Most mutations are not favourable for survival in the wild. However, if a more useful colour is produced (e.g. one that gives an animal better camouflage, or one that is preferred by a plant's pollinator), then the animal or plant has a greater chance to survive and reproduce compared to other individuals of the species: natural selection takes place, and eventually the new form becomes established.

Colour and natural selection

Sometimes animals of different colours are confined to particular populations of a species, separated geographically from each other (or temporally in the case of some insects that produce two differently coloured generations per year), e.g. pale headed rosellas in northern Australia, which have white cheeks in the south and blue cheeks in the north of their range. There are several differently coloured races of humans and many other animals, both vertebrates and invertebrates, and the different colours are usually adaptive, e.g. crested larks in the northern African desert: a dark race lives in the far north nearest the Mediterranean, while a pale race lives in the sandy desert, and a reddish race inhabits the stony desert. Other species of animals may contain differently coloured individuals within the same population, in which case some of the animals will be suitably coloured to match their surroundings at any particular time; e.g. variously coloured chorus frogs live in the Rocky Mountains, a habitat with a great variety of background colours.

Suitably coloured individuals thrive to pass on their genes to succeeding generations in the process of natural selection. A classic case of rapid natural selection for colour is industrial melanism of moths. Peppered moths, well adapted to the colours and patterns of the lichen-covered tree trunks they rested upon, were all but replaced by dark coloured moths during the industrial revolution in Britain in the

PL. 11.31 The adult male yellow spot jewel butterfly.
Photo: J. Landy

Fig. 11.4
Dominant and recessive inheritance in peas. Red is dominant, white recessive. If an individual has one gene for red and one for white it will be red in colour.

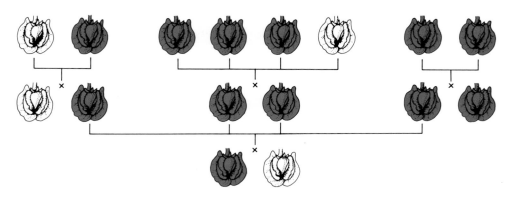

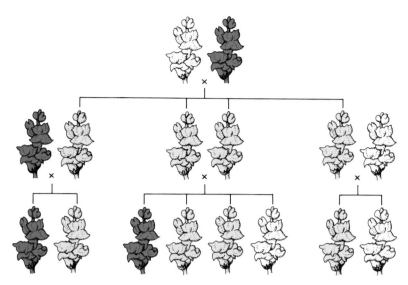

Fig. 11.5
Co-dominance in snapdragons: a cross between red and white individuals produces pink-flowered plants. In these plants the red and white pigments are mixed; however, the genes do not mix and so red and white plants can be bred from pink ones.

nineteenth century. At this time air pollution was extreme and the trees and lichens became dark with soot. The lighter coloured moths became easy for predatory birds to spot, whereas the darker moths survived to breed and pass on their dark genes. With decreasing air pollution and cleaner trees today, there is evidence that the dark moths are now decreasing in numbers.

Animals recognise other animals by their coloration (pl. 11.34); they use colour in a variety of ways. The next chapter examines the role of colour in communication in the natural world.

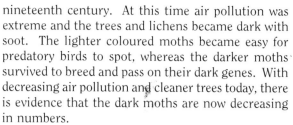

PL. 11.32 Right: Some mongooses are banded because the individual hairs are darker at the base and the bases are more exposed in those parts of the animal's coat where the hairs are sparser. *Photo: W. Farrant*

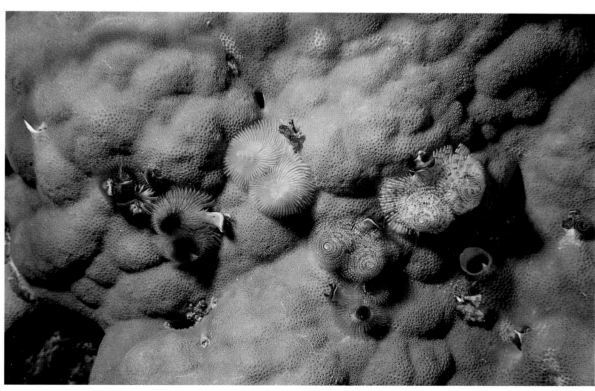

PL. 11.33 Tube worms: the colours of individuals within a population are ultimately due to genetic differences.
Photo: P. Farrant

CHAPTER 12

COLOURS FOR SURVIVAL:
CAMOUFLAGE AND COMMUNICATION

Animals' colours usually play an important role in visual communication between members of the same species and between members of different species. If an animal is conspicuous in its surroundings, its colours enhance communication, help it to be recognised, attract mates or warn off rivals and predators. Different species have characteristic colours and patterns, and individuals within a species may also be recognisable by slight differences in colour and pattern. Animals that are very conspicuous, however, need to have some defence against predators. If an animal blends in with its background, then its colours minimise communication and disguise its presence. Sometimes animals compromise between conspicuousness for social communication and inconspicuousness for camouflage: some have bright colours for only part of the time, some are able to change colour, some can expose colours that are normally concealed, and others have different colour forms within their populations.

CAMOUFLAGE

Camouflage coloration in a broad sense refers to colours which, together with pattern and shape, render an organism inconspicuous in its

PL. 12.1 Right: Stonefish: bottom-dwelling predatory fish often blend in with the background colours.
Photo: R. Berthold

PL. 12.6 Left: Insects that live on leaves are often green, and may even have patterns that resemble the veins of a leaf.
Photo: P. Farrant

surroundings. This can be achieved in several ways: by direct matching of an animal's colours to those around it, by disruptive coloration and linking patterns, by disguise, and by countershading and false shadows. Both predators and prey can have camouflage coloration. Some animals even achieve concealment through symbiotic relationships with plants or with other animals. As animals move in relation to their surroundings, their camouflage coloration must be reinforced by appropriate patterns of behaviour.

Cryptic colours

The easiest way for an organism to conceal itself is to match its surroundings so it is overlooked by both prey and predators. This is known as cryptic coloration.

Animals most likely to have cryptic coloration include those that are: relatively inactive, slow moving or sedentary, such as stonefish (pl. 12.1); weak, young or small, such as the young of ground-nesting birds (pl. 12.2); forced to survive in an exposed habitat, such as birds' eggs; or nocturnal and hide in the open during the day, such as owls and nightjars (pl. 12.3).

Mostly an animal's cryptic coloration relies upon its ability to remain relatively motionless for long periods. This applies to both prey and some predators, although other predatory animals often need to be inconspicuous while moving because they stalk their prey. Cheetahs are particularly well adapted grassland predators: their colours match the yellowish brown of the soil and vegetation, and they move stealthily towards their intended prey, only chasing when they are close enough to outrun the prey over a short distance. Cryptically coloured predators are found in all types of habitats, and include bottom-dwelling fish (pl. 12.4), pelagic fish such as the barracuta, insects such as praying mantises (pl. 12.5) and grasshoppers (pl. 12.6), green tree snakes and tree frogs, fish-hunting herons, blossom spiders and polar bears.

Habitat colours

In most biomes there are animals that are cryptically coloured, usually with an appropriate pattern of blotches, speckles or bands that allows them to blend in with their surroundings. Animals with certain colours tend to be found in particular places. Many white animals such as polar bears and young seals, live in polar regions where they are inconspicuous against the surrounding ice and snow. White animals tend to be young, weak or predatory. Most desert mammals match their backgrounds fairly well, even though they are usually nocturnal. Those without cryptic coloration are usually black or white rather than brightly coloured.

Fish that live close to the surface of the sea tend to be silver, blue or even transparent, so that they match the surrounding water. Glassfish, found in the Indian Ocean, are virtually transparent, with only their gill covers, eyes and skeletons being coloured: they are very difficult to see in their watery habitat. Transparency is not an option for larger species of fish, but these animals usually have scales that reflect

PL. 12.3 Above: Nightjar: nocturnal animals that rest out in the open during the day are usually cryptically coloured. *Photo: W.H. King*

PL. 12.4 Left: Sand flathead: bottom-dwelling fish usually adopt the colours of sand, rocks, coral or seaweed. *Photo: R. Berthold*

the surrounding colours, as well as silvery blue coloration. Cephalopods such as octopuses, squid and cuttlefish, also achieve cryptic coloration through reflection of the colours of their surroundings.

For mammals and birds, cryptic coloration is usually permanent or relatively long-term; for animals that change colour by means of chromatophores, e.g. crustaceans, fish, amphibians, lizards and cephalopods, their cryptic coloration can be changed very quickly to suit changing colours in their environment. This overcomes the disadvantage of moving to a differently coloured background. In all cases, however, an animal's cryptic coloration increases its chances of survival and contributes to the survival of the species as a whole.

Local populations of a species may develop different colour forms, each adapted to different local environments. Differently coloured populations of some lizards, insects and rodents are found in habitats with differently coloured substrates: lighter coloured populations live on sand while dark populations are found on rock. This may lead to the evolution of separate species, when the differently coloured populations eventually cease to interbreed. Although a population of conspicuously coloured animals can survive in some environments if isolated from predators, conspicuously coloured animals are usually

PL. 12.5 Above: Many insects have cryptic coloration. Those that live on twigs, like this praying mantis, are often brown. *Photo: J. Landy*

PL. 12.2 Right: Osprey chicks: the young of ground-nesting birds often have cryptic coloration. *Photo: R. Berthold*

at risk unless their colours are an advertisement for unpalatability.

Disruptive colours

Plain colours, even if they match an animal's surroundings, tend to be much more conspicuous than colours arranged in patterns, especially for animals that move in relation to their background. This is because most environments are patterned with a variety of colours as well as dark and light areas. One of the subtle ways in which colour and pattern can work together to achieve camouflage is through disruptive coloration. Here, the ground colour of the animal's skin or skin products is similar to its surroundings, but a pattern of contrasting (but not vivid) colours helps to divide up the animal's image, so its overall shape is difficult to see and therefore identify. A predator's gaze continues from the animal to its surroundings without stopping at the animal's outline. Predators usually recognise an animal first by its outline, then by individual body parts: if individual parts such as limbs are unrecognisable, it is difficult for the predator to see the animal as a whole. Leopards and cheetahs (pl. 12.7), giraffes (pl. 12.8) and zebras (pl. 12.9) are good examples of disruptive coloration.

Stripes are most effective if they run across an animal's body because, even though they may be somewhat conspicuous, they tend to break up the animal's outline. Many fish have stripes that run in the opposite direction to the general shape of the animals and this helps to disguise their body parts and outlines. Although some animals with disruptive coloration are better camouflaged at rest than when moving, disruptive stripes tend to allow animals to move between differently coloured backgrounds without exactly matching the colours of their background (although it helps if the animal's ground colour matches its surroundings). Disruptive coloration is found in many animal groups besides mammals and fish, e.g. moths that settle on tree bark (pl. 12.10), butterflies whose mottled, dull, lower wing surfaces are displayed when the wings are folded, snakes which have an amazing variety of coloured patterns, and the young of ground-nesting birds.

Other types of coloration may disguise parts of an animal. Some animals have linking patterns, in which parts appear to be joined up by a colour or pattern that extends from one to the other, e.g. some frogs have leg markings that match up with markings on their bodies when they are in a resting position: they look like unrecognisable striped objects. The stripes do not join up when the frogs are actively moving about (pl. 12.11).

The eyes have it!

Disguise of an animal's eyes is probably even more important than disguise of other parts such as limbs. Eyes can be the most conspicuous parts of an animal's body, particularly if they are black, shiny and round. However, there are many ways in which animals' eyes can be camouflaged. Body markings that extend from the general body surface and across the eyes are very common amongst fish (pl. 12.12) and other vertebrates, e.g. the eyes are concealed with black

PL. 12.7 From a distance cheetahs' patterns merge into the ground colour of the animals' coats. *Photo: W. Farrant*

PL. 12.8 If giraffes stand still, it can be difficult to pick out the outlines of individuals against the background. *Photo: W. Farrant*

PL. 12.9 Zebras have disruptive coloration, i.e. colours with abrupt boundaries that disrupt an observer's image of the outline. When zebras are in a herd, it is hard to recognise individual animals from a distance. *Photo: P. Farrant*

lines in the thorny devil and by the masks of some plovers (pl. 12.13).

In snakes and lizards the pattern of facial scales is often carried over into the eyelids, and the same pattern may continue across the lips so that the mouth is disguised. Many mammals have dark patches around their eyes, while in others the eyes are lost among a myriad of dark spots or lines on their faces. The coloration of eyelids also plays an important part in concealing eyes. Some eyelids are covered with scales, as in the chameleon, or feathers,

PL. 12.10 The colours and patterns on the upper surface of this moth's wings match those of the tree's bark. *Photo: J. Landy*

PL. 12.11 Linking pattern: the stripes of this frog appear to continue from body to legs, making it difficult to recognise. *Photo: R. Berthold*

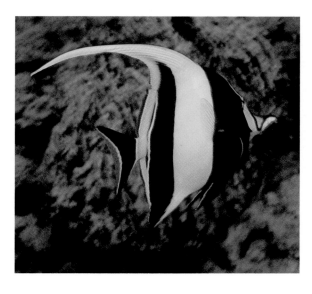

PL. 12.12 Moorish idol: many coral reef fish have body markings that continue across the eyes, making them less conspicuous. *Photo: W. Farrant*

False colours

Some animals not only conceal their eyes but also have false eyes at the tail end of their body, which confuse and distract predators. False eye coloration is common in caterpillars such as the spicebush swallowtail, saturnids (e.g. the giant silkworm and emperor moths), fish, frogs and birds including the peacock. False eyes are not always just simple black spots. Many have lighter coloured borders and even iris-like coloration inside the spot. To a predator, they resemble the fixed and thus aggressive gaze of vertebrates' eyes, and so not only divert the predator's attention away from the real eyes at the head end of the animal, but also frighten it away (pl. 12.14). Whole false heads may occur at the hind end of some caterpillars. These animals therefore derive a further advantage from their coloration and pattern because a predator expects them to move in a particular direction, and is surprised and confused when they appear to go backwards. Animals with false eye and false head coloration are often damaged at their hind ends, an indication that the colours help to protect the more important head ends.

Animals may expose false eyes and false heads only when threatened, while maintaining cryptic coloration under normal conditions. False appendages are also used by some predators for capturing prey: some fish have brightly coloured or even bioluminescent lures that look like worms and attract prey. Some snakes have a brightly coloured tail that looks like a head, but lures a predator's attention away from the real head hidden amongst the body coils: if a predator attacks the false head, the real head is protected and the animal may discharge a noxious substance from its tail region.

Coloration does not necessarily have to resemble eyes or heads in order to divert a predator's attention from its vital parts. Bright colours can do this on their own. Young lizards (and adults of some species) may have brightly coloured tails that they can drop if threatened: the tails break off at a special fracture plane within the animal's vertebrae. Though the lizard sacrifices its tail, the tail grows back again later. Meanwhile the dropped (and still twitching) tail has provided a distraction and perhaps allowed the animal time to escape. Many animals have hidden, brightly coloured areas which they flash when disturbed (pls 12.15, 12.16). Such colours may be important in communication within the animal's own species, such as in mating rituals, and they are not necessarily always for distracting predators.

Countershading

The cryptic coloration of many animals is further enhanced by countershading. Whereas a plain coloured animal is lighter above because most light falls on its upper or dorsal surface, an animal is countershaded by being darker on its upper surface and lighter on its lower or ventral surface. If the natural lighting and the countershading are balanced then an animal appears optically flat and is less conspicuous. Whereas disruptive coloration relies on boundaries between different colours, countershading involves a gradation of colour from

as in nightjars, while in many others a pattern links closed eyes with markings on the face. Such eyes are quite inconspicuous when the animals are resting. Some geckos, birds and fish have irises that are coloured, irregularly patterned or that reflect the colours around them, features which further help to disguise their eyes.

PL. 12.13 Above: The colours and patterns of the thorny devil continue across its eyes. *Photo: W. Farrant*

PL. 12.14 Left: False eyes are common on butterflies and moths. They may frighten predators, or fool them into thinking that the head is at the other end. *Photo: P. Farrant*

top to bottom on an animal's body surface. Countershading is not restricted to plain colours. Patterns can also change gradually, usually from well-defined broad markings above, to thinner, less well-defined markings that merge together below, e.g. zebras' stripes become paler and thinner and leopards' spots become smaller towards the animals' ventral surfaces (pl. 12.17). Many animals that live in open habitats, such as zebras and antelopes, are countershaded. Among vertebrates, many mammals,

birds, reptiles and fish have countershading.

Whereas small fish and other animals that live near the ocean surface are often almost transparent, larger animals must rely on body shape, cryptic coloration and countershading to conceal themselves. Marine fish and other sea creatures such as turtles, tend to have mottled blue or blue-green upper surfaces, silvery sides and white or silver underparts. Thus when they are seen from above they tend to merge in with the dark mass of the water below, but

PL. 12.15 This shingleback lizard flashes its blue tongue when disturbed.
Photo: M. Porteners

PL. 12.16 This moth has a pair of brightly coloured underwings that it can flash to distract predators. *Photo: J. Landy*

PL. 12.17 The leopard's coat is countershaded, i.e. it is darkest on the back and the spots become gradually lighter towards the belly.
Photo: W. Farrant

Fig. 12.1 Countershading and counterlighting in the ocean.

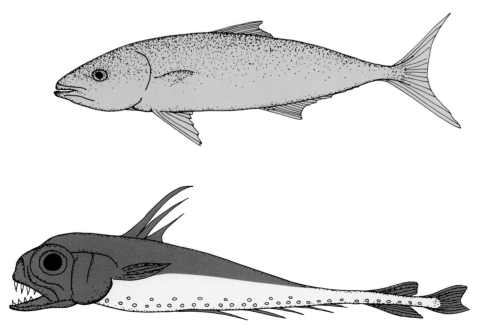

when they are seen from below they merge in with the well-lit surface water. The bioluminescent organs on the under surfaces of deep-sea fish are also thought to have a countershading (or counterlighting) function: when seen from below, these animals are difficult to detect because they merge in with the lighter middle layer of ocean water. The fish light up their ventral photophores when there is light from above and turn them down or off as the light becomes dimmer (fig. 12.1).

Freshwater fish are often countershaded, too, with their upper surfaces mottled in shades of greenish brown so that they blend in well with the colours of river and lake waters. Fish such as the Nile catfish, which swim upside down, have darker colours on their ventral surfaces. Insects that live upside down are shaded in this way too: the caterpillar of the eyed hawkmoth is dark on its ventral surface. As with all countershaded animals, when they are turned upside down from their normal position, the caterpillars become far more conspicuous.

False shadows

No matter how well an animal's coloration matches its background, the distribution of light and shade on its body and its consequent three-dimensionality can render it conspicuous to a predator. An animal's body usually casts shadows and these too can give away its presence, even if it has cryptic coloration. Some animals, e.g. frogs, are coloured in such a way that they have a pattern of false shadows on their bodies, which causes them to appear flatter than they really are (pl. 12.18). Dark and light lines on birds such as bitterns help them to blend in with vertical shadows cast by the vegetation they live in.

Masquerade

One way to match background colours, patterns and textures is to dress up in materials from the background. There are many animals, especially among invertebrates living in both terrestrial and marine environments, that decorate themselves and masquerade in this way (pl. 12.19). Sponge crabs and spider crabs are experts at this type of disguise (pl. 12.20). They use their pincers to cut off pieces of seaweed or sponge, which they then attach to special hooks on their backs. The seaweeds and sponges, as well as other invertebrates such as corals and hydroids, usually continue to grow on the crabs' backs, which are like mobile homes. For animals that depend on moving water to bring nutrients and food, this is not a disadvantage. The only disadvantage is that the crab will probably discard them if they grow too big.

Other animals use materials from their environment in the construction of permanent dwellings, which are either fixed in position or carried around with them. Some caterpillars disguise themselves by attaching pieces of leaves or lichen onto their bristles. Many marine worms live in tubes decorated with pieces of sand and shell, and the only parts of the animal that protrude from the tubes are special food-capturing structures. On the other hand, the twig-like homes of casemoths and the often brightly coloured woollen cases of clothes moth larvae, are carried about by the animals themselves. Even though the animals move about, they are still protected by their homes. When they stop, the homes blend in with the animals' surroundings and make them quite inconspicuous.

There are fewer examples of vertebrates that use masquerade to conceal their presence from predators or prey. The algae and invertebrates that grow on larger marine vertebrates such as sea snakes, turtles, fish and whales, and the symbiotic algae in sloths' fur, no doubt help these animals to blend in with their surroundings. The algae that live in sloths' hair are often specific to particular species of sloth. Birds' nests, which are made from twigs, leaves and grasses, also blend in with the surroundings and help to conceal eggs and young birds. Flatfish and other marine animals that throw sand over themselves are also employing a type of masquerade that conceals them in their surroundings.

COMMUNICATION

While the camouflage coloration of many animals makes them inconspicuous in their environments, the colours of some animals make them extremely conspicuous. Conspicuous coloration in animals usually provides a warning to potential enemies that an animal is poisonous or otherwise harmful and therefore should be avoided. Some other animals gain protection by mimicking the colours of these harmful species. Sudden flashes of conspicuous

PL. 12.18 Spiny-tailed gecko: flattened body and webbed limbs cast little shadow and make the outline harder to recognise. *Photo: R.T. Hoser*

PL. 12.19 Left: This hermit crab's shell is well disguised because of the anemones growing on it. *Photo: R. Berthold*

PL. 12.20 Below: Sponge crabs camouflage themselves by means of masquerade: they attach sessile invertebrates and pieces of seaweed to their shells. *Photo: R. Berthold.*

PL. 12.21 Lionfish: markings extend from the body into the fins, linking these parts visually. *Photo: W. Farrant*

PL. 12.22 The bright red colour of the red-billed hornbill beak probably serves to warn off predators. *Photo: W. Farrant*

PL. 12.23 The puffer fish expands rapidly to further reinforce its warning colours. *Photo: R. Berthold*

Flash coloration

Animals often become conspicuous when they move, either because their cryptic coloration ceases to be effective or because vividly coloured parts that were formerly hidden now become visible. A cryptically coloured bird sitting on a nest becomes visible when it moves away from the nest, but a predator's attention is drawn to the moving adult bird rather than to the still cryptically coloured nest of eggs or young birds. An animal may stay in one place but move some part of its body to reveal vivid colours: in this way the animal is using flash coloration as an element of surprise, to repel predators, distract prey or attract a mate.

Flash coloration is shown by animals in many groups: frogs and toads, e.g. the firebelly toad that shows its coloured belly by suddenly rolling over; fish such as gurnards that spread brightly coloured breast fins; moths and locusts that expose a second underlying pair of brightly coloured front wings or wings with false eyes; snakes, lizards and some birds that show brightly coloured mucus membranes when they open their mouths; birds such as the frigatebird that inflate coloured air sacs; mammals such as the African crested rat, whose stripes become exposed when the hair stands on end; and other mammals that expose brightly coloured skin patches.

This type of flash coloration is often caused by an animal's moods and is often associated with breeding, especially for males. Males use their colours to attract and court females and also to defend females or territory from rival males. If flash coloration is related to an animal's reproductive cycle, the colours may be limited to the breeding season. Though bright colours might make an animal more conspicuous to predators at this time of the year, if the colours are hidden most of the time and if they are directional in

colours may frighten and distract enemies. Conspicuous colours in animals may also help individuals to recognise other members of the same species, especially during the breeding season if there are closely related species living in the same area.

nature and only visible close up, then the risk is not so great.

The directional nature of flash coloration makes it useful for signalling to other members of a species. The white patches underneath the wings of black swans in flight, the bobbing white tails of rabbits, the white rumps of deer, the flicking white tails of leopards and swamphens, the coloured beaks of parent birds and the coloured throats of the young birds, all serve a signalling function.

The types of colours that animals use for flash coloration are often similar to those displayed by animals that have more or less permanent warning colours: red, yellow, orange, black and white are common. However, in the case of flash coloration, the colours serve as a distraction rather than a warning because the animals are usually only bluffing. These animals rely on the element of surprise to frighten or confuse a predator and thus gain enough time to escape. In a similar way, octopuses, squid and cuttlefish may secrete an ink screen as a decoy to momentarily distract or repel an enemy and allow the cephalopod time to escape. Sometimes, however, an animal's warning colours are more permanent, especially when it is not bluffing.

Warning coloration

Some animals have permanently conspicuous colours that warn potential predators of their distastefulness. This is known as aposematism. Warning colours are usually bright and striking, occurring in contrasting combinations and simple patterns that are quickly recognised. The most widespread warning colours are combinations of yellow, orange and black. Combinations of black and white may also warn off crepuscular and nocturnal species: these colours provide the greatest possible contrast and therefore are the most conspicuous colours for low light levels at dawn, dusk and night, when colour vision is not possible. Particular striped or spotted patterns are often shared by a variety of unpalatable species, so that other animals readily recognise them. The behaviour of animals with warning coloration is usually distinctive: they tend to move rather more slowly than similar species without warning coloration.

Animals with warning coloration usually have ways of protecting themselves from enemies. The pink, red, white and black colours of lionfish tend to make them conspicuous as they swim slowly around rocks or coral outcrops in shallow water, but if a lionfish is attacked, it can deliver a deadly poison through the spines of its fins (pl. 12.21). Brightly coloured boxfish can protect themselves with poisonous secretions. Cone shells with brightly coloured patterns lie conspicuously in the sand, but can fire harpoons filled with deadly toxin into an approaching predator. Sea snakes, renowned for the strength of their poisons, have bright or contrasting colours to warn off predators. The yellow and black European salamander has poison glands, as do many other amphibians that have warning coloration. The red cross of the black widow spider and the red markings on some millipedes probably warn off predatory birds.

The bright colours in the claws of fiddler crabs and in toucans' beaks, which are brightly coloured both inside and out, may reinforce and warn predators of the strength of these structures (pls 12.22, 12.23).

Poisonous insects

While warning coloration is widespread among both vertebrate and invertebrate animals generally, it is particularly common in the insect world. Birds avoid red and black ladybirds; they know that yellow and black wasps and bees are liable to sting them, and that brightly coloured caterpillars and butterflies are likely to have an unpleasant taste (pl. 12.24). Sometimes birds appear to have an innate sense about insects with warning colours, and they avoid these insects without any prior contact being necessary. Usually, however, it seems that birds need to learn by their mistakes. Young birds need to sample some of the insects in the population before they learn to avoid them. The insects' stings or poisons may be unpleasant or they may make the bird ill, but they are not usually sufficiently strong to kill young birds. Some insects do not even have to be touched, let alone eaten, to repulse attackers: they squirt unpleasant smelling substances and warn predators in the same manner as skunks.

For warning coloration to be effective, animals within a population cannot be scattered over a wide area: if a potential predator did not come in contact with many individuals then the sampling-learning process would not work as effectively. The process seems to work best for those insects that live close together in large populations, such as monarch butterflies which have poisonous body fluids. The massed colour of monarch butterflies probably helps

PL. 12.24 Red velvet mite: bright colours, especially red or yellow, sometimes with black, often serve to warn predators that an animal is poisonous or distasteful. *Photo: W. Farrant*

PL. 12.25 Leaf insects are conspicuous but unlikely to be recognised because they look like leaves. *R. Berthold*

to deter predators. These butterflies, like many others, derive their poisons from the plants, in this case milkweeds, eaten by the caterpillars. Poisonous plants may also have warning colours: fruits that are yellow and black, or red and black, are often poisonous to birds. In nature there are always exceptions to the rules, so most species that are seemingly protected by warning coloration and poisons or stings, usually have highly specialised enemies for which their defences fail to work. Though most other birds will not attack bees, for instance, these insects form an important part of the diet of rainbow birds.

Confusing colours

Swiftly moving iridescent animals vary in colour as they swim, run or fly. Since they show no colour at all at some viewing angles, it is difficult for a predator to follow them when they move. When an iridescent butterfly alights, it folds its wings vertically; the predator is still looking for the iridescent colours and overlooks the now cryptically coloured undersurface of the butterfly's wings. Some moths flash a brightly coloured pair of underwings when they alight, and immediately cover them up, thus disrupting a predator's search pattern. Groups of fish with very reflective scales, and birds with reflective feathers (e.g. hummingbirds and sunbirds), can also confuse their predators by apparent colour

changes as they turn in and out of sunlight.

Mimesis and mimicry

While many animals are inconspicuous because they blend in with their surroundings, and others are conspicuous because they stand out, another large group of animals protects itself by deception. These animals are said to be involved in mimesis if they resemble and therefore imitate a particular object in their environment. However, if the animals imitate another species of animal, this is known as mimicry. In both cases the animals are mimicking or imitating something else which they resemble in colour, pattern and shape.

Animals often seem to imitate plants or parts of plants, though they may also resemble inanimate objects such as stones. Animals can mimic leaves (including living and healthy leaves, diseased, torn, eaten and dead leaves), flowers, flower parts such as petals, groups of flowers or inflorescences, twigs, branches, bark, lichen and even tree trunks (pls 12.25, 12.26).

There are numerous examples of mimesis in the animal world and insects provide many spectacular examples. Some of the best known are stick insects that resemble twigs, loopers that not only resemble twigs but also sit at the same angle as the twigs around them (pl. 12.27), mantises that look like flower petals, tree hoppers that look like thorns,

PL. 12.26 This grasshopper has the same colours and patterns as the grass and could easily be overlooked. *Photo: J. Landy*

PL. 12.27 Loopers not only resemble the colours of the twigs that they sit on, but they also rest at a similar angle. *Photo: P. Farrant*

grasshoppers (pl. 12.28) that resemble leaves in colour and shape and even have veins and fungal spots, and different colour forms of plant hoppers that alight on a branch and look like unopened buds at the top and older red flowers below. The wings of some butterflies have tattered edges so they look like insect-attacked leaves: a half-eaten leaf does not look appetising to a leaf-eater. Some insects resemble inanimate objects, e.g. Chinese character moths resemble bird droppings (pl. 12.29), and some grasshoppers look like stones. Mimesis is also common among fish, amphibians, reptiles and birds (pls 12.30-12.32).

Muellerian and Batesian mimicry

Mimicry is the type of camouflage in which an animal imitates another animal species which has warning coloration, so that predators associate the colours with unpleasantness and avoid both species. Two types of mimicry are recognised. One is simply a type of aposematism and is known as Muellerian mimicry: two or more different species share the

PL. 12.28 This grasshopper mimics a dead leaf in its coloration and general body shape. *Photo: J. Landy*

PL. 12.29 Right: Caterpillars that look like bird droppings are conspicuous, but not at all attractive to predators. *Photo: R. Berthold*

PL. 12.30 Below: Leatherjacket: some fish that live in seaweeds have similar coloration to the weeds. *Photo: P. Farrant*

same warning colours (and often other characteristics as well) and receive extra protection by being part of a large group. In Muellerian mimicry, both or all species are harmful, e.g. related species of tropical American snakes.

The second type of mimicry, known as Batesian mimicry, involves two or more species with similar warning coloration, only one of which is actually harmful. The harmful animal is known as the model (pl. 12.33) and the animal that imitates it is known as the mimic (pl. 12.34). Often mimics reinforce their imitation of models' colour and behaviour by producing similar sounds and odours.

The viceroy butterfly is a Batesian mimic of the toxic monarch butterfly. There are many examples of Batesian mimicry amongst butterflies and moths and insects generally. Some species of butterfly are sexually dimorphic mimics, i.e. only individuals of one sex, usually the female, mimic the other harmful species, e.g. the black swallow butterfly. The males and females are coloured differently and the males do not receive the added protection that the females obtain through their mimicry.

Both Muellerian and Batesian mimicry are widespread and found in many animal groups, especially invertebrates, but also some fish and birds. Mimicry occurs amongst plant-eating animals as well as carnivorous animals. Even some plants seem to

PL. 12.31 Above: Red Indian fish: some fish are inconspicuous because they resemble floating leaves. *Photo: P. Farrant*

PL. 12.32 Left: Even a large animal like a crocodile can gain some degree of inconspicuousness by resembling a drifting log. *Photo: W. Farrant*

engage in mimicry (see BOX 1), apparently to encourage animals to eat their fruits or visit their flowers: this is in direct contrast to animals which engage in mimicry to avoid being eaten. Some plants appear to mimic animals, while others seem to mimic other plants or, more rarely, inanimate objects.

Having examined how animals use colour for camouflage and communication, the next chapter looks at how humans use the colours of nature.

PL. 12.33 Right: The soft-bodied beetle (*Metriorrhynchus* sp.) has coloration that warns it is harmful. *Photo: J. Landy*

PL. 12.34 Far right: The jewel beetle (*Stigmodera* sp.) is a harmless mimic of the harmful soft-bodied beetle (*Metriorrhynchus* sp.). *Photo: J. Landy*

CAMOUFLAGE AND COMMUNICATION IN PLANTS

Plants are rarely cryptically coloured. Their leaves are almost always green (or sometimes red) and they are exposed to sunlight in order to photosynthesise. The most obvious examples of cryptic coloration in plants are those of immature flowers and fruits. Before the pollen is ready to be released by the anthers of a flower, the flower is usually closed and protected by its outermost whorl of green sepals. Green buds are far less conspicuous to hungry animals than colourful petals that indicate when the reproductive structures are mature. Green buds blend in with foliage. Some plants even produce green flowers, which have the advantage of attracting only specialist pollinators (usually birds) that are adapted to searching for them.

Immature fruits are usually green and inconspicuous against green foliage. Fruit-eating animals are not attracted to them at this stage, and in fact animals generally avoid eating green fruit because it can be unpalatable or even poisonous. Immature flowers and fruits which are inconspicuously coloured usually become brightly coloured and conspicuous when mature.

When several plant species growing together have flowers of a similar colour that are relatively unspecialised and attract a range of insects, this can be thought of as a type of Muellerian mimicry that enhances the individual species' chances of pollination. This also applies to plants visited by migratory birds: migratory hummingbirds, for instance, seem to be attracted to different plant species that occur along their migratory path in North America, and these plants usually have red bell-shaped flowers. Non-migratory hummingbirds in Central America, however, are more likely to visit flowers of several different colours.

Colour mimics

Presumed examples of Batesian mimicry amongst plants include flowers with similar coloration to those of a nearby species: the flowers of the mimic attract pollinators that visit the model, but only the models provide any reward. Some orchids appear to mimic legume flowers in this way. The female flowers of tropical gourd vines mimic the male flowers: butterflies visit the male flowers for their pollen but the female flowers have nothing to offer them. In the same way, some plants have fruits or seeds that do not contain any reward, but which are eaten and dispersed by birds largely because they resemble the nutritious fruits or seeds of another nearby species. Some plants have non-toxic leaves that are similar in colour and shape to the toxic leaves of nearby non-related species: mimicking the toxic species helps to protect the plant from leaf-eating insects. Some plants even have protuberances on their leaf surfaces that are similar in colour to insect eggs and these spots probably deter other insects from laying their eggs on the 'occupied' leaves. The brownish red pitchers of carnivorous pitcher plants even seem to mimic the colours of rotting meat and this may help to attract insects and other prey.

Sometimes plants mimic inanimate objects. The stone plants of southern Africa each consist of only two flat-topped succulent leaves that are similar in colour to the brown, grey and whitish stones around them. Animals searching for moisture would probably overlook stone plants. The most bizarre occurrences of mimicry in plants, however, are the flying duck orchids that have flowers which are similar in colour, shape, pattern (and odour) to the female of particular bees or wasps. The males are attracted to, and attempt to mate with the flower, and in so doing they accidentally pick up pollen which they may subsequently transfer to another plant (pl. 12.35).

PL. 12.35 Some orchids imitate female insects in order to attract male insects; the males attempt to mate with the flower and inadvertently pick up pollen and transfer it to another flower in the process. *Photo: W.H. King*

CHAPTER 13

COLOUR, NATURE AND HUMANS

PL. 13.11 Left: Many plants like coleus are grown for their colourful foliage.
Photo: R. Berthold

Colour is important in practically every field of human endeavour, including our observation of the natural world, and our recording of it by means of colour photography (see BOX 1). For centuries people have brought the colours of nature into their lives in some way. In gardening, agriculture, the production of textiles and other artefacts, the colours of nature have been observed, enjoyed, borrowed, developed and extended until we now have immensely complex systems for classifying and accurately describing colours. Nowhere is the human fascination with colour more apparent than in the pursuit of paradise on earth, gardening.

COLOUR IN THE GARDEN

For thousands of years, civilisations have created gardens by taking plants out of their natural habitats and growing, selecting and breeding them. The ancient Egyptians had formal gardens with highly prized flowers, fruit trees and exotic plant collections brought back from expeditions into Africa. The Babylonians, Chinese, ancient Greeks and Romans all had gardens for pleasure, food and medicines. Medieval gardens contained methodically arranged crops and medicinal plants, so the gardens that developed for pleasure were quite formal, often symmetrical, with topiary shrubs and heraldic colours: gold, silver, purple, green, black, blue and

red. Later parterre gardens used blocks of vivid colour like those still used today in council gardens and parks. A most important impact on the use of colour in the garden was made by Gertrude Jekyll (1843-1932), an English painter and horticulturist. Jekyll used flowers and foliage to create gardens in which colour harmonies were far more important than colour contrasts. Her garden borders, in which she used artists' aerial perspective (see below), were designed so any part would be colourful for several months of the year; they showed a mastery of horticulture combined with aesthetics.

Many of Jekyll's ideas are still used by gardeners who prefer subtle colour harmonies. However, many other gardeners like to use contrasting colours that are novel and exciting. Collections of plants from remote parts of the world continue to provide exotic colours and forms. Plant collections reached a peak last century when conservatories were built in Europe to house tropical plants. That era of plant collecting saw the establishment of university and botanic gardens in the western world. With an increasing range of natural plant material to work with, plant breeders are continuing to produce plants with more vivid flower and foliage colours. With hybridising, these colours are becoming more removed from colours found in nature (pls 13.1-13.3). Despite this, gardening has become one of the most popular hobbies around the world.

A wheel of colour

In order to understand the fundamental concepts behind colour in modern gardens, we need to look at the colour wheel, a concept devised by Michel Chevreuil of the French Gobelin Tapestry factory and published in 1854. The colour wheel is a circular arrangement of colours in their spectral sequence which demonstrates harmonic relationships. It shows the primary pigment colours (red, blue and yellow), the secondary colours (purple, orange and green — obtained by mixing two primary colours), and the

PL. 13.1 Vivid flower colours are eagerly sought after by gardeners, so breeding for colour is a big business.
Photo: P. Farrant

PL. 13.2 Right: Orchid enthusiasts are constantly striving to improve the colours, especially of yellow and green flowers. *Photo: P. Farrant*

PL. 13.3 Far right: Vivid foliage colours, as well as vivid flower colours, have a ready market amongst gardeners.
Photo: P. Farrant

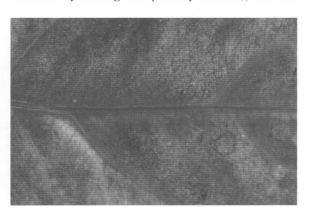

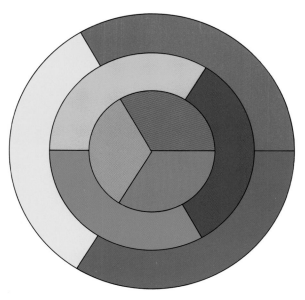

Fig. 13.1 The colour wheel.

tertiary colours (russet, olive and citrine — made from a mixture of two secondary colours) (fig. 13.1).

A pure spectral colour, which does not contain any white, grey or black, is known as a hue, its intensity or degree of saturation is termed its chroma, and its degree of lightness or darkness is known as its value. A colour that is not at full intensity is known as a tone. The value of a colour can be changed by adding black or white to a hue: shades are obtained by adding increasing amounts of black, and tints are obtained by adding increasing amounts of white (fig. 13.2). The millions of permutations of these factors result in an enormous range of colours.

Analogous colours are those that share a common hue, such as orange and violet (fig. 13.3), while complementary colours are those directly opposite each other on the colour wheel (fig. 13.4). Contrasting colours, which include complementary colours, are those which do not share a common hue. Complementary colours intensify each other, and may harmonise if they are similar in tone, just as a red rose stands out against green leaves (pl. 13.4). This effect is enhanced by colour contrast and

the eye's ability to produce an after-image: both of these are psychological sensations of the human brain that produce a strong complementary colour to the one being observed.

The interpretation of colours by an observer has some interesting psychological aspects. Humans have an ability called colour constancy which allows us to see objects as the same colour even though their actual colour changes from time to time. Colours can affect physiological functions such as heart rate, muscular tension, breathing and even reproduction. Colours also have emotional effects and we have inherited a number of associations between colours, concepts and emotions. White has always been associated with purity and goodness, black with darkness, fear and evil, blue with serenity and depression, green with freshness and youth, and red with blood and strength.

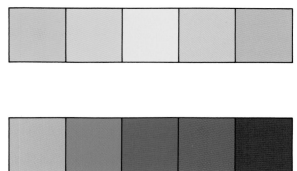

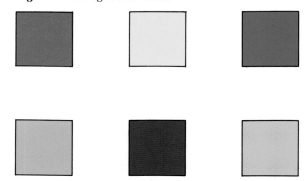

Fig. 13.3 Analagous colours.

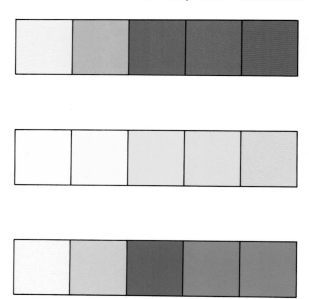

Fig. 13.2 Tints and shades.

Fig. 13.4 Complementary colours.

PL. 13.4 Complementary colours, like red and green, do not share a common hue, but will harmonise if they are similar in tone. *Photo: P. Farrant*

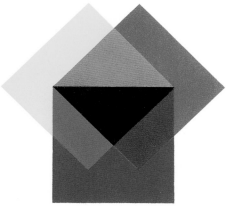

Fig. 13.5
Additive primaries (physical primaries of light) mix to give white (left), whereas the subtractive primaries (chemical primaries of pigments) mix to give black (right).

PL. 13.5 Below right: Warm coloured yellow-green plants tend to appear closer than they really are. Hiroshima, Japan. *Photo: P. Farrant*

PL. 13.6 Below : Cool colours give the illusion of distance. Butchart Gardens, Vancouver Island. *Photo: J. Lush*

Subtractive and additive primaries

The colour wheel demonstrates the chemical nature of colour. The three primary pigment colours are said to be subtractive because a mixture of the three primaries filters all wavelengths of white light to produce black; a mixture of any two is always darker than either component. While the subtractive (or pigment) primaries are produced by pigments, the so-called additive (or physical) primaries are produced by light (fig. 13.5). The three primary colours of light (red, green and blue) are said to be additive because a mixture of these three differently coloured wavelengths of light produces white light. Any two colours of light that produce white when they are mixed together are called complementary colours: cyan is the complementary of red, magenta is the complementary of green, and yellow is the complementary of blue.

These relationships between colours on the colour wheel are often used to lay down guidelines on the design of a colour scheme for a garden. The three primary colours, red, yellow and blue, should not be used together or the effect will be jarring; if two are used together, then the intervening secondary colour should be used as well. Two secondary colours will harmonise if they contain a primary in common, e.g. orange and purple, which have red in common. Analogous colours used together, such as pinks and mauves, yellows and oranges, will blend and harmonise. Contrasting colours will harmonise if they are alike in intensity and tone, like the red rose against green leaves. Some plants already have colour schemes like these in their flowers! In some gardens a compromise is reached where a basically harmonious scheme of analogous colours contains accents of complementary or even more dramatic contrasting colours.

Distant blues

Warm colours such as red, orange and yellow are said to be advancing colours because, when placed beside cool colours, they appear closer and larger in area than they really are. The cool or receding colours will appear further away and smaller in area. Our eyes naturally focus upon yellow-green, which is the most conspicuous colour of the spectrum for human eyes (pl. 13.5). To look at reds and blues at the two ends of the spectrum, we need to adjust the focus of our eyes slightly, closer for reds and further away for blues. The fact that blues seem to recede is probably further enhanced by our association of distance with blue in the landscape, an effect due to Rayleigh scattering.

The illusion of distance given by cool colours is known by artists as aerial perspective and can be put to good use in the garden (pl. 13.6). Garden beds can appear deeper if they are planted with bright, strong, warm colours at the front, then with increasingly cooler and lighter colours behind. Or, if more space is available, drifts of warm then cool colours, repeated several times, will tend to lead the eye off into the distance. The effect can be enhanced further if plant height increases with distance. Tall blue spruces and evergreens at the far border of a garden will tend to make it look larger. On the other hand, yellow-green spruces and larches will draw the eye inward and a garden with only warm colours will give the eye no means of escape.

The blueness of shadows is another atmospheric effect caused by Rayleigh scattering, and must also be considered when planning a colour scheme for the garden. Cool colours will be hardly noticeable in shadows, whereas warm, bright colours will stand out.

Colour harmonies and colour clash

As in all aspects of design, when planning a garden simplicity often gives the best results. Gertrude Jekyll was a strong advocate of single-colour gardens or garden beds. Though a single colour may sound monotonous, we need only think of the huge variety of foliage greens to realise that single colour schemes can really contain a multitude of different varieties of that colour. Nonetheless, many gardeners would add an accent colour for a more dramatic effect. Two-colour gardens, such as green and white, blue and grey, green and gold and so on, can also be quite stunning.

Clashing colours in a garden can more often than not be solved by separating the magenta shades of red (bluish reds) from the scarlet shades of red (orange-reds). The bluish reds will go well with white or pale blue. Though the orange-reds present

PL. 13.7 Above: Colourful display, Butchart Gardens, Vancouver Island. *Photo: J. Lush*

PL. 13.8 Left: Bright colours in blocks are often used in parks. *Photo: P. Farrant*

PL. 13.10 Below left: Foliage plants provide the colours for this lawn planting. *Photo: P. Farrant*

PL. 13.9 Below: Massed tulips. *Photo: R.J. King*

the most problems because they tend to appear hard against green foliage, they can be relieved somewhat if combined with white, pale yellow or pale orange. In a similar way, bright oranges can be relieved with white or even light blue. Purples and mauves can also be a problem, as they look harmonious with silver, but not with gold or golden red. Unlike purple, pure blue seems to go well with both silver and gold.

Colours in a garden change with the seasons and this needs to be taken into account during the planning process. A garden can be designed for a single spectacular flowering event once a year, in different beds or over the whole garden. Alternatively, colour can be provided by flowers that bloom at various times, so the garden has some colour throughout the year, or a different colour scheme for each season. Strong colours tend to have most impact if they are confined to a short period or a small area of the garden (pl. 13.7). If they are planted densely over large areas, as in council gardens and parks (pls 13.8, 13.9) then the impact is also great but the effect is completely artificial: intense colour in nature usually covers a very small area or if it covers a larger area, then it is modified by less intense background colours.

Foliage colours

Foliage provides background colour at times when flowers or fruits are out and often for the rest of the year when they are not. Many plants are grown specially for their colourful foliage and have flowers that are either dull or inconspicuous. Foliage plants provide an enormous range of greens in the garden, as well as many of the whites, silvers, greys, pinks, purples, reds and yellows (pls 13.10, 13.11). Warm foliage colours can make a garden feel warmer while cool coloured foliage can relieve the impact of hot coloured flowers, those colours between red and yellow on the colour wheel, which do not contain any blue. Dark foliage tends to make a garden feel enclosed, whereas lively foliage colours tend to make

the garden feel more open. Variegated foliage can introduce contrast and variety to a garden (pl. 13.12). So, too, can brightly coloured fruits that follow flowers, and many garden plants are grown for their attractive autumn berries (pl. 13.13).

The different colours of foliage are further enhanced by differences in leaf texture. Differently textured leaves, ranging from the metallic and the smooth, glossy, dark green leaves of tropical species to the thin, matt, paler leaves of deciduous trees, to the waxy, blue-green leaves and the hairy or felted grey leaves of species from dry sunny regions, all reflect sunlight in different ways.

PL. 13.12 Right: Plants with variegated foliage are popular for gardens. Many families of plants contain species that produce variegated foliage.
Photo: P. Farrant

PL. 13.13 Autumn berries: many plants are grown in the garden for the colours of their fruits.
Photo: P. Farrant

The direction and amount of light should be considered when planting particular species in a garden. For instance, reds and yellows appear richer in the reddish yellow light of early morning and at sunset. Blue flowers will be lost in shadows whereas strong colours can be used together in the shade. Yellow and white flowers stand out best in the shade and at night. Bright colours should be used in gardens in tropical areas. While soft colours tend to appear dull in the strong light of the tropics, bright colours may appear garish in temperate areas. Pastels, those lighter reds and blue-reds tinted with white or grey, are better suited to gardens in temperate regions where the atmosphere is often misty and the light muted and soft.

Breeding for colour

Colour is one of the characteristics of plants and animals that breeders are continually improving or extending. While collections of plant species from around the world have provided much raw material for breeders, individual plants of common species, which have unusual characteristics that might lessen their chances of survival in the wild, are also collected, cared for under artificial conditions and used for breeding. White-flowered plants of species that are normally coloured, for instance, may be useful in breeding if they have white pigments: these pigments often function as co-pigments, brightening other colours. Plants with variegated leaves that frequently do not have sufficient chlorophyll to survive in nature, are also kept for their novelty value. As well as selecting unusual mutant plants from the wild, plant breeders also induce mutations, select unusual characteristics and combine them with other plant features. With modern genetic engineering techniques, plant and animal breeders may soon be able to insert their choice of genetic material into the make-up of plants and animals.

The colours of most popular flowers are often the result of hundreds of years of selection and hybridising (pls 13.14-13.17). Modern hyacinths have been bred in a variety of colours from a single original blue species from the Middle East. Indeed, cut flowers in novel colours are just as popular today: Australian breeders are attempting to develop a white or pale pink Sturt's desert pea for the Japanese market.

COLOUR IN OUR DAILY LIVES

The quality and ripeness of agricultural and food products such as flour, fruits, oil, sugar, spices, wool and so on are often judged by their colours. Raw

PL. 13.14 Above: Roses are probably the most popular garden flowers. Roses were grown by the Moors in Spain and in monasteries throughout Europe, and the Crusaders introduced new roses from the East. Old-fashioned roses, which tend to flower only once a year, are mostly pink or white. These were the only colours available in Europe until crimson and pale yellows were introduced from China at the end of the eighteenth century.
Photo: P. Farrant

PL. 13.15 Left: Rich yellows, derived from the Austrian briar rose, were not successfully incorporated into roses until the end of the 19th century.
Photo: W. Farrant

PL. 13.16 Above: It was only comparatively recently that the orange-red colour of pelargonidin was introduced to roses. Modern roses have incorporated all these colours, and more, so that there is a wide range of colours available today, including striped and multicoloured varieties.
Photo: P. Farrant

PL. 13.17 Roses are included in the never-ending quest for novel flower colours. They have no relatives with blue genes, so breeding a true blue has proved difficult. *Photo: P. Farrant*

PL. 13.18 Many attractively coloured fruits, like these blueberries, owe their colours to anthocyanin pigments. *Photo: R.J. King*

PL. 13.19 Many different colours of capsicums and chillies are available due to selection and breeding: red coloration is caused by carotenoids. *Photo: R. Berthold*

PL. 13.21 Right: Leaves that are diseased or deficient in one or more mineral elements tend to be blotchy or have abnormal coloration. *Photo: P. Farrant*

foods derive their colours from the pigments they contain (pl. 13.18). These colours are attractive to humans in the same way that the plants' ancestors would have been attractive to the animals that ate and dispersed them in the wild: e.g. grapes, cherries, plums and blackberries, which are all coloured by anthocyanins, and peppers (chillies and capsicums) coloured by carotenoids (pl. 13.19). Many have been selected and bred with colours that are attractive to humans, e.g. red cabbage and the various, differently coloured cauliflowers.

We rely on colour. The natural changes in colour as a fruit or vegetable ripens tell us when it is at its peak for eating (pl. 13.20). Fruits and vegetables change colour again after they have passed through the stage of peak ripeness. Many of the changes in colour during storage and processing of foods are caused by chemical changes, usually oxidations, which also result in changes of flavour and texture and make the foods far less attractive, and sometimes poisonous.

Raw foods also change colour when they are cooked due to degradation of the natural plant and animal pigments, and we use these colour changes to judge whether food is cooked. Since we have come to rely on colour as an indication of quality, the colours of many processed products are nowadays enhanced by added food colorants. Similarly, food colours may be altered to make them more attractive, e.g. white rice, white bread and white sugar. The various food spoilage bacteria and fungi produce an enormous range of vividly coloured spots and patches on foods if the conditions are suitable.

Just as we judge agricultural produce by colour, farmers and gardeners use leaf colour as a diagnostic tool in maintaining the health of their plants. Although mineral deficiencies produce different coloration in different species, leaves that turn white, yellow, brown or red, especially in blotches or between the veins, are likely to be deficient in one or more mineral elements (pl. 13.21).

PL. 13.20 We judge the ripeness of many fruits and vegetables by their colour. *Photo: R.J. King*

BOX 1

Recording the Colours of Nature

The camera records colours more accurately than the human eye because the latter is influenced by the brain, which can correct and compensate. Some modern colour films are even designed to make the more popular colours appear brighter than they really are. Modern colour photography is based on a method whereby three differently coloured images are recorded (in black-and-white) and combined to give a final image.

Colour reversal films

With colour slide or transparency films, three emulsions are coated one above the other on a film backing, the whole being known as a tripack. The emulsions are basically like black-and-white film, but each is sensitive to and absorbs only one colour: red, green or blue, and allows the other two to pass through (fig. 13.6).

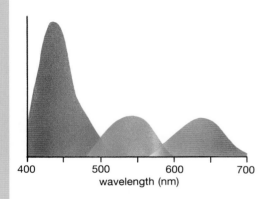

Fig. 13.6 Absorption by the three light-sensitive pigments in colour film.

Three separate images are formed simultaneously when the film is exposed, so that when the film is processed these become three separate negatives. The film is then developed a second time, and the undeveloped emulsions provide positive images. Because of this second development, it is known as a reversal process. During the second development, the developer combines with couplers to produce coloured dyes. The dyes that are formed are cyan, magenta and yellow. When all chemicals except the dyes are washed from the film, the three differently coloured images (cyan, magenta and yellow) combine to give the final fully coloured image on the slide (fig. 13.7).

Colour negative films

Colour negative films, which are used for making colour prints on paper, have the same basic

components as colour slide films. However, they are only developed once, and so the final cyan, magenta and yellow images are complementary to the original reds, greens and blues and they are negatives rather than positives (fig. 13.8). As well, the dyes are formed during the first and only development. Colour negative films can have more than ten different layers, though they usually have at least a blue-sensitive emulsion, a yellow filter, a green-sensitive emulsion and a red-sensitive emulsion. The yellow filter causes negatives to appear yellowish orange and, together with the extra thickness of the overall product, this makes reproduction somewhat less sharp than with colour transparency film. In general, colour prints do not have as long a lifespan as colour transparencies.

Problems with colour matching

It is not possible to obtain perfect colour rendition in colour photographs, for several reasons. First, the dyes or pigments in the subject and in the film do not match, e.g. the pigments in fabrics differ from the dyes in films. Second, brightness is lost, e.g. fabrics are usually duller in photographs. Third, film is sensitive to reflected colours that we do not perceive because of colour constancy; a white garment may be slightly blue because of reflection from a blue sky. Fourth, film is sensitive to reflected colours in the far-red part of the spectrum, which we cannot perceive; this may cause a blue subject to appear pink in a photograph. For critical colour matching it is necessary to include on the film a photograph of a colour control reference card film; a professional photographic laboratory can match the colours as accurately as possible, though the colour match will never be perfect.

Colour films are designed for reproducing the colours seen in full sunlight in the middle of the day. Hence we cannot expect the colour balance to be perfect at other times.

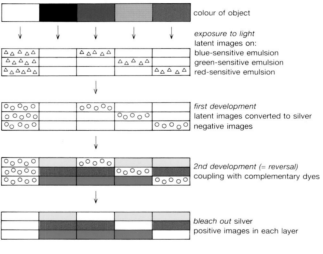

Fig. 13.7 Colour reversal process.

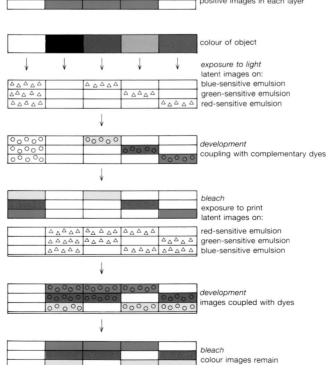

Fig. 13.8 Colour negative process.

Natural pigments and dyes

Early civilisations first used natural pigments for body painting and clothing: white came from chalk or gypsum; black from charcoal and manganese oxide; green from malachite, terreverte, chrysocolla and copper verdigris; blue from lapis lazuli, ultramarine and compounded copper salts; browns and reds from realgar, red ochre, iron oxide and clay; and yellow from orpiment, yellow ochre, iron oxide and various coloured clays and lime. Many of these pigments have since been replaced with synthetic ones.

These would have been the same pigments used for artwork (pls 13.22, 13.23) and decoration of ceramics. When they were applied to fabrics, however, the pigment particles would have been dislodged easily from the fibres, by washing or even handling the fabrics. Dyes, on the other hand, discovered by early people during the Bronze Age, are coloured substances applied in solution to a fabric, so that the colouring matter adheres more strongly to the cloth fibres.

The earliest dyes were probably organic, made by extracting substances from brightly coloured flowers or animals in a watery solution. Such a solution applied to cloth would probably have washed out fairly readily in the same way that pigments did. How the important ingredient for fixing a dye more or less permanently to cloth was discovered is not known, but it was either a very fortunate or a very ingenious discovery. This important step in the dyeing process is called mordanting and it involves pretreating the cloth to be dyed with a mordant such as alum (aluminium hydroxide) or other metal salts. When the dye is applied to the pretreated fabric, the mordant causes it to become insoluble and adhere to the fibres of the fabric.

In the red

Mordanting was probably first used with madder, to produce a red dye. The way in which early people discovered dyes such as madder is as intriguing as how they discovered mordants: the colour of most early dyes was not related to the colour of the plants and only became apparent after considerable treatment of the raw plant material. The dye substance produced from the dried ground roots of madder is a glucoside that is hydrolysed to alizarin when the dried ground root material is fermented. Whereas madder itself is a mixture of various substances, alizarin is a single substance. Turkey Red is a madder dye, which, depending on the type of mordant used, can produce a variety of red, orange and violet colours. Today madder is cultivated in the Middle East and southern France, and the dye is used to produce a particular red watercolour paint.

Though madder is probably the most important red dye from plants, many others are used in various parts of the world, e.g. haematoxylin from the Mexican logwood tree, brazilien from sappanwood, annatto, henna, and safflower. The dye litmus, prepared from lichens, is used as an indicator because its colour varies from rose red through purple to blue depending on conditions of acidity or alkalinity. Three of the four important dyes derived from animals are red and they all are anthraquinones from scale insects (family Coccidae): lac, kermes and cochineal. Cochineal, the most brilliant of the three dyes, comes from the dried bodies of female cochineal insects, which feed on various Central and South American cacti. This dye has many uses in cosmetics, watercolours, microscopy and food colouring.

The other important natural dye derived from animals is Tyrian purple, a purple dye secreted by certain species of mollusc. Each animal produces such a tiny amount of the precursor, however, that thousands of animals were used by the Phoenicians for dyeing cloth, and purple coloured robes were restricted to the aristocracy in Rome, with only the Emperor having an entirely purple outfit.

Blue and yellow dyes

It is also fascinating to imagine how early people discovered the blue dye indigo. Whole plants of indigo or the European woad are fermented for about a week, during which the glucoside indican, contained in the leaves, is hydrolysed to a yellow material, indoxyl. The indoxyl is drained and beaten, oxidising in the air to produce indigo. Like madder, indigo is applied to cloth pretreated with a mordant. Indigo dyes cloth blue and with repeated dyeing gives blue-black and eventually black. Used in conjunction with yellow fabric (natural yellow wool or fabric dyed yellow), a green colour is obtained. The best indigo comes from species of *Indigofera*, as the European woad produces rather variable results. Another deep blue-black dye called xagua, used by Amazon Indians for dyeing and body painting, is derived from the marmalade box tree, the green fruits of which produce a juice that oxidises in air to a blue-black colour.

Although many plants provided yellow dyes in early times, most yellow dyes were fugitive because of their instability in light. The surest way was to use yellow wool. Early yellow dyes came from safflower, saffron, weld, turmeric, dyers' broom and the yellow dye quercetin came from vine leaves and dyers' chamomile. The yellow dye used for the silk robes of Buddhist monks in south-east Asia and India is gamboge, derived from the resin of the south-east Asian tree *Garcinia hanburyi* by tapping its cut bark. The colour fades in sunlight. Different mordants can be used to give various yellow dyes tints of yellow, gold and brown.

Browns and blacks

Brown and black dyes were derived from tannins extracted from bark (especially oak) and from walnut shells. Whereas tree bark extracts need a mordant like other dyes, the brown dye from walnuts is one of the few direct plant dyes that does not need a mordant.

Tannins, yellow to brown substances derived from wood and bark, have been used for a long time for tanning, the process that renders leather impervious to water. The bark and wood of particular species of tree, such as the American red quebracho and the Australian black wattle, yield especially large concentrations of tannins. Tannins from the autumn leaves of some species of sumac are used to colour the fine leathers used to bind books, and tannins from bark, wood, fruits and leaves of many other species are also used commercially.

In recent years there has been a resurgence of interest in home-made artefacts and many home dyers are experimenting with plants and discovering new dyes: the colours of these are usually more delicate than the vivid colours discovered earlier.

WHAT'S IN A NAME?

Ancient civilisations did not have the range of colours that are available to us today from artificial dyes and pigments and so early people did not have as large a vocabulary of colour words as we have. Apart from the enormous range of colours, the subjectiveness of how individuals perceive colour presents problems in its measurement and specification. Various systems have been devised for measuring and specifying colours.

The Munsell system is an American system of defining colours in terms of their hue, saturation and brightness. Soil colour is described using this system. The ISCC-NBS (Inter-Society Colour Council — National Bureau of Standards) system also divides colours on the basis of hue, saturation and brightness. In the ICI (International Commission on Illumination) system of scientific measurement and specification of colour, colours are defined in terms of three primaries (red, green and blue) and three light sources (daylight, sunlight, incandescent). The P.M. (Perry Marthin) system is a Swedish system in which each colour is defined by its height of tone and its reflection factor. The C.I.E. (Commission Internationale de l'Eclairage) Colour Triangle is a system in which each colour is defined by co-ordinates in a triangle according to its black body colour temperature; white lies at the centre of the triangle.

Precise measurement of colours in plants and animals is even more difficult because of the variation inherent in the natural world. Rarely is a petal, a hair or a feather even in colour or texture. Robert Ridgway in 1912 devised a reference for naturalists that contained far too many colours (1 115) to be workable. Ridgway's reference was replaced in 1974 by Frank Smithe's *Naturalist's Colour Guide*, a more useable handbook that contains swatches of 86 colours as well as a text that cross-references these colours with those of other systems.

Plants' colours are widely used by botanists and gardeners in the identification of different species and cultivars. Amongst both plants and animals there are many thousands of species whose names incorporate some Greek or Latin colour words, such as *melas* (= black or dark), *flavum* (= yellow) and *leukos* (= white). Many words in the vocabulary of colour are derived from plants and other coloured objects in nature: e.g. apricot, gold, violet, lavender and lilac. Whereas early people had relatively few words to describe colours, today in many fields we often need to specify colours exactly from the multitude of synthetic dyes and pigments available.

The Royal Horticultural Society (London) provides a colour chart to which a plant's colour can be matched and then described in a standard way. The chart, reprinted in 1966, includes 800 separate colour patches arranged in a systematic order. Other more recent publications specify colours in terms of Munsell co-ordinates: an azalea might have vivid yellowish pink flowers with vivid yellow-orange blotch, and the corresponding Munsell number is given for each. Specifying plant colours by means of such a system is far more accurate than relying upon colour photographs in books and catalogues: these tend to be rather inaccurate, especially in the cyan (blue-green) range.

IN SUMMARY

Colour has a crucial role on our planet. Colour for camouflage, communication or attractiveness plays a part in the survival of every species of plant and animal, each beautifully adapted to the colours of its own habitat.

An understanding of colour in the solar system, in Earth's atmosphere and on the planet itself, can provide us with a key to understanding the mysteries of our extraordinary universe.

PL. 13.24 Tree frog *(Litoria Chloris)*. Photo: R. T. Hoser

GLOSSARY OF TERMS

absorption: conversion of light energy into heat by colorants

absorption spectrum: colours (wavelengths) of light absorbed; dark lines on a continuous background where atoms have absorbed certain wavelengths

accessory pigment: pigment that helps chlorophyll by harvesting some light for photosynthesis, but which cannot drive photosynthesis on its own

accommodation: change of focus of the eye

achromatic lens: lens free from colours caused by splitting of white light

actinolite: bright green crystalline mineral

action spectrum: colours (wavelengths) of light that are active in promoting a particular process

adaptation: characteristic which improves chances of survival and ultimately of leaving descendents

additive primary colours: primary colours of light: red, green and blue

aerial perspective: illusion of distance due to cool colours

aerosol: group of small particles floating in the air

afterglow: coloured glow in the western sky after the sun has set

after-image: illusion of an image just seen

agamid: lizard in the family Agamidae

agate: precious stone with colours in stripes or bands, or blended

air sac: thin-walled air-filled extension of bird lung

albedo: ratio of radiation reflected by a non-luminous body to the amount incident upon it

albinism: lacking development of skin pigments

albino: animal or plant without normal pigmentation

Alexander's dark band: dark region of sky between primary and secondary rainbows

algae: simple non-vascular photosynthetic organisms

algal bloom: concentration of planktonic algae usually producing a discoloration of water

alizarin: red pigment from madder root

alleles: (allelomorphs) different forms of a gene, occupying the same relative position on chromosomes

alloy: mixture of metals

altostratus: high sheet-like cloud

alum: whitish transparent mineral salt (sulfate of aluminium) used as a mordant for pre-treating fabric to be dyed

amber: gem, fossil resin or gum produced by coniferous trees

ammonia: colourless gas with pungent smell, common in atmospheres of outer planets

amphibians: group of vertebrates containing frogs, toads, newts and salamanders

anaerobic: living in absence of free oxygen

analogous colours: colours that share a common hue

angiosperm: flowering plant

annatto: pigment from fleshy pulp around seeds of *Bixa orellana*

anther: terminal part of a stamen, containing pollen

anthocyanin: water-soluble flavonoid pigment occurring in plant vacuoles and causing many of the red, purple and blue colours of plants

anthoxanthin: cream or yellow plant pigment, a type of flavonoid

anthraquinone: animal pigment, usually red

aperture: opening through which light enters a camera

aposematism: warning coloration

aril: brightly coloured fleshy edible outgrowth of a seed

ashen light: see *earthshine*

astacin: oxidised product of the carotenoid astaxanthin

asteroid belt: region between Mars and Jupiter containing asteroids

asteroids: group of objects orbiting the sun between Mars and Jupiter

astoxanthin: carotenoprotein, e.g. in crustaceans

astronomy: the study of the stars and planets and other objects in space

atmosphere: the layer of gases which surrounds a planet or star: Earth's atmosphere is air

atom: the smallest unit of a chemical element

atomic number: number of protons or electrons in an atom

augite: dark greenish black mineral containing alumina

aureole: disc of light bordering an object

aurora: coloured light emission in the sky when electrically charged particles interact with air

aurora australis: aurora in southern hemisphere

aurora borealis: aurora in northern hemisphere

auroral zone (auroral oval): ring of Earth's surface approximately 20° south or north of the poles where auroral activity is greatest

axis: an imaginary straight line from the top to the bottom of e.g. a spinning object such as Earth

azurite: copper-containing blue mineral

backscattering: scattering of radiation in reverse direction

bacteria: microscopic organisms, simpler than plants and animals

barb: lateral branch from the shaft of a feather

barbule: lateral branch from the barb of a feather

bark: protective tissue of dead cells on the outside of stems and roots of woody plants

basalt: fine-grained igneous rock, black or greenish black, rich in iron, magnesium and calcium

Batesian mimicry: type of mimicry in which one of two species is harmful and has warning coloration and the other is harmless but gains protection by having the same coloration

bauxite: mineral containing varying proportions of alumina, the main commercial source of aluminium

bedrock: layer of rock underlying horizons or layers of soil

bee purple: mixture of ultraviolet and yellow, seen by bees as a separate colour in the same way that we see purple as a separate colour

beryl: transparent precious stone; known as emerald when chromium is present

beta-carotene: orange carotenoid pigment found in autumn leaves; an accessory pigment for photosynthesis

betacyanins: group of red, purple and blue water-soluble pigments found in only a few plants

bilateral symmetry: symmetry about one axis

bilin: yellow animal pigment

bilirubin: yellow bilin pigment that causes the colour of human bile

biliverdin: green bilin pigment that occurs in the gall bladders of frogs and birds

binocular vision: vision in which the image of an object falls on the retinas of both eyes, giving three-dimensionality

bioluminescence: light emission by living organisms

biome: main ecological community of plants and animals extending over large natural region

bipolar cell: double-ended nerve cell

bivalve mollusc: animal with a shell in two parts hinged together, e.g. oyster

black: colour perceived if an object absorbs or transmits all wavelengths of white light

black body colour: colour of light or other radiation of a hypothetical perfect absorber and radiator at a given temperature

black hole: the remains of a star, invisible because it has such strong gravity that it even sucks in light

black light: ultraviolet radiation

blackwater river: river with black or dark brown water due to large amount of undecomposed organic matter from surrounding well-vegetated catchment

blue: colour perceived when an object reflects high energy, short wavelength light

blue haze: blue colour of distant vegetated mountains due to scattering of sunlight by molecules of plant origin in the atmosphere

blue moon: blue coloured moon due to scattering of moonlight by particles of a particular size, like volcanic dust, high in the atmosphere

bond: region between atoms of a molecule in which electrons are shared

bonellin: green pigment occurring only in some worms

bract: specialised leaf enclosing a flower or inflorescence

brain: anterior part of central nervous system of most bilaterally symmetrical animals

brazilien: purplish red dye from the wood of the sapponwood tree

Brochenspectre: see *glory*

brown dwarf: dim star with low mass, emitting mainly infra-red radiation

brown haze: pollution haze coloured brown by nitrogen dioxide

bryophyte: group of small plants without vascular tissue, including mosses and liverworts

calcareous: containing calcium carbonate

calcite: form of calcium carbonate

calcium carbonate: compound containing calcium, carbon and oxygen: $CaCO_3$

camera eye: eye with components similar to camera components: iris, pupil, lens and retina

camouflage: disguise or concealment so that an organism is inconspicuous against its surroundings

canopy: layer of foliage at the top of a rainforest

capacitor: device able to store a charge of electricity

carbohydrate: compound containing carbon, hydrogen and oxygen, the main stored food of plants, e.g. starch

carbon: element contained in all organic compounds

carbonate: mineral composed of carbon, oxygen and other elements

carbon dioxide: a gas without colour or smell, found in the air on Earth and in the atmospheres of some other planets

carbon monoxide: noxious compound of carbon and oxygen, produced in vehicle emission

carotene: carotenoid plant pigment

carotenoids: yellow, orange or red plant pigments located in chloroplasts or other plastids; in animals it is derived from plant food

carotenoprotein: carotenoid molecule linked to a protein molecule

caterpillar: soft-bodied larva of certain insects, e.g. butterflies

C.C.D.: see *charge coupled device*

cell: unit of which living organisms are composed

cell sap: liquid contents of plant vacuole

cephalopods: group of mollusc invertebrate animals including squids, cuttlefish, octopuses and nautilus

chalk: sedimentary rock composed of remains of calcareous micro-organisms

charge coupled device: electonic device that uses a silicon chip to produce images of celestial objects as video signals

charged particle: particle with positive or negative electric charge

chemical primary colours: see *subtractive primary colours*

chitin: nitrogen-containing polysaccharide present in and giving mechanical strength to animal cuticle

chlorocruorin: iron-containing green respiratory pigment in blood of some worms

chlorophyll: magnesium-containing green pigment found in chloroplasts, responsible for light capture in photosynthesis

chloroplast: chlorophyll-containing plant plastid, the site of photosynthesis

choroid: layer containing blood vessels and pigment, outside retina in vertebrate eye

chroma: intensity or degree of saturation of a colour

chromatic aberration: defect of lenses in which the different wavelengths or colours of light are separated because they are bent by slightly different amounts

chromatophore: animal cell containing granules of pigment in the cytoplasm; contraction and dispersal of pigment granules changes the colour of the cell

chromium: metallic element which forms brilliantly coloured compounds

chromosomes: thread-shaped bodies in the nuclei of plant and animal cells containing the genetic material

chromosphere: part of the sun's atmosphere that lies between the bright surface or photosphere and the outer corona

chrysocolla: green mineral, silicate of copper

chrysomelids: yellow beetles, *Coptocycla* spp.

chrysopsin: yellow rod pigment found in eyes of some deep-sea fish

cirro-cumulus cloud: high level cloud in stable air, in sheets or layers with small-scale billows or ripples

cirrostratus cloud: semi-transparent veil of fibrous or smooth cloud

cirrus cloud: high wispy cloud

clay: fine inorganic mineral found in soils and rocks

clearwater river: river that has transparent water because it carries almost no sediment load

cloud: large aggregation of water droplets or ice crystals in the atmosphere

cochineal: red dye from the dried bodies of cochineal insects

co-dominant: two alleles of a gene have equal effect, i.e. neither is dominant or recessive

coelenterates: group of simple aquatic animals which are more or less radially symmetrical, with a coelenteron (gut) with a single opening; includes jellyfish, corals, anemones

cold-blooded: blood temperature varies with that of surroundings

colorant: colouring matter or pigment

colour: depends upon which wavelengths of light are reflected by an object to the eyes of an observer

colour-blindness: inability to differentiate one or more colours from grey

colour constancy: ability to perceive the colour of an object as constant even though it may alter

colour contrast: adjacent colours do not share a common hue; psychological sensation of seeing a contrasting colour

colour print (negative) film: photographic film which produces images in negative form, from which a print is made

colour transparency film: photographic film which produces the colour image directly

colour vision: ability to perceive different wavelengths of light as colours rather than as greys

colour wheel: circular arrangement of pigment colours in their spectral sequence

coma: hazy patch around the nucleus of a comet

comet: a ball of dust and ice which travels around the the sun, with the dust streaming out behind to form one or more tails

commensal: members of different species living in close association

complementary colours: colours which mix to produce white light; colours opposite each other on the colour wheel

compound: union of chemical elements

compound eye: eye of insects and crustaceans, consisting of a number of units or ommatidia

cone: light sensitive cell found in the retina of vertebrates

cone lens: cone-shaped cell acting as lens in ommatidium of compound eye

conifer: cone-producing plant typical of temperate regions, e.g. pine, spruce, cedar

coniferous forest: forest in which most trees are conifers

constellation: a group of stars as seen from Earth

continent: a large mass of dry land on Earth

continuous spectrum: spectrum not broken into lines or bands

cool colours: colours at the blue end of the spectrum

co-pigmentation: loose combination of pigments resulting in a change in hue or intensity of colour

coproporphyrin: reddish brown pigment found in human faeces

corals: coelenterate animals, usually colonial, usually producing calcareous skeleton

core: the very centre of something; the central zone of a star

cornea: transparent layer at the front surface of the eye of vertebrates, overlying iris and lens

corneal lens: outer transparent cell acting as lens in ommatidium of compound eye

corona: the outermost layer of the sun's atmosphere; coloured aureole around the sun or moon produced by diffraction; type of auroral display

corpuscles: tiny particles

corundum: mineral which is known as ruby when it contains chromium

cosmic rays: high energy radiation, passing mainly through space

counterglow: a very faint glow in the night sky opposite the position of the sun

counterlighting: similar to countershading except that the gradation in darkness is caused by light-producing organs rather than by the animal's colour

countershading: gradation in darkness of an animal's colour in opposite direction from the gradation occurring on a plain surface in the natural light of the animal's habitat

counter-twilight: a coloured border above the eastern horizon, before sunset, showing transitions to orange, yellow, green and blue

coupler: connecting substance

crepuscular: active or occurring at twilight

cross pollination: transfer of pollen from a different plant of the same species

crust: outer zone of Earth

crustaceans: group of invertebrate animals that includes shrimps, crabs and lobsters

crystal: solid body with regular atomic structure and flat external surfaces

cumulus: heaped, rounded masses of cloud with horizontal base

current: a movement of water or air

cuticle: outer non-cellular layer covering an animal or plant

cyan: greenish blue colour

cyanidin: a bluish red anthocyanin pigment found in red roses

cyanism: variant with bluish coloration

cysteine: an amino acid; component of proteins

cytochrome: protein and iron-containing pigment involved in cell respiration

cytoplasm: cell contents excluding the nucleus, containing organelles such as plastids

dark adapted: eye that has pigments necessary for night vision

dark nebula: nebula containing dust that is so thick that no light penetrates

deciduous: plant that sheds leaves in autumn

delphinidin: blue anthocyanin pigment found in delphiniums

density: mass per unit volume of a substance

depth of focus: range of distances away from eye within which objects are all in focus

dermis: inner layer of skin of vertebrates, beneath epidermis

desert: hot or cold arid region with little vegetation

destructive interference: waves which are out of phase cancel each other out

dew bow: coloured bow similar to a rainbow but formed on a horizontal surface such as a lawn

diamond: colourless gem of carbon that has brilliance because of internal refraction and reflection of light

diaphragm: device for varying aperture of lens in camera

diffraction: deflection of light rays by an opaque object or a narrow opening

diffraction grating: series of narrow openings that cause diffraction of light rays passing through

diffusion colour: see *Tyndall blue*

dimorphic: occurring in two forms

dinoflagellate: single-celled brown alga that swims by means of a flagellum or tail

disc: circle of light from celestial objects that are large (e.g. the sun) or close (e.g. planets)

discolor: upper and lower leaf surfaces are different in colour

dispersal: distribution away from parent plant

disruptive coloration: colour and pattern that disrupt an animal's outline making it hard to identify

dissolved material: material that has become part of a liquid

dolerite: coarse basaltic rock

dominant: allele of a gene which produces a character when present doubly (two dominant alleles) or singly (one dominant, one recessive)

dorsal: the back of an animal

double bond: pair of bonds between two atoms

double star: two stars that appear to be close together; binary stars if actually associated

dune: a high bank of sand which is built up by the wind

dwarf star: a very small star, about 100 times smaller than the sun

earthshine: (ashen light) the faint luminosity of the night side of the moon

echinochrome: brownish purple quinone pigment found in some sea urchins

echinoderms: group of invertebrate animals that contains seastars, sea urchins and sea cucumbers

eclipse: the shadow caused by one object blocking off the light of another: in an eclipse of the sun, the moon comes between the sun and the Earth: in an eclipse of the moon, the shadow of Earth falls across the moon

ecliptic: sun's apparent path around Earth during the year

electric charge: imbalance of electrons, too few giving positive charge, too many giving negative charge

electromagnetic field: region under the influence of electromagnetic forces

electromagnetic radiation: full range of radiation: gamma-rays, X-rays, ultraviolet, visible light, infra-red, and radio waves

electron: tiny negatively charged particle of matter in orbit around the nucleus of an atom

electron cloud: region around an atom or molecule in which atoms orbit

element: substance composed of only one type of atom

elliptical galaxy: oval-shaped galaxy

embryo: immature plant (in the seed) or unborn animal

emerald: bright green precious stone, a type of beryl

emission: sending out radiation

emission (line) spectrum: spectrum consisting of bright lines or bands

emission nebula: nebula sending out its own radiation

endoderm: inner layer of cells usually lining an animal's gut

energy: ability of matter or radiation to do work

epidermis: outermost layer of cells of an animal or plant

epiphyte: plant growing on and supported by another plant

equinox: time at which the sun crosses the equator, making day and night of equal length in all parts of Earth (March 21 and September 21)

eumelanin: dark brown or black melanin pigment found especially in skin and skin products of animals

evergreen: bearing leaves year-round

excitation: raising of electrons to a higher orbit within an atom

excited state: high energy state of an electron

eye: light receptor organ

eyeshine: mirror-like glow from an eye illuminated at night

eyespot: light-sensitive pigmented organelle of single-celled organism

eyestalk: crustacean appendage upon which the eye is located

facet: flat surface on a cut gem

falling star: see *meteor*

false eye: pattern on an animal's surface that resembles an eye

false shadow: pattern on an animal's surface that resembles a shadow and makes the animal appear flatter than it really is

false sun: see *mock sun*

family: a group used in the classification of organisms; consists of a number of related genera

far red: infra-red radiation with longer wavelength than red light

feldspar: very abundant mineral in soils and rocks, consisting of compounds of aluminium and silicates

ferns: group of spore-bearing, vascular plants that do not produce flowers

fertilisation: the union of male and female cells in sexual reproduction

field of view: area that the eye, telescope or microscope sees at any one time

filament: stalk of a flower's stamen

firefly: bioluminescent beetle

flash coloration: brightly coloured part of an animal that is usually hidden but which can be exposed suddenly and briefly

flat spectrum: see *continuous spectrum*

flavone: glucoside, parent molecule of some flavonoid pigments

flavonoid: water soluble plant pigment, usually blue, purple or red (anthocyanins) or white to yellow (anthoxanthins)

flower: specialised reproductive shoot of an angiosperm

flowering plants: (angiosperms) plants that produce flowers, and seeds enclosed in fruits

fluorescence: emission of light during exposure to radiation of shorter wavelength such as ultraviolet

fluorite: (fluorspar) yellow, green, blue, purple or colourless mineral

focus: sharpness of an image

fog: thick white mist caused by water droplets in the air

fog bow: white rainbow caused by very small water droplets in the atmosphere

foliage: leaves

forest: large tree-covered region

fossil: remains or impression of ancient plant or animal preserved in rocks

fovea: part of retina of some vertebrates where vision is most acute

Fraunhofer lines: absorption lines crossing the spectrum of sunlight

freshwater: water of lakes and rivers that is not salty

fruit: ripened ovary of a flower that encloses the seeds

fucoxanthin: brown carotenoid pigment present in brown algae

fugitive: quickly fading

full moon: the moon when the whole of the surface we see is lit by the sun

fungi: group of simple organisms that do not contain chlorophyll; includes mushrooms, moulds and yeasts

galaxy: group of millions of stars, all loosely held together by gravity, e.g. the Milky Way

gamboge: gum resin from various East Asian trees, used as yellow pigment

gamma rays: very short wavelength radiation emitted by radioactive substances

ganglion cell: nerve cell that is part of an larger assemblage (e.g. enlargement of nerve, or central nervous system)

gas: a substance like air that is lighter than a liquid

gastropod mollusc: molluscs that are usually enclosed in a spiral shell, e.g. snails

gecko: lizard in the family Gekkonidae

Gegenscheim: see *counterglow*

Gelbstoffe: see *yellow substance*

gem (gemstone): precious mineral, usually crystalline in structure

gene: unit of inheritance, located on a chromosome

genetic engineering: deliberate modification of hereditary features by transfer of genes

genus: group used in classification of organisms, contains a number of related species

germinate: to produce shoots,to sprout

giant star: a very large star, much bigger than the sun

glacial lake: lake formed in depression left by glacier

glacial river: river of water from a melting glacier

glacier: a mass of slowly flowing land ice

glory: a coloured aureole of light around an observer's shadow

glow-worm: beetle whose wingless female emits light from the end of the abdomen

glucoside: compound that gives sugar and other product(s) in reaction with water

goethite: yellow-brown iron compound known as yellow ochre

gourd: large fruit of plant in the family Cucurbitaceae

granite: a crystalline rock with coarse and medium grains, consisting essentially of feldspar and quartz

graphite: crystalline form of carbon

grassland: region where grasses dominate the vegetation and there are few trees

gravitational field: the space surrounding a body within which its gravity, the force that pulls objects towards each other, affects other bodies

gravity: the force that pulls objects towards each other

Great Red Spot: region of atmospheric disturbance in the atmosphere of Jupiter's southern hemisphere

green: colour between red and blue in the visible spectrum

green flash: brief green coloration sometimes seen as the top of a setting sun drops below the horizon

ground state: normal energy state of electron

guanine: white excretory product of some animals, also occurs as a reflective substance in guanophores

guanophore: (leucophore) reflective cell containing guanine or related compound

gum arabic: gum exuded by some acacias

gypsum: mineral, hydrated calcium sulfate

habitat: environment inhabited by organism(s)

haematite: iron-containing mineral common in soils and rocks, known as red ochre

haematoxylin: red dye from Mexican logwood tree

haemerythrin: iron-containing red respiratory pigment found in some invertebrates

haemocyanin: blue copper-containing respiratory pigment in blood of some invertebrates

haemoglobin: red iron-containing respiratory pigment in red blood cells of vertebrates and in some invertebrates

hair bulb: basal expanded root of hair

hair follicle: pit in mammal epidermis surrounding root of hair

halo: a coloured ring appearing at 22° or 46° around the sun or moon when ice crystals are present in the atmosphere

haze: obscuring of atmosphere by fine particles of water, smoke or dust

heartwood: dead non-functional tissue in centre of tree trunk

helium: gas found in stars and in outer space

henna: tropical shrub, shoots and leaves of which are used as reddish dye

herbaceous plant: plant with no persistent parts above ground

herbivore: plant-eating animal

hibernate: become dormant through winter

high energy state: see *excited state*

honeyguide: marking on a petal which leads a pollinating animal towards a flower's nectar or pollen

horizon: the distant line where the sky and sea or land seem to meet

hormone: organic substance produced in small amount in one part of an organism and transported to other parts where it exerts a profound effect

hue: spectral colour

humic acid: acid found in humus or derived from it

humus: complex organic matter resulting from decomposition of plant and animal tissue in soil; gives the surface layer of soil its characteristically dark colour; holds mineral nutrients and prevents them leaching away

hydrocarbon: compound of hydrogen and carbon

hydrogen: the lightest gas of all, found in stars and in outer space; combined with oxygen in water

hydrolysis: chemical reaction with water

hydroxide: compound of atom(s) with hydroxyl (hydrogen and oxygen)

ice: water in its solid state

igneous rock: rock cooled from molten magma or lava

image: optical appearance of an object

impurity: minor amount of foreign element in a mineral

incandescent: emitting light when heated

incident: falling on or striking

indican: glucoside from which the blue dye indigo is obtained

indigo: blue dye obtained usually from plants of the genus *Indigofera*; colour between blue and violet in the spectrum

indoxyl: yellow hydrolysis product of indigo

inflorescence: flowering shoot

infra-red rays: rays with a wavelength longer than visible light

inkscreen: dark fluid expelled by cephalopds, which confuses predators

inorganic: substances not formed by living organisms

in phase: peaks and troughs of waves coincide

integument: skin

interference: the mutual action of two waves or systems of waves, in reinforcing or neutralising each other

interference bow: see *supernumerary bow*

interstellar gas and dust: gas and dust derived from exploding stars in galaxies

interstellar reddening: reddening of light coming from stars etc. due to scattering of blue light by interstellar dust

invertebrate: animal without backbone, e.g. jellyfish, sponge, worm, seastar, snail

ion: atom or molecule that has a positive or negative electric charge

ionisation: conversion into ions

iridescence: interference of many light waves reflected from layers within an object to produce intense colours

iridescent clouds: coloured clouds around the sun or moon caused by diffraction of light

iridocyte: (iridophore) iridescent cell containing layers of crystals of guanine or similar compounds

iridophore: see *iridocyte*

iris: the coloured part of the human eye**iron:** most abundant and useful metallic element

irregular galaxy: galaxy that has an irregular shape

jade: hard stone, usually green, blue or white, used as ornament

jaundice: yellowness of skin caused by obstruction of bile

juglone: dark yellowish brown quinone pigment found in walnuts

katydid: type of large green grasshopper

keratin: tough fibrous protein occurring in epidermis of vertebrates, e.g. in hair, feathers, scales, nails

kermes: red dye from dried bodies of female *Kermes ilicis* insects

labradorite: mineral which shows a brilliant variety of colour when turned in the light

lac: dark red resinous substance produced on certain trees by the insect *Coccus lacca*

lake: enclosed body of fresh water

lamp shell: belonging to a small phylum of animals (Brachiopoda) which have two-valved shells

lapis lazuli: deep blue mineral

larval stage: immature form of an animal that undergoes metamorphosis
lateritic soil: red soil of hot wet tropics
lava: hot, liquid rock that flows from a volcano or fissure in Earth's surface
leaching: removal of minerals from soil by water
leaf: green photosynthetic organ of plants
lens: piece of glass or other material that is curved to bend light rays and focus light
leucemism: whiteness due to structure or pigment
leucophore: see *guanophore*
lichen: organism formed by the symbiotic association of a fungus and an alga
light: visible part of the electromagnetic spectrum
light adapted: eye that has pigments necessary for day vision
lightning: light emission as electrical balance is re-instated within clouds
light-sensitive cell: cell that contains light sensitive pigments for absorbing light and transforming its energy to chemical energy
light-sensitive pigment: pigment that absorbs light energy and converts it into chemical energy
limestone: sedimentary calcareous rock
limonite: yellow-brown iron-containing clay mineral found in soils and rocks
linking pattern: pattern which appears to link body parts when an animal is at rest, making the animal difficult to recognise
lipochrome: term formerly used for animal carotenoid pigment
litmus: blue colouring material from lichens that turns red with acid and is restored to blue by alkali
llanos: South American grassy plain
luciferase: enzyme that aids the light-producing reaction of luciferin with oxygen
luciferin: substance in bioluminescent organisms which reacts with oxygen to cause the emission of light
luminescence: light emission not due to heat
luminous: emitting light; bright, shining
lunar eclipse: Earth lies between the moon and the sun, blocking light from the sun to the moon
lustre: gloss
lutein: yellow xanthopyll pigment found in green leaves
lycopene: red carotenoid pigment found in tomatoes

madder: red dye from root of herbaceous plant *Rubia tinctorum*
magenta: coloured like magenta, a brilliant crimson aniline dye
magma: molten rock below Earth's surface
magnesium: metallic element
magnetic field: field originating inside Earth due to Earth spinning on its axis and the mantle and crust rotating relatively faster than the core
magnetic pole: one of the points on Earth near the north and south poles to which the needle of a compass points
magnetite: magnetic iron oxide
malachite: bright green mineral, hydrated copper carbonate
malvidin: reddish purple pigment from mallow plants
mantis: type of insect; praying mantis holds forelegs in position resembling prayer
mantle: outer fold of skin enclosing mollusc's body
marble: metamorphic rock formed from limestone
marsupial: pouched mammal
masquerade: disguise by attaching objects from surroundings
mass: the amount of matter in an object
matter: physical substances in general
medium: intervening substance
melanin: dark pigment in animals which in different concentrations gives black, brown and yellow coloration
melaniridocyte: composite structure of melanophore and iridocyte
melanistic: black
melanocyte: melanin-producing cell of mammal
melanoma: tumor of melanocytes
melanophore: chromatophore containing melanin
melanosomes: granules of melanin
melatonin: substance secreted by pineal gland that acts on an animal's chromatophores
membrane: flat sheet-like structure
mesophyll: internal chlorophyll-containing tissue of leaves
mesosphere: layer of upper atmosphere approximately 50-80 km above Earth's surface

metal: metallic mineral
metamorphic: changed rock or mineral
meteor: piece of rock from space which burns up when it strikes the layer of gases around a planet; then it is known as a falling star
meteorite: larger piece of rock from outer space (probably asteroid belt) that is able to reach ground-level without being destroyed
methane: gaseous hydrocarbon: CH_4
microwave: type of radiation longer than infra-red
Mie scattering: scattering of light by particles that are relatively large compared to the wavelengths of light
Milky Way: the galaxy containing Earth
mimesis: protective similarity of an animal species to an object in its environment
mimicry: protective similarity of one species of animal to a different species
mineral: naturally occurring solid chemical compound
mineral deficiency: lacking an essential mineral
minor planets: see *asteroids*
mist: water vapour in the atmosphere consisting of smaller and more densely aggregated droplets than those in rain
mock sun: bright area of the sky that looks like another sun, caused by refraction of light by ice crystals in the air
molecule: smallest amount of a compound having all the chemical properties of that compound
molluscs: group of soft bodied animals, often with shells, including snails, octopuses, oysters
monochromatic: having one colour only
monsoonal: region with alternation of wet and dry seasons
moon: small body that travels around a planet
moonlight: sunlight reflected from the surface of the moon
mordant: substance serving to fix colouring matter onto another substance
mosaic virus: virus causing plant disease, symptom being patchiness of colour
moss: simple spore-producing plant found in damp habitat
mother-of-pearl: iridescent inner shell layer of some molluscs
mother-of pearl cloud: (noctilucent cloud) cloud high in the atmosphere (c. 80 km) formed from meteoritic dust, seen at night after sunset
moult: shedding of feathers, hair, shell etc.
mucus membrane: moist lining tissue of animal
Muellerian mimicry: two species gain protection by having the same warning coloration
multi-celled: consisting of many cells
Munsell: system for defining colours
mutant: organism bearing altered gene

nacreous shell: mother-of-pearl shell of mollusc
nanometre: one millionth of a millimetre
natural: not affected by humans
natural selection: mechanism of evolutionary change in which organisms with successful variations have a greater chance to survive and pass on their genes
nature: the features and products of the universe and Earth itself, in contrast with those of human civilisation
nautilus: shelled cephalopod related to octopuses and squids
nebula: a cloud of gas and dust in space that emits or reflects light
negative charge: the kind of electrical charge carried by electrons
nematode: slender unsegmented worm-like animal
nerve: bundle of nerve cells that conduct impulses or messages from one region of the body to another
nerve cord: central nervous system of lower animals
nerve net: network of nerve cells distributed through tissue of some animals, e.g. coelenterates
neutron: neutral particle in the nucleus of an atom
neutron star: very small fast-spinning core of a star that has blown up
new moon: moon's phase when none of its sunlit surface is visible from Earth
nitrogen: a gas found in the atmosphere of some planets, without colour taste or smell
nitrogen dioxide: toxic brown gas in the atmosphere that gives the colour to brown pollution haze
noctilucent cloud: see *mother-of-pearl cloud*
nocturnal: active mostly at night
normal state: normal energy state of electron
northern lights: aurora borealis of the northern hemisphere

North Pole: the furthest point north on a planet

nuclear reaction: change in the make up of atoms, occurring in stars

nucleus: centre of an atom, including the protons and neutrons; central region of galaxy or comet; material in the centre of a pearl, around which layers develop

nutrient: inorganic or organic compounds or ions used primarily in the nutrition of primary producers

obsidian: black volcanic glass

ocellus: simple light receptor of some invertebrates

ochre: iron and clay mixture, providing yellow and red pigments

oil droplet: coloured droplet of oil acting as filter in the light sensitive cells of some animals' eyes

olivine: olive-green mineral, magnesium iron silicate

ommatidium: element of the compound eye of insects and crustaceans

ommatin: dark granular pigment found in invertebrates; shielding pigment in insects' eyes

opal: gem composed of silica and water and deriving its iridescent colours from interference of light

opalescence: colours reflected from milky opals

opaque: letting no light pass through

optic nerve: major nerve between eyes and brain of vertebrates

orange: colour between red and yellow in the visible spectrum

orbit: the path through space of one object going around another

ore: rock or mineral deposit yielding a metal

organ: multicellular region of an organism which forms a structural and functional unit

organelle: structure within a cell having specialised function

organic: substances based on hydrocarbons, existing naturally in organisms

organic molecule: carbon-containing molecule found in living organisms

organism: organised body with connected interdependent parts sharing common life

orient: lustre of a pearl

orpiment: arsenic trisulphide as mineral, used as yellow dye and artist's pigment

out of phase: the peaks of one wave coincide with the troughs of another wave, so the two cancel each other

ovary: female part of flower which produces ovules

over-exposed: photograph that has received too much light

ovule: structure in a seed plant that develops into a seed after fertilisation

oxide: mineral composed of oxygen and other elements

oxidation: reaction in which an element combines with oxygen

oxygen: gas found in air and water, important to all plants and animals

ozone: gas composed of O_3 molecules (3 atoms of oxygen) found in the atmosphere in minute quantities; most of it originates in the stratosphere, some in thunderstorms

pampas: large South American treeless plain, especially in Argentina

parasitic: living on and deriving food from another organism

parhelium: see *mock sun*

parterre: leval space in garden occupied by flower-beds

particle: a small portion of matter

pastel: light, subdued colour

pearl: gem produced inside the shell of bivalve mollusc by concretion around a foreign body

pearlescent: slightly iridescent, as in a pearl

peat: accumulated dead plant material that has remained incompletely decomposed owing mainly to lack of oxygen in waterlogged area

pebble: small rounded stone

pelargonidin: red anthocyanin pigment found in geraniums

pencil ice crystal: atmospheric ice crystal that is pencil shaped (long, and hexagonal in cross section)

perennial: plant that continues to grow from year to year

petal: sterile part of a flower, usually conspicuous and colourful

phaeomelanin: orange or light brown melanin pigment found especially in skin and skin products

pharynx: part of vertebrate gut between mouth and oesophagus

phases: the changes in the apparent shape of a moon or planet according to amount of illumination

phosphorescence: emission of light after exposure to short wavelength radiation (light lasts for a longer time than in fluorescence)

photochemical smog: brown pollution haze

photomorphogenic process: process of plant growth, development or differentiation triggered by specific wavelengths of light

photon: unit particle of light

photophore: light-producing cell

photoreceptor: receptor that detects light

photosphere: the bright surface of the sun

photosynthesis: the manufacture of carbohydrate food from carbon dioxide and water using energy absorbed from sunlight by chlorophyll; oxygen and water are also produced

physical colour: see *structural colour*

physical primary colours: see *additive primary colours*

phytochrome: plant pigment present in very small amounts which, when activated by red light, initiates various processes of growth and development

phytoplankton: plants of plankton

piebaldism: skin of two colours, usually black and white, irregularly arranged

pigment: a colouring substance

pigment cell: cell that contains pigment

pigment colour: colour produced by chemical means (i.e. pigments) rather than by light

pineal gland: gland involved in control of pigment concentration and dispersion in melanophores

planet: a large object that moves around a star and shines by reflecting the light of the star

planetary nebula: a thin shell-like layer of gas given off into space by a dying star

plankton: passively drifting or weakly swimming organisms

plastid: organelle in the cytoplasm of a cell, containing pigment or food reserves

plate ice crystal: atmospheric ice crystal shaped like a thin hexagonal plate

platelet: tiny plate-shaped body

play of colours: colours of an opal come from within and change randomly as it is turned from side to side

plumage: birds' feathers

plutonic: formed as igneous rock by solidification beneath Earth's surface

polar cap: polar region of planet when capped e.g. with ice

polarised light: light that vibrates only in one plane

polarising filter: filter that only lets through light vibrating in one plane

polar region: region at or near either pole of Earth or other celestial body

poles: the most northern or southern points on a star, planet or moon, the end points of its axis

pollen grain: male reproductive product of flowering plants

pollen tube: long outgrowth to ovary from germinating pollen grain

pollination: transfer of pollen from an anther to a stigma

pollinator: animal that transfers pollen from an anther to a stigma

pollution: spoilage of Earth and its atmosphere with waste and poison

pollution haze: pollutants in the atmosphere scatter light and nitrogen dioxide colours the air brown

polychaetes: segmented worms with many bristles

polymorphism: having a number of different forms

polyp: individual animal within a coelenterate colony

porphyrin: pink or reddish animal pigment

porphyropsin: purplish pigment in the eyes of tadpoles and lampreys

positive charge: the kind of electrical charge carried by protons (opposite to that carried by electrons)

powder: light coloured particles on birds' feathers that soften the underlying colour

prairie: large treeless region of level or undulating grassland in North America

precursor: substance from which another is formed

predator: animal that feeds on other animals but is not a parasite

prey: animal that is fed upon by other animals or predators

primary bow: intense rainbow, occurring at an angular radius of 42°

primary pigment colours: see *subtractive primary colours*

primates: group of placental mammals that includes man, apes and monkeys

prism: glass block with flat surfaces inclined to one another

protochlorophyll: colourless precursor of green chlorophyll

proton: elementary positively charged particle in nucleus of atom

pterin: colourless, red or yellow pigment found especially in butterflies

pupal stage: stage of passive development of insect following larval stage

pupil: opening in iris at front of eye

pyrite: (fool's gold) sulfide mineral

quantum: the smallest amount of light energy which can be transmitted at a given wavelength

quartz: mineral consisting of silica or silicon dioxide

quebracho: South American tree yielding very hard timber

quercetin: yellow plant pigment, e.g. from vine leaves

quill: hollow stem of feather

quinones: group of yellowish plant pigments, also found in animals

radial symmetry: symmetry about every line or plane through a centre

radiant energy: energy of rays, e.g. rays of light

radiation: rays sent out, e.g. visible light rays

radio wave: ray with very long wavelength

rainbow: arc of spectral colours in the sky caused by refraction and reflection of sunlight by water droplets in the atmosphere

rainforest: closed, usually humid, temperate or tropical forest

ray: beam or straight line in which the radiant energy propagated to any given point

Rayleigh scattering: preferential scattering (and polarisation) of blue light by tiny particles

realgar: arsenic sulphide mineral used as brownish red pigment

receding colours: cool colours that give the impression of distance

recessive: allele of a gene which is not expressed in the presence of a dominant allele

red: colour of long wavelength, low energy visible light

red flash: fleeting red light sometimes seen at the base of the sun's disc at sunset

red giant: very large, relatively cool star

red ochre: haematite, mineral of clay and hydrated ferric oxide, used as pigment

red shift: a movement of the lines in the spectrum of light towards the red end, by a receding object

Red Spot: see *Great Red Spot*

red supergiant: a huge red star, over 100 times the size of the sun

red tide: a red or reddish brown discoloration of surface waters by certain pigmented algae

reflection: the process whereby a surface turns back part of the incident radiation into the medium through which it approached; image of surrounding landscape seen on calm water surface

reflection nebula: nebula which is seen because of the starlight it reflects

reflectivity: degree to which a surface throws back or reflects light

refraction: the process by which the direction of an oblique wave is changed or bent by an obstacle in its path

reptiles: group of vertebrate animals that contains turtles, snakes, lizards and crocodiles

resolution: ability to detect as separate two objects that are close together

respiratory pigment: pigment involved with the transport of oxygen for respiration

retina: layer of light sensitive cells in an eye

retinula cells: cells surrounding rhabdom in compound eye

reversal film: colour slide or transparency film

rhabdom: central cell in ommatidium of compound eye, containing light-sensitive pigments

rhodopsin: visual purple, light sensitive pigment in the rods of vertebrate eyes

rod: type of light sensitive cell in vertebrates responsible for night vision and peripheral vision

ruby: gem of corundum with colour varying from deep crimson to purple and pale rose

run-off: water running off the land surface following rain

rutile: titanium dioxide as reddish mineral

safflower: thistle-like plant with petals yielding reddish dye

salamander: tailed amphibian

sand: small mineral grains, usually quartz

sandstone: sedimentary rock composed mainly of sand

sapphire: transparent blue gem of corundum

sapwood: outer living region of xylem of tree trunk

satellite: an object in space which moves in orbit around another object

savannah: grassy plain with few or no trees in tropical and subtropical regions

scarab: dung beetle

scattering: the dispersion of light when a beam strikes small particles suspended in air or water; known as Rayleigh scattering when the particles are small relative to the wavelength of light, and as Mie scattering when the particles are larger

scheelite: calcium tungstate in native crystalline form

sea hare: slug-like gastropod mollusc with internal shell

sea pen: colonial coelenterate shaped like a quill

seaweed: large red, brown or green marine alga

secondary bow: paler of the two rainbows, with an angular radius of 51°

secondary pigment colours: colours formed when pairs of primary pigment colours are mixed

sediment: particulate organic and inorganic matter which accumulates in a loose unconsolidated form

sedimentary rock: rock formed by deposition and compression of minerals and organic matter

seed: product of a fertilised ovule containing embryo of new plant

sensory cell: cell that receives stimuli and passes impulses to other cells for eventual response

sepal: outer sterile part of a flower, usually green and leaf-like

sex-linked: gene carried on the X-chromosome and more likely to be expressed in males

shade: colour made darker by the addition of black

shade-leaf: leaf formed in shade by a plant that produces different types of leaves in sun and in shade

shadow: dark area where light does not reach because an obstacle blocks light from the source

silicate: mineral composed of silicon, oxygen and other elements, found in sand

silicon: non-metallic element found in silica

silt: particles between sand and clay in size

simple eye: eye with narrow window or lens to bend light

single bond: sharing of one pair of electrons

single-celled: organism consisting of only one cell

slate: metamorphic rock formed from shale or mudstone

smog: brown pollution haze

smoke: atmospheric particles produced by burning

snow: atmospheric vapour frozen into ice crystals and falling to Earth in light white flakes

soil: broken and decomposed rock and decayed organic matter

solar flares: brilliant outbreaks in the outer part of the sun's atmosphere which send out electrified particles

Solar System: the sun and all the objects that are in orbit around it

solar wind: a steady flow of atomic particles streaming from the sun in all directions

southern lights: aurora australis of the southern hemisphere

South Pole: the furthest point south on a planet or star

space: the area between the planets and the stars, almost empty except for tiny amounts of gas and dust

species: the smallest unit of classification commonly used for living things, a breeding group of plants or animals

spectral class: colour group into which a star is classified

spectral colour: one of the colours of the spectrum, seen when white light is split

spectroscope: an instrument which is used to obtain information about e.g. the composition of a substance, by splitting light that the substance emits or absorbs

spectroscopy: use of spectroscope to determine the composition of objects in the universe

spectrum: range of electromagnetic rays, such as gamma rays, X-rays, ultraviolet rays, visible light, infrared and radio waves; the spectrum of visible light includes all the colours of the rainbow

spinochrome: brownish pink quinone pigment found in sea urchins

spiral galaxy: a kind of galaxy which has a flattened shape and arms curving out from the centre

spore: microscopic reproductive body that detaches from parent and gives rise to a new individual

stalactite: deposit of calcium carbonate hanging down from the roof of cave

stalagmite: deposit of calcium carbonate standing on floor of cave

stamen: pollen-producing organ of a flower

star: a glowing ball of gas that gives off its own heat and light, like the sun

star cluster: a group of stars which are very close together

star trail: circular line of star's apparent movement across the sky in a time-exposed photograph

stem: aerial axis of a plant, bearing leaves and reproductive structures e.g. flowers

stigma: expanded part of style (female part of flower) that receives pollen

stratus: continuous horizontal sheet cloud

streak: colour of powdered mineral

stroma: connective tissue e.g. of iris of eye

structural blue: blue coloration caused by structure rather than pigments

structural colour: colour caused by surface structure rather than pigments

style: filamentous structure of female part of flower, linking ovary to stigma

subtractive primary colours: primary pigment colours: red, blue and yellow

sulfur: a hard, brittle, yellow substance that burns with a blue flame and forms an unpleasant-smelling gas (also spelt 'sulphur')

sulfuric acid: a liquid chemical that can destroy living things and eat through metals

sumac: shrub of genus *Rhus*, dried and ground leaves of which are used in tanning and dyeing

sun: the star that gives Earth its heat and light

sunburn: skin condition involving expansion of blood vessels and breakdown of dermis, caused by excess ultraviolet radiation

sundog: see *mock sun*

sunfleck: transient spot of direct sunlight beneath a canopy

sun-leaf: type of leaf produced in the sun by a plant that produces different leaves in the sun and shade

sunlight: radiation emitted by the sun

sun spot: dark area on the surface of the sun corresponding to an intense magnetic field

suntan: darkening of skin due to an increased amount of melanin after exposure to ultraviolet radiation

supergiant: a huge star, over 100 times the size of the sun

supernova: the explosion of a very big star at the end of its life

supernumerary bow: (interference bow) additional bow inside the primary rainbow caused by interference of light

suspended material: particles not dissolved in water, but small enough not to settle out

symbiotic: living in association with a dissimilar organism to mutual advantage

tail: region of a comet containing ionised gases or dust, and pointing away from the sun

tannin: one of a group of complex organic compounds containing phenols, hydroxy acids or glucosides, found in plants e.g. in bark and leaves

tapetum: reflecting layer of eye

tarnish: surface alteration of metallic mineral

telescope: an instrument for looking at distant objects

terpene: unsaturated hydrocarbon occurring in plant oils and resins

terreverte: soft green earth used as pigment

tertiary pigment colours: colours obtained by mixing pairs of secondary pigment colours

thermosphere: region of the atmosphere greater than 80 kilometres above Earth's surface

tide: a rising and falling in the level of the oceans caused by the pull of the gravity of moon and sun

tin leaf: leaf with a surface that is so shiny it appears metallic

tint: colour made lighter by addition of white

tissue: a large number of cells working together to perform a function

tone: tint or shade of a colour

tourmaline: boron aluminium silicate mineral of various colours

tracheae: air conducting tubes of insects

transition elements/metals: group of eight elements that are mainly responsible for the colours of gems (titanium, vanadium, chromium, manganese, iron, cobalt, nickel and copper)

translucent: letting only some light pass through

transmission: passage through a medium

transparent: letting all light pass through

transpiration: loss of water vapour by terrestrial plants

tremolite: white or whitish green mineral

tripack: a pack consisting of layers of three light-sensitive photographic films in one

tropics: regions of Earth between 23°N and 23°S

troposphere: the inner layer of the atmosphere, varying in altitude between

9.5 km and 19 km, within which there is a steady decrease of temperature as altitude increases; all weather occurs in this layer

Turkey Red: scarlet pigment made from madder

turquoise: opaque or translucent sky-blue or greenish blue precious stone, hydrated copper aluminium phosphate

twilight: time after sunset that the sky is still lit by the sun's light

twinkling: the apparent flashing of a star due to Earth's air

Tyndall blue: structural blue coloration due to tiny particles in an animal's surface

Tyrian purple: bromine-containing pigment derived from secretion of certain gastropod molluscs

tyrosinase: enzyme involved in the synthesis of melanin

tyrosine: amino acid from which melanin is derived

ultramarine: blue pigment from lapis lazuli

ultraviolet radiation: radiation with a shorter wavelength than the visible violet light occurring in sunlight

under-exposed: photograph that has not received sufficient light

universe: all of space and everything in it

upwelling: the process by which water rises from a lower to a higher depth

uric acid: almost insoluble, nitrogen-containing compound, the main excreted product of some animals

urobilin: brown pigment in oxidised human faeces

urobilinogen: yellow pigment in human faeces

uroporphyrin: pink, red or brown pigment found in mollusc shells; first discovered in human urine

vacuole: fluid-filled region within the cytoplasm of a cell, surrounded by a membrane

value: degree of lightness or darkness of a colour

variegation: variation of colour of plant organs, inherited or due to disease

ventral: side of an animal which faces downward with reference to gravity

verdigris: green crystallised substance formed on copper by action of acetic acid and used as a pigment

vertebrates: animals with backbones, including fish, amphibians, reptiles, birds and mammals

violet: colour seen at the opposite end of the spectrum from red, produced by slight mixture of red with blue

virus: sub-microscopic agent that infects plants and animals

visible light: light within the range of wavelengths to which the eye is sensitive

visible spectrum: that part of the electromagnetic spectrum that is visible to us as light

visual cortex: part of the brain where a visual image is built up

volcanic: produced by a volcano

volcanic dust: fine particulate matter ejected into the atmosphere by a volcano

volcano: a type of mountain, formed when very hot liquid rock, forced up from deep inside a planet, cools and leaves a mountain of rock

volume: the three-dimensional space taken up by a solid object, liquid or gas

warm-blooded: able to maintain high and constant body temperature

warm colour: (advancing colour) colour such as red, orange or yellow, which appears to be closer to an observer than it really is

warning coloration: conspicuous coloration of poisonous or distasteful animals or plants

water vapour: water in the form of a gas

wave: a disturbance which moves through or over the surface of the ocean, earth or air

wavelength: horizontal distance between successive wave crests

weathering: destruction of rock by thermal, chemical or mechanical processes

white: not absorbing any wavelengths of white light

white dwarf: the remains of a dead star which is very small

white light: sunlight, containing all the wavelengths or colours of light

whitewater river: river that contains a large sediment load and appears brown or white as a result

xagua: deep blue to black plant dye

xanthophore: cell containing yellow pigment

xanthophyll: brownish yellow carotenoid plant pigment

x-ray: a type of ray which has a very short wavelength, given out by super-hot gases in space

yellow: colour between green and orange in the spectrum
yellow ochre: goethite, yellowish brown mineral of clay and hydrated ferric oxide, common in many soils; used as pigment
yellow substance: general term used to denote the pigmented products or organic decomposition which absorb blue and violet light in coastal waters, causing the water to be most transparent to yellow light

zodiac: twelve constellations in the sky that the sun, the moon and the planets appear to cross as Earth orbits
zodiacal light: a cone of light rising from the horizon and stretching along the ecliptic, seen at certain times when sun is below the horizon

SCIENTIFIC NAMES OF PLANTS AND ANIMALS IN EACH CHAPTER

Chapter 1
Algae from coral (*Symbiodinium microadriaticum*)
Black coral (Class Anthozoa, Order Antipatharia)
Brittle star (Class Ophiuroidea)
Cheetah (*Acinonyx jubatus*)
Coral fish (*Chaetodon* sp.)
Cuttlefish (*Sepia* sp.)
Daisies (*Craspedia* spp.)
Featherstar (Class Crinoidea)
Fish (Class Pisces)
Hydroid (Class Hydrozoa)
Luminous bacteria (*Photobacterium* sp.)
Nudibranch (Class Gastropoda, Subclass Opisthobranchia)
Pandanus (*Pandanus* sp.)
Pigeon (Family Columbidae)
Pouch fungus (*Aseroe rubra*)
Scallop (Class Bivalvia, Family Pectinidae)
Sea dragon (*Phyllopteryx taeniolatus*)
Sea fan (Class Anthozoa, Order Gorgonacea)
Sea pen (Class Anthozoa, Order Pennatulacea)
Seaweed (Division Rhodophyta)
Sea whip (Class Anthozoa, Order Alcyonaria)
Soft coral (Class Anthozoa, Order Alcyonaria)
Spider (Class Arachnida)
Sponge (Phylum Porifera)
Temperate coral (*Plesiastrea versipora*)
Waratah (*Telopea* sp.)

Chapter 4
Algae (Division Chlorophyta)
Floating fern (*Azolla pinnata*)

Chapter 5
Agamid lizards (Family Agamidae)
Anemones (*Anemone* spp.)
Angelfish (Family Pomacanthidae)
Antelope (Family Boviidae)
Ants (Family Formicidae)
Barracuta (*Scomberomorus commerson*)
Bats (Order Chiroptera)
Bears (Family Ursidae)
Bee-eater (*Merops* sp.)
Bees (Order Hymenoptera, Super-Family Apoidea)
Beetles (Order Coleoptera)
Birches (*Betula* spp.)
Birds of paradise (*Paradisaea* spp.)
Bison (*Bison bison*)
Blackbirds (*Turdus merula*)
Bluebells (*Scilla* spp.)
Blue bird of paradise (*Paradisaea rudolphi*)
Bluebush (*Maireana* spp.)
Blue flying fish (*Cypselurus melanocercus*)
Bottle tree (*Brachychiton* sp.)
Bowerbirds (*Ptilonorhynchus violaceus*)
Breadfruit trees (*Artocarpus* sp.)

Bustards (Family Otididae)
Buttercups (*Ranunculus* spp.)
By-the-wind sailors (*Velella lata*)
Cactus wrens (*Campylorhynchus brunneicapillus*)
Cassowaries (*Casuarius casuarius*)
Cats (*Felis catus*)
Chameleon (*Chamaeleo* spp.)
Cheetahs (*Acinonyx jubatus*)
Clams (Family Tridacnidae)
Clownfish (*Amphiprion* spp.)
Cocoa plant (*Theobroma cacao*)
Coffee plant (*Coffea arabica*)
Corals (Class Anthozoa, Order Scleractinia)
Crayfish (Family Parastacidae)
Crows (*Corvus* spp.)
Cuipo (*Cavanillesia platanifolia*)
Deer (*Cervus* spp.)
Desert geckos (Family Gekkonidae)
Desert grasshoppers (Order Orthoptera)
Desert locusts (Order Orthoptera)
Desert peas (*Swainsona formosa*)
Eagles (Family Accipitridae)
Edelweiss (*Leontopodium alpinum*)
Egyptian cobra (*Naja hafe*)
Elephants (*Loxodonta africana*)
Elms (*Ulmus* spp.)
Epiphytic bromeliads (Family Bromeliaceae)
Eucalypts (*Eucalyptus* spp.)
Evening primroses (*Oenothera* spp.)
Ferns (Order Filicales)
Figs (*Ficus* spp.)
Firs (*Abies* spp.)
Flame tree (*Brachychiton acerifolius*)
Flies (Order Diptera, especially Family Muscidae)
Floating sea slugs (*Glaucus atlanticus*)
Flower mantises (Family Mantidae)
Flycatchers (Family Muscicapidae)
Frogs (Order Anura)
Gentians (*Gentiana* spp.)
Giant caladium (*Alocasia cuprea*)
Giant groundsel (*Senecio* sp.)
Giant lobelia (*Lobelia* sp.)
Glow-worms (Family Lampyridae, Family Mycetophildae)
Grasshoppers (Order Orthoptera)
Hares (*Lepus* spp.)
Harvestmen (Order Phalangida)
Hatchetfish (Family Sternoptychidae)
Hedgehogs (*Erinaceus* spp.)
Jerboas (*Paradipus* spp.)
Kangaroo rats (*Dipodomys* spp.)
Katydid leaf insects (Order Orthoptera)
Larches (*Larix* spp.)
Lilies (*Lilium* spp.)
Lillypilly trees (*Syzygium* spp.)
Lions (*Panthera leo*)

Lizards (Order Squamata, Suborder Sauria)
Long-tongued hawk moth (*Xanthopan morgani*)
Madagascan orchid (*Anagraecum sesquipedale*)
Magnolias (*Magnolia* spp.)
Maples (*Acer* spp.)
Mice (Family Muridae, especially the genus *Mus*)
Millepedes (Class Diplopoda)
Mosquitoes (Family Culicidae)
Mosses (Class Musci)
Oaks (*Quercus* spp.)
Orchids (Family Orchidaceae)
Ostriches (*Struthio camelus*)
Owls (Order Strigiformes)
Ozark cave salamanders (*Typhlotriton spelaeus*)
Phalaropes (Family Phalaropodidae)
Philodendron (*Philodendron* spp.)
Pigeon (*Hemiphaga novaeseelandiae*)
Pines (*Pinus* spp.)
Plovers (Family Charadriidae)
Polar bears (*Thalarctos maritimus*)
Portuguese man o' war (*Physalia physalis*)
Possum (Family Phalangeridae)
Pouch fungus (*Thaxergaster porphyreum*)
Praying mantises (Family Mantidae)
Ptarmigan (*Lagopus* spp.)
Purple ocean snails (*Janthina* spp.)
Pygmy possums (Family Burramyidae)
Python (*Chondropython viridis*)
Reindeer (*Rangifer* spp.)
Robins (Family Muscicapidae)
Salamanders (*Salamandra* spp.)
Salmon (Family Salmonidae)
Saltbush (*Atriplex* spp.)
Sand monitors (Family Varanidae)
Scorpions (Order Scorpionida)
Sea anemones (Class Anthozoa)
Sea snakes (Family Hydrophiidae)
Seastars (Class Asteroidea)
Sea urchins (Class Echinoidea)
Snowdrops (*Galanthus* spp.)
Southern sea lion (Order Pinnipedia)
Spathiphyllums (*Spathiphyllum* spp.)
Spinifex (*Triodia* sp.)
Spruces (*Picea* spp.)
Squirrels (*Sciurus* spp.)
Stick insects (Order Phasmatodea)
Sticklebacks (Family Gasterosteidae)
Swifts (Family Apodidae)
Terns (Family Laridae)
Thrashers (*Toxostoma* spp.)
Thrushes (Family Turdidae)
Titmice (Family Paridae)
Tortoises (Order Chelonia)
Treecreepers (*Climacteris* spp.)
Tulip tree (*Liriodendron tulipfera*)
Violas (*Viola* spp.)

Whales (Order Cetacea)
Wildebeest (*Connochaetes* spp.)
Wolves (*Canis lupus*)
Wood anemones (*Anemone* spp.)
Woodpeckers (Family Picidae)
Yew (*Taxus baccata*)

Chapter 6
Acacias (*Acacia* spp.)
Alpine anemones (*Pulsatilla alpina*)
Azaleas (*Azalea* spp.)
Bamboo (Family Gramineae)
Beets (*Beta* spp.)
Begonias (*Begonia* spp.)
Bromeliads (Family Bromeliaceae)
Brown seaweeds (Division Phaeophyta,
   Order Dictyotales)
Buttercups (*Ranunculus* spp.)
Caladiums (*Caladium* spp.)
Carrots (*Daucus* spp.)
Cave mosses (*Schistostega* spp.)
Coleus (*Coleus* spp.)
Cordylines (*Cordyline* spp.)
Daffodils (*Narcissus* spp.)
Ferns (Order Filicales)
Fungus (*Amanita muscaria*)
Fungus - yellow (*Cyttaria gunni*)
Green seaweed (*Caulerpa* sp.)
Japanese maples (*Acer palmatum*)
Larch (*Larix* spp.)
Lichen (alga-fungus association)
Liquidambar (*Liquidambar styraciflua*)
Liverworts (Class Hepaticae)
Mosses (Class Musci)
Oaks (*Quercus* spp.)
Orchid (*Gastrodia cunninghamii*)
Peacock plant (*Selaginella willldenovii*)
Philippine spoon lily (*Alocasia micholitziana*)
Red seaweeds (Division Rhodophyta)
Rhododendrons (*Rhododendron* spp.)
Sacred lotus (*Nelumbo nucifera*)
Sedges (Family Cyperaceae)
Tomatoes (*Lycopersicon esculentum*)
Tulips (*Tulipa* spp.)
Walnuts (*Juglans regia*)
West Malaysian iridescent begonia
   (*Begonia pavonina*)

Chapter 7
African sunbirds (Family Nectariniidae)
Almonds (*Prunus dulcis*)
Ants (Family Formicidae)
Apple trees (*Malus* spp.)
Aroids (Family Araceae)
Aspens (*Populus* spp.)
Banksia (*Banksia* sp.)
Bats (Order Chiroptera)
Bees (Order Hymenoptera, Super-Family Apoidea)
Beetles (Order Coleoptera)
Beetroot (*Beta vulgaris*)
Blackberries (*Rubus fruticosus*)
Blackbirds (*Turdus merula*)
Black grapes (*Vitis* spp.)
Bottlebrush (*Callistemon* spp.)
Bougainvillea (*Bougainvillea spectabilis*)
Broadbills (Family Eurylaimidae)
Bromeliad (Family Bromeliaceae)
Buttercups (*Ranunculus* spp.)
Cassowaries (*Casuarius casuarius*)
Cherries (*Prunus* spp.)
Chrysanthemums (*Chrysanthemum* spp.)

Clover (*Trifolium* spp.)
Copper cups (*Pileanthus* sp.)
Cornflowers (*Centaurea cyanus*)
Crocus (*Crocus* sp.)
Daffodils (*Narcissus* spp.)
Daisies (Family Compositae)
Delphiniums (*Delphinium* spp.)
Dragons blood tree (*Dracaena* spp.)
Edelweiss (*Leontopodium alpinum*)
Elephants (*Loxodonta africana*)
Eucalypt (*Eucalyptus macrocarpa*)
Figs (*Ficus* spp.)
Flamingo flowers (*Anthurium* spp.)
Flies (Order Diptera, especially Family Muscidae)
Forget-me-nots (*Myosotis alpestris*)
Fruit bats (Suborder Megachiroptera)
Fuchsia (*Fuchsia* spp.)
Geebung (*Persoonia* sp.)
Geraniums (*Pelargonium* spp.)
Giant water lily (*Victoria amazonica*)
Gloxinia (*Sinningia* spp.)
Gorillas (*Gorilla gorilla*)
Gorse (*Ulex* spp.)
Gumnuts (from *Eucalyptus* spp.)
Hawthorn (*Crataegus* spp.)
Heather (*Calluna vulgaris*)
Honeyeaters (Family Meliphagidae)
Honeysuckle (*Lonicera* spp.)
Hornbills (Family Bucerotidae)
Hyacinths (*Hyacinthus* spp.)
Hydrangeas (*Hydrangea* spp.)
Kangaroo paws (*Anigozanthos* spp.)
Lilies (*Lilium* spp.)
Lobelias (*Lobelia* spp.)
Lotus (*Nelumbo* spp.)
Madagascan poinciana (*Delonix regia*)
Mayweed (*Tripleurospermum inodorum*)
Mesquites (*Prosopis* spp.)
Monkeys (Order Primates)
Morning glory (*Ipomoea learii*)
Myrtle (*Myrtus* spp.)
Nasturtiums (*Tropaeolum* spp.)
Nightshade family (Fam. Solanaceae)
Nutmeg (*Myristica fragrans*)
Oranges (*Citrus* spp.)
Orchids (Family Orchidaceae)
Petunias (*Petunia* spp.)
Pigeons (Family Columbidae)
Poinsettias (*Euphorbia pulcherrima*)
Possums (Super-Family Phalangeroidea)
Proteas (*Protea* spp.)
Primroses (*Primula* spp.)
Radishes (*Rhaphanus sativus*)
Raspberries (*Rubus* spp.)
Red cabbage (*Brassica oleracea*)
Red flowering gum (*Eucalyptus ficifolia*)
Red grapes (*Vitis* spp.)
Red hot poker (*Kniphofia thomsonii*)
Red pepper (*Capsicum* spp.)
Rose (*Rosa* spp.)
Rowan (*Sorbus aucuparia*)
Scribbly gums (*Eucalyptus* spp.)
Sea grasses (marine Angiosperms)
South African heath (*Erica coccinea*)
Sturt's desert pea (*Swainsona formosa*)
Sunflower (*Helianthus* sp.)
Sweet peas (*Lathyrus odoratus*)
Sweet potato (*Ipomaea batatas*)
Thrushes (Family Turdidae)
Tomatoes (*Lycopersicon esculentum*)
Toucans (Family Ramphastidae)

Tulips (*Tulipa* spp.)
Walnuts (*Juglans regia*)
Wasps (Order Hymenoptera)
Water lilies (*Nymphaea* spp.)
Wattle (Mimosa) (*Acacia* spp.)

Chapter 8
Bees (Order Hymenoptera, Super-Family Apoidea)
Bittern (Family Ardeidae)
Brown falcon (*Falco berigora*)
Butterflies (Order Lepidoptera)
Cats (*Felis catus*)
Cave fish (Family Amblyopsidae)
Chameleons (*Chamaeleo* spp.)
Cheetahs (*Acinonyx jubatus*)
Clams (Family Tridacnidae)
Cormorants (Family Phalacrocoracidae)
Crabs (Suborder Brachyura)
Crocodile fish (Class Pisces)
Crocodiles (*Crocodylus* spp.)
Cuttlefish (*Sepia* spp.)
Dingoes (*Canis familiaris dingo*)
Dogs (*Canis familiaris*)
Dragonflies (Order Odonata)
Eagles (Family Accipitridae)
Elephants (*Loxodonta africana*)
Feather duster worm (Family Sabellidae)
Fireflies (Family Lampyridae)
Flatworms (Class Turbellaria)
Flies (Order Diptera, especially Family Muscidae)
Frogs (Order Anura)
Geckos (Family Gekkonidae)
Goanna (*Varanus varius*)
Goldfish (*Carassius auratus*)
Grasshopper (Order Orthoptera)
Hermit crab (Family Paguridae)
Huntsman (*Isopoda* sp.)
Hyrax (Family Procaviidae)
Jackson's chameleon (*Chamaeleo jacksoni*)
Kingfishers (Family Alcedinidae)
Koala (*Phascolarctos cinereus*)
Lizards (Order Squamata, Suborder Sauria)
Lobsters (Family Palinuridae)
Mantis shrimp (Order Stomatopoda)
Marine segmented worms (Class Polychaeta)
Monkeys (Order Primates)
Moths (Order Lepidoptera)
Nautilus (*Nautilus* sp.)
Newts (*Triturus* spp.)
Nudibranchs (Class Gastropoda, Subclass
   Opisthobranchia)
Octopuses (*Octopus* spp.)
Ostrich (*Struthio camelus*)
Owls (Order Strigiformes)
Oysters (Family Ostreidae)
Penguins (Family Spheniscidae)
Piranhas (Subfam. Serraeosalminae)
Polar bears (*Thalarctos maritimus*)
Possums (Super-Family Phalangeroidea)
Prairie dogs (*Cynomys ludovicianus*)
Prawns (Family Penaeidae)
Rabbits (*Oryctolagus cuniculus*)
Rays (Order Batoidei, Order Myliobatiformes)
Salamanders (*Salamandra salamandra*)
Scallops (*Pecten* spp.)
Sea anemones (Class Anthozoa)
Seastars (Class Asteroidea)
Single celled organism (*Euglenia gracilis*)
Slugs (Class Gastropoda)
Snails (Class Gastropoda)
Soft corals (Order Alcyonacea)

Soles (Family Soleidae)
Spiders (Order Arachnida)
Squirrels (*Sciurus* spp.)
Starlings (Family Sturnidae)
Stingrays (Order Batoidei, Order Myliobatiformes)
Toads (*Bufo* spp.)
Tree frogs (Family Hylidae)
Turtles (Order Chelonia)
Vultures (Family Vulturidae)
Wallabies (Family Macropodidae)
Wildebeest (*Connochaetes* spp.)
Wolverines (*Gulo gulo*)
Woodcock (*Scolopax rusticula*)

Chapter 9
American fox squirrel (Family Sciuridae)
Aphids (Family Aphididae)
Ascidian (Class Ascidiacea)
Atlantic soft coral (*Alcyonarium palmatum*)
Australian feather star (*Comatula pectinata*)
Birds' eggs (*Larus novaehollandiae*)
Black aphids (Family Aphididae)
Black beetles (Order Coleoptera)
Bloodworm (*Chironomus* spp.)
Blue arctic foxes (*Alopex lagopus*)
Blue coral (*Heliopora coerulea*)
Bubble shell (*Hydatina physis*)
Burrowing tube anemones (*Cerianthus* spp.)
Butterfly (Order Lepidoptera)
Capybara (*Dolichotis patagonica*)
Cockerel (*Gallus gallus domestica*)
Crabs (Suborder Brachyura)
Crayfish (Family Parastacidae)
Cuttlefish (*Sepia* spp.)
Dark sea urchins (Class Echinoidea)
Dragonflies (Order Odonata)
Earthworms (*Lumbricus terrestris*)
Echiurid worm (Family Echiuridae)
Emu (*Dromaius novaehollandiae*)
Feather star (Class Crinoidea)
Flamingoes (*Phoenicopterus* spp.)
Frogs (Order Anura)
Glacier bears (Family Ursidae)
Goldfish (*Carassius auratus*)
Grasshoppers (Order Orthoptera)
Hippopotamus (*Hippopotamus amphibius*)
Jaguar (*Panthera onca*)
Kangaroo (*Macropus* sp.)
Ladybirds (Family Coccinellidae)
Lampreys (*Lampetra* spp.)
Lamp shells (Phylum Brachiopoda)
Lobsters (Family Palinuridae)
Marine snails (Class Gastropoda)
Molluscs (Phylum Mollusca)
Monkeys (Order Primates)
Nudibranchs (Class Gastropoda, Subclass Opisthobranchia)
Octopuses (*Octopus* spp.)
Orange pipe coral (*Tubipora musica*)
Oysters (Family Ostreidae)
Parrotfish (Family Scaridae)
Pipefish (Order Syngnathiformes)
Planktonic snails (*Janthina* spp.)
Plant lice (Family Aphididae)
Polychaete worms (Order Polychaeta)
Prawns (Family Penaeidae)
Precious coral (*Corallium rubrum*)
Rhino (*Diceros bicornis*)
Salmon (Family Salmonidae)
Scale insects (Family Coccidae)
Scallops (Pecten spp.)

Scorpions (Order Scorpionida)
Sea anemones (Class Anthozoa)
Sea urchins (Class Echinoidea)
Sea whip (Class Anthozoa, Order Alcyonaria)
Shrimps (Family Penaeidae)
Snails (Class Gastropoda)
Spanner crab (*Ranina ranina*)
Spiders (Order Arachnida)
Sponges (Phylum Porifera)
Starfish (Class Asteroida)
Tree frog (*Litoria caerulea*)
Trout (*Salmo* spp.)
Turkey (*Meleagris gallo-pavo*) .
Wasps (Order Hymenoptera)
Wrasses (Family Labridae)

Chapter 10
Abalone (*Haliotis* sp.)
Angelfish (Family Chaetodontidae)
Anglerfish (Family Antennariidae)
Beetles (Order Coleoptera)
Birds of paradise (*Paradisaea* spp.)
Blue eared glossy starling (*Lamprotornis chalybaeus*)
Blue morpho (*Morpho didius*)
Blue-ringed octopus (*Hapalochlaena maculosa*)
Blue winged kookaburra (*Dacelo leachii*)
Boa constrictor (*Constrictor constrictor*)
Budgerigars (*Melopsittacus undulatus*)
Butterflies (Order Lepidoptera)
Cabbage butterflies (*Pieris rapae*)
Cats (*Felis catus*)
Centipedes (Class Chilopoda)
Cephalopods (Class Cephalopoda)
Chrysomelid beetles (*Coptocycla* spp.)
Cicadas (Family Cicadidae)
Clam (*Tridacna* spp.)
Commensal shrimps (Family Penaeidae)
Corals (Class Anthozoa)
Cranes (Family Gruidae)
Cuttlefish (*Sepia* spp.)
Dragonfish (Family Stomiatidae)
Dragonflies (Order Odonata)
Ducks (Family Anatidae)
Earthworms (*Lumbricus terrestris*)
Echinoderms (Phylum Echinodermata)
Fan mussel (*Pinna* spp.)
Fireflies (Family Lampyridae)
Firefly squid (Order Teuthoidea)
Fish (Class Pisces)
Flies (Order Diptera, especially Family Muscidae)
Floating sea slug (*Glaucus atlanticus*)
Freshwater limpet (*Latia* sp.)
Glow-worms (Family Lampyridae, Family Mycetophildae)
Goatfish (Family Mullidae)
Golden mole (Family Talpidae)
Green birds (*Nestor notabilis*)
Green dragon (*Diporiphora superba*)
Hatchetfish (Family Sternoptychidae)
Herrings (Family Clupeidae)
Horses (*Equus caballus*)
Kingfishers (Family Alcedinidae)
Lanternfish (Family Myctophidae)
Lemurs (*Lemur* spp.)
Lilac breasted roller (*Coracias caudata*)
Mackerels (*Scomber* spp.)
Marchfly (Order Diptera)
Mayflies (Order Ephemeroptera)
Millipedes (Class Diplopoda)
Molluscs (Phylum Mollusca)
New Zealand glow-worms (*Arachnocampa luminosa*)

Octopuses (*Octopus* spp.)
Orange tailed blue demoiselle (*Glyphidodontops cyamens*)
Ostracod crustaceans (*Cypridina* spp.)
Peacock (*Pavo cristatus*)
Pheasants (*Phasianus* spp.)
Pigeons (Family Columbidae)
Pineapple fish (*Cleidopus gloriamaris*)
Porcupines (Family Erethizontidae)
Rainbow trout (*Salmo gairderii*)
Rays (Order Batoidei, Order Myliobatiformes)
Riflebirds (*Ptiloris* spp.)
Rollers (Family Coraciidae)
Salps (Family Salpidae)
Sea anemones (Class Anthozoa)
Siamese fighting fish (*Betta splendens*)
Snails (Class Gastropoda)
Spiders (Order Arachnida)
Sponges (Phylum Porifera)
Star eaters (Family Astronesthidae)
Starlings (Family Sturnidae)
Sunbirds (Family Nectariniidae)
Swans (Subfamily Cygninae)
Tetras (Family Characinidae)
Transparent shrimp (Family Penaeidae)
Urania moth (*Urania* sp.)
Viperfish (Family Chauliodontidae)
Vulturine guinea fowl (*Acryllium vulturinum*)
Wasps (Order Hymenoptera)

Chapter 11
Birds of paradise (*Paradisaea* spp.)
Blossom spiders (Family Sparassidae)
Bushbuck (*Tragelaphus scriptus*)
Cabbage white butterlies (*Pieris rapae*)
Chameleon (*Chamaeleo* spp.)
Chorus frogs (Order Anura)
Cicada (Family Cicadidae)
Cleaner wrasse (*Labroides dimidiatus*)
Crabs (Suborder Brachyura)
Crested larks (*Galrida cristata*)
Crimson banded wrasse (*Pseudolabrus gymnogenus*)
Cuttlefish (*Sepia* spp.)
Deer (Family Cervidae)
Dogs (*Canis familiaris*)
Dotterels (Family Charadriidae)
Ducks (Family Anatidae)
Eels (Family Anguillidae)
Emus (*Dromaius novaehollandiae*)
Eurasian bustard (*Otis tarda*)
Fiddler crabs (*Uca* spp.)
Flamingoes (*Phoenicopterus* spp.)
Flounder (Family Pleuronectidae, Family Scophthalmidae)
Frogs (Order Anura)
Geckos (Family Gekkonidae)
Geometrid moths (*Nemoria arizonaria*)
Gorillas (*Gorilla gorilla*)
Gropers (*Choerodon* spp.)
Hercules beetles (*Dynastes hercules*)
Kangaroos (*Macropus* sp.)
Leeches (Class Hirudinea)
Lion (*Panthera leo*)
Lizards (Order Squamata, Suborder Sauria)
Locusts (Order Orthoptera)
Lyrebirds (*Menura* spp.)
Madagascan chameleon (*Chamaeleo parsoni*)
Mongoose (*Herpestes* sp.)
Mosquito fish (*Gambusia affinis*)
Mountain grasshoppers (*Acripeza reticulata*)

North American sage grouse (*Centrocercus urophasianus*)
Oaks (*Quercus* spp.)
Ostrich (*Struthio camelus*)
Peacocks (*Pavo cristatus*)
Peppered moths (*Biston betularia*)
Phalaropes (Family Phalaropodidae)
Pheasants (*Phasianus* spp.)
Pipits (Family Motacillidae)
Polar foxes (*Vulpes* sp.)
Ptarmigans (*Lagopus mutus*)
Salamanders (*Salamandra salamandra*)
Scarab beetles (Family Scarabaeidae)
Sea hares (*Aplysia* spp.)
Seahorses (*Hippocampus* spp.)
Seals (Suborder Piniipedia)
Sea urchins (Class Echinoidea)
Sloth (*Bradypus griseus*)
Snapdragons (*Anthirrhinum* spp.)
Snow hares (*Lepus timidus*)
Soles (Family Soleidae)
Spekes weaver (*Ploceus spekei*)
Springbok (*Antidorcas marsupialis*)
Starlings (Family Sturnidae)
Stick insects (Order Phasmida)
Stoats (*Mustela erminea*)
Surgeonfish (*Acanthurus* spp.)
Swans (*Cygnus* spp.)
Tasmanian devil (*Sarcophilus harrisii*)
Tinamous (Family Tinemidae)
Tree frogs (Family Hylidae)
Tubeworms (Family Sabellidae)
Waterbuck (*Kobus ellipsiprymnus*)
Weaver birds (Family Ploceidae)
Wrasses (Family Labridae)
Yellow eyed penguin (*Megadyptes antipodes*)
Yellow spotted jewel butterfly (*Hypochrysops* sp.)

Chapter 12
African crested rat (*Lophiomys ibeanus*)
Antelopes (Family Boviidae)
Barracuta (*Scomberomorus commerson*)
Black swallow butterfly (Order Lepidoptera)
Black widow spider (*Latrodectus mactans*)
Blossom spiders (Family Sparassidae)
Boxfish (Family Ostracionidae)
Casemoths (Family Psychoidae)
Cheetahs (*Acinonyx jubatus*)
Chinese character moths (*Cilix glaucata*)
Clothes moth larvae (Family Tineidae)
Coneshells (*Conus* spp.)
Crocodiles (*Crocodylus* spp.)
Cuttlefish (*Sepia* spp.)
Deer (Family Cervidae)
Eyed hawkmoth (*Smerinthus ocellata*)
Fiddler crabs (*Uca* spp.)
Firebelly toad (*Bombina bombina*)

Flatfish (numerous families)
Frigatebird (*Fregata* spp.)
Frogs (Order Anura)
Geckos (Family Gekkonidae)
Giraffes (*Giraffa camelopardalis*)
Glassfish (Family Centropomidae)
Grasshoppers (Family Acrididae)
Gurnards (Family Triglidae)
Hermit crab (Family Paguridae)
Herons (Family Ardeidae)
Hummingbirds (Family Trochilidae)
Jewel beetle (*Stigmodera* sp.)
Ladybirds (Family Coccinellidae)
Leaf insect (Order Orthoptera)
Leatherjacket (*Brachaluteres jacksonianus*)
Leopards (*Panthera pardus*)
Lionfish (*Pterois volitans*)
Lizards (Order Squamata, Suborder Sauria)
Loopers (Family Geometridae)
Mantids (Order Dictyoptera)
Milkweeds (*Asclepias* spp.)
Monarch butterflies (*Danaus plexippus*)
Moorish idol (*Zanclus cornutus*)
Moth (Order Lepidoptera)
Nightjar (*Eurostopodus guttatus*)
Nile catfish (*Synodontis batensoda*)
Octopuses (*Octopus* spp.)
Orchids (Family Orchidaceae)
Osprey (*Pandion haliaetus*)
Owls (Order Strigiformes)
Peacock (*Pavo cristatus*)
Pitcher plants (*Nepenthes* spp.)
Polar bears (*Thalarctos maritimus*)
Praying mantis (Family Mantidae)
Puffer fish (Family Tetrodontidae)
Rabbits (*Oryctolagus cuniculus*)
Rainbow birds (*Merops ornatus*)
Red billed hornbill (*Tockus erythrorhynchus*)
Red indian fish (Class Pisces)
Red velvet mite (Family Trombidiae)
Salamanders (*Salamandra salamandra*)
Sand flathead (*Platycephalus* sp.)
Saturnids (Family Saturniidae)
Seals (Suborder Piniipedia)
Sea snakes (Family Hydrophiidae)
Shingleback (*Trachydosaurus rugosus*)
Soft bodied beetle (*Metriorrhynchus* sp.)
Spicebush swallowtail (*Papilio troilus*)
Spider crabs (*Leptomithrax sternocostulatus*)
Spiny tailed gecko (*Diplodactylus ciliaris*)
Sponge crabs (Family Dromiidae)
Stick insects (Order Phasmatodea)
Stonefish (*Synanceja* spp.)
Stone plants (*Lithops rubra*)
Sunbirds (Family Nectariniidae)
Swamphens (*Porphyrio porphyrio*)
Thorny devil (*Moloch horridus*)

Toucans (Family Ramphastidae)
Tree frogs (Order Anura)
Tree hoppers (Family Membracidae)
Tree snakes (Family Colubridae)
Turtles (Order Chelonia)
Viceroy butterfly (*Brasilarchia archippus*)
Wasps (Order Hymenoptera)
Whales (Order Cetacea)
Zebras (*Hippotigris* spp.)

Chapter 13
American red quebracho (*Schinopsis* spp.)
Annatto (*Bixa orellana*)
Australian black wattle (*Acacia mearnsii*)
Austrian briar (*Rosa foetida*)
Bilberries (*Vaccinium* spp.)
Blackberries (*Rubus fruticosus*)
Blueberries (*Vaccinium* spp.)
Blue rose (*Rosa* cv. Blue Moon)
Capsicum (*Capsicum* spp.)
Cauliflower (*Brassica oleracea* var. *botrytis*)
Cherries (*Prunus* spp.)
Chillies (*Capsicum* spp.)
Cochineal insects (*Dactylopius coccus*)
Coleus (*Coleus* spp.)
Dyers' broom (*Genista tinctoria*)
Dyers' chamomile (*Anthemis nobilis*)
European woad (*Isatis tinctoria*)
Fig (*Ficus* spp.)
Grapes (*Vitis* spp.)
Henna (*Lawsonia inermis*)
Hyacinths (*Hyacinthus* spp.)
Indigo (*Indigofera tinctoria*)
Kermes insects (*Coccus ilicus*, *Lecanium ilea*)
Lac insects (*Coccus laccae*, *Tachardia lacca*)
Madder (*Rubia tinctorum*)
Marmalade box tree (*Genipa americana*)
Mexican logweed tree (*Haematoxylin campechianum*)
Molluscs (especially *Murex* and *Purpura* spp.)
Orchids (Family Orchidaceae)
Peppers (*Capsicum* spp.)
Plums (*Prunus* spp.)
Potatoes (*Solanum tuberosum*)
Red cabbage (*Brassica oleracea* var. *capitata*)
Safflower (*Cathamus tinctorius*)
Saffron (*Crocus sativus*)
Sappanwood (*Caesalpinia sappan*)
Scale insects (Family Coccidae)
South east Asian tree (*Garcinia hanburyi*)
Sturt's Desert Pea (*Swainsona formosa*)
Sumac (*Rhus* spp.)
Tulips (*Tulipa* spp.)
Turmeric (*Curcuma longa*)
Walnuts (*Juglans regia*)
Weld (*Reseda luteola*)

SELECTED BIBLIOGRAPHY

Abercrombie, M., Hickman, C.J. and Johnson, M.L. (1973) *A dictionary of biology*. 6th edn. Penguin, England.

Allen, Oliver E. (1983) *Planet Earth atmosphere*. Time-Life Books, Alexandria, Virginia.

Ayensu, Edward S. (1980) *Jungles*. Jonathan Cape, London.

Ayensu, Edward S., Heywood, Vernon H., Lucas, Grenville L. and Defilipps, Robert A. (1984) *Our green and living world*. Cambridge University Press, Cambridge.

Bailey, Jill (1988) *Mimicry and camouflage*. Hodder & Stoughton, London.

Bender, Lionel (ed.) (1989) *World of science*. Equinox, Oxford.

Benzing, David H. (1980) *The biology of the Bromeliads*. Mad River Press, Eureka, California.

Bille, Rene Pierre (1974) *The Guinness guide to mountain animals*. Guinness Superlatives, England.

Birren, Faber (1982) *Light, color and environment*. Revised edn. Van Nostrand Reinhold, New York.

Bjorn, Lars Olof (1976) *Light and life*. Hodder & Stoughton, London.

Bodin, Svante (1979) *Weather and climate*. Blandford, England.

Bown, Deni (1988) *Aroids, plants of the Arum family*. Century, London.

Bown, Deni (1989) *Alba — the book of white flowers*. Unwin Hyman, Great Britain.

Boynton, Robert M. (1979) *Human colour vision*. Holt Rinehart & Winston, New York.

Breathnach, A.S. (1971) *Melanin pigmentation of the skin*. Oxford Biology Readers. Oxford University Press, London.

Burton, Robert (1987) *Eggs. Nature's perfect package*. Facts on File Publications, New York.

Burtt, Edward H. Jr (1979) *The behavioural significance of color*. Garland, New York.

Caes, Charles J. (1988) *Studies in starlight. Understanding our universe*. TAB Books, Blue Ridge Summit, P.A.

Caras, Roger (ed.) (1972) *Protective coloration and mimicry. Nature's camouflage*. Westover, New York.

Chalmers, Oliver (1979) *The observer's book of rocks and minerals of Australia*. Methuen Australia, Sydney.

Chamberlin, G.J. and Chamberlin, D.G (1980) *Colour, its measurement, computation and application*. Heyden, London.

Cox, Jeff and Cox, Marilyn (1985) *The perennial garden. Color harmonies through the seasons*. Rodale Press, Emmaus, Pennsylvannia.

DeLuca, Marlene A. and McElroy, William D. (eds) (1981) *Bioluminescence and chemiluminescence. Basic chemistry and analytical applications*. Academic Press, New York.

Downer, John (1988) *Supersense. Perception in the animal world*. BBC Books, London.

Echternacht, Arthur C. (1977) *How reptiles and amphibians live*. Elsevier-Phaidon, Oxford.

Fairley, Alan (1984) *Australian seasons. Summer and autumn*. Methuen, Melbourne.

Fogden, Michael, and Fogden, Patricia (1974) *Animals and their colours*. Crown Publishers, U.S.A.

Fox, H.M., and Vevers, G. (1960) *The nature of animal colours*. Sidgwick & Jackson, London.

Freeman, Michael (1984) *The wildlife & nature photographer's field guide*. Nelson, Melbourne.

Gerritsen, Frans (1975) *Theory and practice of color. A color theory based on laws of perception*. Van Nostrand Reinhold, New York.

Goulding, Michael (1989) *Amazon, the flooded forest*. BBC Books, London.

Graham, F. Lanier (ed.) (1975) *The rainbow book*. The Fine Arts Museum of San Francisco in association with Shambhala, Berkeley, California.

Griesbach, R.J. (1985) *Biochemistry of flower colour*. In: Proceedings of the Eleventh World Orchid Conference, March 1984. Maimi, Florida, U.S.A.

Gross, M. Grant (1972) *Oceanography: a view of the earth*. Prentice Hall, New Jersey.

Hamilton, William J. III (1973) *Life's color code*. McGraw-Hill, New York.

Hart, J.W. (1988) *Light and plant growth*. Unwin Hyman, London.

Haworth-Booth, Michael (1984) *The hydrangeas*. 5th Edn. Constable, London.

Henbest, Nigel (1985) *Comets, stars and planets*. Multimedia Publications, U.K.

Henderson, S.T. (1977) *Daylight and its spectrum*. 2nd edn. Hilger, Bristol.

Heran, Ivan (1976) *Animal coloration. The nature and purpose of colours in vertebrates*. Hamlyn, London.

Herring, Peter J. (ed.) (1978) *Bioluminescence in action*. Academic Press, London.

Hess, Lilo (1970) *Animals that hide imitate and bluff*. Blackie, London.

Hingston, R.W.G., Major (1933) *The meaning of animal colour and adornment*. Edward Arnold, London.

Jekyll, Gertrude (1982) *Colour schemes for the flower garden*. 8th edn. Antique Collectors' Club, London.

Jolivet, Pierre (1986) *Insects and plants*. Parallel evolution and adaptations Flora & Fauna Handbook No. 2. Brill, New York.

Jolly, V.H. and Brown, J.M.A. (1975) *New Zealand lakes*. Auckland University Press, Auckland.

Kerrod, Robin (1979) *Gems and minerals*. Franklin Watts, London.

Lambert, David and McConnell, Anita (1985) *Seas and oceans*. Colour Library of Science. Orbis, London.

Lancaster, Michael (1989) 'Colour and plants'. *Landscape Design,* April 1989: 33-36.

Lee, David W. (1977) 'On iridescent plants'. *Gardens' Bulletin Singapore*, 30: 21-29, 2 plates.

Lee, R. and Fraser, A. (1990) 'The light at the end of the rainbow'. *New Scientist* September 1990: 32-36.

Leeper, G.W. (1967) *Introduction to soil science*. Melbourne University Press, Melbourne.

Lewington, Anna (1990) *Plants for people*. Natural History Museum Publications, London.

Lloyd, Christopher (1985) *The well-tempered garden*. Revised edn. Viking, London.

Lloyd, Christopher (1990) 'Bits of brilliance'. *Horticulture,* April 1990: 36-40.

Lythgoe, J.N. (1979) *The ecology of vision*. Clarendon, Oxford.

Malin, David, and Murdin, Paul (1984) *Colours of the stars*. Cambridge University Press, Cambridge.

Mayer, Wolf (1976) *A field guide to Australian rocks, minerals & gemstones*. Rigby Ltd., Adelaide.

McLaren, K. (1986) *The colour science of dyes and pigments*. 2nd edn. Hilger, Bristol.

Meglitsch, Paul A. (1972) *Invertebrate zoology*. 2nd edn. Oxford University Press, London.

Minnaert, M. (1954). *The nature of light and colour in the open air*. Dover Publications, New York.

Mitchell, James (ed.) (1982) *The illustrated reference book of the Earth*. Colporteur Press, Sydney.

Moore, Patrick (1984) *The new atlas of the universe*. Mitchell Beazley, London.

Moore, Patrick (1980) *Stars of the Australian and New Zealand skies*. George Philip and O'Niel, Victoria.

Moore, Patrick (1987) *Stars and planets*. Golden Press, Drummoyne, Australia.

Murdin, Paul and Murdin, Lesley (1985) *Supernovae*. Cambridge University Press, Cambridge.

Murray, Bruce, Malin, Michael C. and Greeley, Ronald (1981) *Earthlike planets. Surfaces of Mercury, Venus, Earth, Moon, Mars*. Freeman, San Francisco.

Nations, James D. (1988) *Tropical rainforests. Endangered environment*. Franklin Watts, New York.

Needham, Arthur E. (1974) *The significance of zoochromes.* Springer-Verlag, Berlin.

New, Timothy R. (1988) *Associations between insects and plants.* New South Wales University Press, Kensington, New South Wales.

Newbigin, Marion I. (1898) *Colour in nature — a study in biology.* John Murray, London.

O'Connor, John (1967) 'Autumn colour'. *Journal of Royal Horticultural Society* 92(2):90-95.

Overheim, R.D., and Wagner, D.L. (1982) *Light and colour.* Wiley, New York.

Parker, George Howard (1948) *Animal colour changes and their neurohumours. A survey of investigations 1910-1943.* Cambridge University Press, Cambridge.

Pearsall, W.H. (1949) 'Autumn colours'. *Endeavour,* October 1949: 157-162.

Prance, Ghillean T. and Lovejoy, Thomas E. (eds) (1984) *Amazonia.* Pergamon Press, Oxford.

Proctor, John and Proctor, Susan (1978) *Nature's use of colour in plants and their flowers.* Cassell Australia, Stanmore.

Raven, P.H., Evert, R.F. and Curtis, Helena (1976) *Biology of plants.* 2nd edn. Worth, New York.

Rebelo, Tony (1988) 'Erica flower colours. Pollination, polychromatism, polymorphism and populations'. *Sagittarius,* September 1988, p12-17.

Reidy, David and Wallace, Ken (1987) *The southern sky. A practical guide to astronomy.* Allen & Unwin, Sydney.

Ridpath, Ian (ed.) (1989) *Norton's 2000.0 star atlas and reference handbook.* 18th edn. Longman, New York.

Roberts, Jeremy A. and Hooley, Richard (1988) *Plant growth regulators.* Blackie, Glasgow.

Roberts, M.B.V. (1974) *Biology — a functional approach.* Nelson, London.

Rossotti, Hazel (1983) *Colour.* Penguin, Harmondsworth, England.

Royal Horticultural Society London (1966) *Colour chart.* Royal Horticultural Society, London.

Russell, Sir Frederick S. and Yonge, Sir Maurice (1975) *The seas.* 4th edn. Frederick Warne, London.

Schaefer, Bradley E. (1992) 'The green flash'. *Sky & Telescope,* February 1992: 200-203.

Schaeffer, Vincent J. and Day, John A. (1981) *A field guide to the atmosphere.* Houghton Mifflin, Boston.

Seddon, Tony (1988) *Animal eyes.* Hodder & Stoughton, Kent, UK.

Sherman, Irwin W. and Sherman, Vilia G. (1970) *The invertebrates. Function and form.* 2nd edn. MacMillan, New York.

Simon, Hilda (1971) *The splendor of iridescence — structural colours in the animal world.* Dodd, Mead & Company, New York.

Simon, Hilda (1973) *Chameleons and other quick change artists.* Dodd Mead, New York.

Simpson, A.G.W. (1988) *Growing annuals.* Kangaroo Press, Kenthurst.

Sinclair, Sandra (1985) *How animals see. Other visions of our world.* Facts on File Publications, New York.

Smith, Anthony (1970) *The seasons. Rhythms of life: cycles of change.* Weidenfeld & Nicolson, London.

Smithe, Frank B. (1974) *Naturalists color guide and supplement.* The American Museum of Natural History, New York.

Sparkes, John and Soper, Tony (1987) *Penguins.* Facts on File Publications, New York.

Sparkes, John and Soper, Tony (1989) *Owls. Their natural and unnatural history.* Facts on File Publications, New York.

Stowar, John (1989) 'The phenomenon of autumn colour'. *Garden Journal,* Autumn 1989: 154-155.

Street, Philip (1977) *Colour in animals.* Penguin, England.

Taburiaux, Jean (1985) *Pearls, their origin treatment and identification.* NAG Press, Ipswich, Suffolk.

Taylor, R.M. (1983) *Soils, an Australian viewpoint.* CSIRO. Academic Press, Melbourne.

Thomas, Graham Stuart (1986) *Shrub roses of today.* Dent & Sons, Melbourne.

Time-Life (eds) (1973) *Life library of photography. Colour.* Time Inc., U.S.A.

Verity, Enid (1967) *Colour.* Leslie Frewin, London.

Verity, Enid (1980) *Colour observed.* Macmillan, London.

Vevers, Gwynne (1977) *Octopus, cuttlefish and squid.* Bodley Head, London.

Vevers, Gwynne (1982) *The colours of animals.* Edward Arnold, London.

Vines, A.E. and Rees, N. (1972) *Plant and animal biology.* 4th edn, 2 vols. Pitman Publishing, London.

Von Frisch, Otto (1973) *Animal camouflage.* Collins, London.

Wells, M.J. (1978) *Octopus. Physiology and behaviour of an advanced invertebrate.* Chapman & Hall, London.

Whitehead, Peter (1975) *How fishes live.* Elsevier Phaidon, London.

Williamson, S.J. and Cummins, H.Z. (1983) *Light and colour in nature and art.* John Wiley, New York.

Wilson, E.O., Eisner, T., Briggs, W.R., Dickerson, R.E., Metzenberg, R.L., O'Brien, R.D., Susman, M. and Boggs, W.E. (1977) *Life, cells, organisms, populations.* Sinauer, Massachusetts.

INDEX